# DAYS AND NIGHTS IN CALCUTTA

*Part One is for*
*Dodoo, Chhoto-mamu, and Manik-da,*
*three givers of Bengal.*


*Part Two is dedicated to*
*Bina, Ranu, Mira, Saudamini Sarujabala,*
*Nita, Preeti, Roma, Shanti, Iti,*
*Aroti, Jijabai, Namita, Archana,*
*Mother John Baptist, Mother Joseph Michael,*
*Mother Damien, and Mother Stella.*

# DAYS AND NIGHTS
# IN CALCUTTA

Clark Blaise and
Bharati Mukherjee

 **Hungry Mind Press**

# Days and Nights in Calcutta

Clark Blaise and Bharati Mukherjee met when they were graduate students at the University of Iowa's Writers Workshop. They were married two years later in 1963 on their lunch hour, a far cry from the elaborate ritual for Bengali brides.

Clark Blaise now heads the International Writing Program at the University of Iowa. He is the author of six works of fiction and a 1993 memoir, *I Had A Father: A Post-Modern Autobiography*. Bharati Mukherjee was born in Calcutta. She is a winner of the National Book Critics' Circle Award and author of *The Holder of the World*, published in 1993. She is a professor at the University of California at Berkeley. The authors have two sons.

# CONTENTS

# PROLOGUE

# CLARK BLAISE

Revisiting your younger self in a time and place that have vanished carries the pleasure and some of the risk of time travel. *Days and Nights in Calcutta* has been dead in this country for nearly twenty years. Calcutta was an unorthodox subject back then. I had the feeling that I was reporting something still slightly exotic (the kind of thing that would drive me to Mongolia or Albania if I were doing it today). Now Calcutta has subways and Five-Star hotels. Patrick Swayze has made a Calcutta film. The Communists are back in power. Easy allusions (including my own) to dysfunctional, septic Calcutta (which were never justified) or anarchic, collapsing India (which were obviously premature) are no longer sustainable in a world where universal homelessness, drugs, violence, gangs, clan warfare, ethnic and religious strife have become commonplace.

The India of 1973–74 described in this book has vanished. The people who had given me their India, Bharati's parents and Satyajit Ray, have passed on. My parents are gone, our children are grown. We're no longer young Montrealers with beckoning futures and perfect jobs in the same city; we're American authors in our mid-fifties in a strained, permanent

commute between Iowa City and Berkeley. Bharati has become one of
America's best-known novelists and short-story writers; my world has retreated to ever-tighter, French-Canadian circles. None of that was apparent
twenty-one years ago. Back then, I was full of imperial confidence. Want to
know about India, about Calcutta, about Hinduism? Be right with you.
Bharati was the autobiographer. She was the injured and distrustful one.

While this vision of India has been lying fallow for a generation, India
has added the equivalent of a full United States and Canada to its population. A prime minister has been lost to assassination, her son to another. It
has fought, and continues to wage, a brutal and repressive civil war against
its major religious minorities, Sikh and Muslim. (Eight years ago, Bharati
and I teamed up for another book, *The Sorrow and the Terror*, on the
Canadian Sikh community and the role of violent factions within it in carrying out the bloodiest terrorist act of modern times, the bombing of an Air
India 747 off the coast of Ireland in June, 1985.) Ancient unresolved in-
equities of caste, dowry and female infanticide, festering communal suspi-
cions and separatist movements, and the newer corrosive force of
corruption, together have wiped out the innocent hope that a fusion of ancient teachings, parliamentary democracy, socialism and now the free
market, could hold a disparate society together.

More than ever, India seems poised for rupture, yet the nightmare future that was so easy to predict twenty-one years ago never materialized, at
least not in the dramatic form I'd expected. India is poor and fragile, but
it is also rich and robust; the problems have always been the unequal distribution of wealth and the disparities between urban and village
economies. It must be understood that India has the largest middle class
in the world.

Contemporary, cosmopolitan Bombay has spread for miles from the
narcissistic outposts of Nariman Point and Marine Drive, outposts we described in this book. Small apartments in the center of Bombay, their
prices driven upward by Arab money and the new international corporate
culture, are now the most expensive real estate in the world ($600,000, not
counting bribes, can get you modestly installed). Bharati's relatives on this
side of the world complain that a lifetime of American savings cannot buy
a decent retirement apartment in Poona.

When I was last in Bombay—dull, materialistic Bombay—a little over
a year ago, I gave a reading at the American Cultural Center on a night
when the German, French and British Councils were also shuttling au-

thors through. At the opening of a new photographic gallery, my responses were solicited by a society news television reporter.

Bangalore, India's Silicon Valley, is even more transformed; India is now second only to the U.S. in software exports. San Jose engineers are returning, bringing their children home before America corrupts them completely.

Servants are gone, the old leisure of India is gone. Aggressive business practices, naked corruption and a debased political dialogue have taken their place. Urban, middle-class India is no more alien than Germany or France. Bharati's sister and her husband in Baroda, who once despaired of being able to afford a car, have both risen to the status and income their talents and efforts would have earned them in the U.S. or anywhere else.

Societies evolve, families and individuals flare, then disappear. I was the beneficiary of extraordinary guides who lavished care and love upon me. I was the avid young stranger who'd wandered into their village, the intimate alien who'd become family. Now the older members of the family have died, the cousins have scattered and are no longer in contact. Some of Bharati's classmates (including a passenger on that Air India flight) and even more of their husbands, are gone. The gurus are gone. Only our contemporaries are left, and we're alike in the quality of our loss. What remains, I realize now, is this book, the record of vanished times. You knew Satyajit Ray? young Bengalis ask me. You actually met old Raj Kapoor? You knew Shobha De (now a scandalous, best-selling novelist) when she was just a movie gossip columnist?

The thing that changed our life most profoundly is only hinted at in this text: the distant rumble of Canadian racism that would explode upon us and finally force us to leave just five years later. The realization that we were not just a lucky young professional couple, but somehow marked by history and society and by race, became for Bharati the liberation of all her talents, and for me, the end of my precocious sophistication.

I read this book now with grim amusement and with chagrin at my own misdirected apocalyptic expectation. While I confidently projected the collapse of a whole subcontinent, I failed to see the collapse of the only world—my fragile and constructed Canadian identity (see my 1993 autobiography *I Had A Father*)—that had fed my sense of purpose and lent me that confident perspective on something larger than my own childhood and adolescence.

*PART ONE*

·॰॰] I

1

Eight months later in an ancient courtyard outside the city of Baroda, in the Indian state of Gujarat, in hot, dry, still, postmonsoon October, I would be sitting barefoot, at the card table of a bearded *sadhu* in dingy robes named Joshi-boa, his shoulder-length hair and breast-long beard all the whiter for its streaks of yellow. And he would be telling me (through my sister-in-law, Ranu, who translated from Marathi and Gujarati into English) that I had passed through a very bad phase, a nearly fatal phase, between December of the year before and my birthday, this past April. Danger of death, of paralysis on the left side. "Amazing," I said. But now all was fine. Many books, I would write. "Big bank balance," he kept saying in English, turning to me for approval.

"When will I die?" I asked, it being the question that haunts my waking hours, the one question all my writing was trying to ask, or answer, and now was the first time I'd come so close to believing another's vision: *When will I die?* And without hesitation he began at length in Marathi, as Ranu nodded and I stared at the mosquitoes drinking from my wrist (disrupt them and I might lose twenty years, I thought). I scanned the rows of gods that hung like country calendars along the roofless courtyard walls: Ganesh, the elephant-headed, bounteous fat-boy god, god of the kitchen, enthroned with dishes of sweets at his feet, and in the mixture of the extravagant and the literal that is Hinduism and that I am constantly misjudging, realistic rats, his avatars, are pictured lapping the milk and sweets.

"You will die at eight-one," Ranu says.

The *sadhu* holds on tightly. He must be seventy, but his hands are prize-fighter wide, thick, and hard. Mine slip like crumpled tissues in his palms. "He wants to know if you are healthy," she asks.

"Reasonably."

"Heart, kidneys, stomach—"

"Tell him I fart a lot."

She giggles but doesn't translate. "He says do not travel unnecessarily over water. He says in five years, *big bank balance*, you will be known by everyone." The *sadhu* chuckles, nods, repeats, *Big bank balance, saab.*

He has absolutely no way of knowing that I write. I don't look like a writer, my Indian connections are properly businesslike, and Baroda is never visited by foreign writers. There are college girls giggling nervously out beyond the courtyard, their schoolbooks resting in the dry fountain's pool. It is examination time and fortune-tellers are busy. I slip him ten rupees—a little over a dollar—which seems to please him, and we find a scooter-rickshaw to take us home.

Eighty-one. Big bank balance. Last year, between December and April, as Joshi-boa said, I had nearly died. Perhaps, in that metaphorical way that is more real to me than any injury, I did die. There is no way for him to know that he was precisely right, that I had passed through shadows that tinge my nightmares red. Every phone call, every knock on the door, every time I start up the car, I hear the broken sobs, smell smoke, smell bone, and begin to shake. Between December and April I collected on every insurance policy I carried, and I became, in fact as well as in imagination, disaster-prone. I feared I had used up my good luck, my inheritance, any unearned advantages. From this moment on, I would view myself as a *bad risk*. In our culture, it is the ultimate disgrace.

On December 4 I had fallen on ice outside a student's apartment and broken my left hand.

But by late February I was riding higher than I'd ever ridden. My first book, *A North American Education,* had come out two weeks earlier and I was still coasting on the strength of reviews. The Canadian bureau of *Time* had sent someone out to the house two days before for pictures ("Author Blaise in his Montreal home") and I'd seen the prints that morning of Author Blaise in his white leather armchair flanked by the rows of his nearly human avocados. And there I sat in my office at four in the afternoon, my older son, Bart, in Vermont for the week skiing with friends, and my younger son, Bernie, at home with the baby-sitter. It was nearly time for me to leave and prepare for a television appearance at seven that evening. My wife, Bharati, was at a McGill meeting. The office phone rang.

It had been getting ridiculous, the joys of authorship in a small literary culture like Canada's. All my calls had been long-distance, reviews being read to me from Toronto and New York. Every intrusion a welcome distraction from teaching. Eagerly I answered in the manner that seemed least offensive to my rapidly vanishing modesty. "Clark Blaise speaking."

The voice took awhile to speak. I could hear breathing, the long suck of air, then the moan. "Oh, Mr. Blaise . . . I am so sorry."

Micheline had been working for us nearly three months. She would come at about two-thirty, be there when the children got home from school, do light housework, and cook their supper. I would leave my office around five, drive or walk over to McGill to pick up Bharati, and be home by six. After nine years of marriage, parenthood, and a double career, it was the first year of full professionalism Bharati and I had been able to afford. But this week Bart was away and Micheline was in all day since it was a school vacation for the children, and the five-year-old, Bernie, was with her. We hadn't let him go to Vermont, because we thought he'd miss us. Suddenly I could picture him only on a snapshot, a memory preserved.

A few words pushed through tears and hysterics, "I'm so sorry, I'm so sorry."

A new voice, "Give me that!" A neighbor's shrill English voice. "Mr. Blaise. Get over here right away. There's been a fire."

"How's Bernie? Has anything happened to Bernie?"

"No, nothing's happened to your Bernie. Can't you get it through your head your house is burning down and maybe my house is going up next? This girl is useless—get over here right away."

WASP disapproval, bottled up for three years, all spilling out. Too far to get my car at McGill; I ran to the office of my closest friend. "Drive me home, Ed. My house is burning down."

It was a subfreezing, cloudy, late winter day. My thoughts were all on Bernie. Bart had always seemed a miracle, something provisional, but Bernie was our reality principle, our success story. On Côte-St.-Antoine, the only approach to the house, fire trucks had blocked the road four blocks from our intersection. I got out and began running. House fires were common all over Westmount; many a time in the past five years I'd detoured around closed streets, read of deaths of people we'd vaguely known, and seen their stately brick houses with just the tell-tale, fatal plywood over the windows. Westmount fires were swift and deadly, but always discreet.

You see the trucks, the hoses, the odd pieces of equipment parked around corners and down the block, and you hear chopping and smashing of glass—your glass—and somehow you cut through those lines of firemen that are holding dozens of other people back (they seem, all of them, to recognize your claim, your special right to push through their barriers; their eyes are keen, they know authorship when they see it). There are firemen on the roof chopping holes, others on ladders breaking the upper-story windows. My manuscripts are there. Bharati's manuscripts. Our Indian paintings from a brief visit three years earlier, rugs, all the new furniture we'd just started buying, two thousand books, my plants, the indoor lime and orange trees that after two years were just bearing fruit, the gerbils Bart and Bernie liked to hold as they watched the children's shows after school. Bernie and I had just changed their bedding the night before. He was out on the sidewalk, held by Micheline, wrapped in her coat. In penance, she stood, dazed and shivering, in her T-shirt.

You see flames and smoke consuming all that you own and have so patiently accumulated since graduate school; and you see the firemen casually attacking the shell of your ownership (we'd rented it advantageously when Quebec was at its lowest political ebb, but it still cost us. It reflected us). You feel a trembling rage at fate, your frailty, and even the forces of protection. The next-door neighbor who called me is loudly complaining to the fire chief about what "our" fire is doing to her trees and hedges; Micheline is rapidly going into shock; and only Bernie can give his usual rational account: "I was watching *Sesame Street* and Micheline was upstairs and I looked into the kitchen and I said, 'Oh-oh, the house is on fire.'"

It burns not to the ground, it being brick, but everything is lost. We showed up that night at the TV studios, endured ten minutes of "Hear your book is selling like a house afire," then checked into a hotel. At midnight we had to go back to the ruin to take official repossession of the house, and that was when we had our first look.

It was like identifying the body of your child or wife. The floors were already thick with ice, and a fine hoarfrost glittered in the flashlight beam, sifting down from the smashed skylight high over the stair well. Our Indian tapestries and our paintings lay crumpled or curled in the matted ice. The shelves of plants had wilted like the frozen celery crops I remember as a child in Florida. I saw the gerbil cage, empty, up high on the mantel where the firemen had tossed it. The kitchen, where the pot of boiling french fries oil had hit the heating coil and exploded, was only a cave, missing a back wall where a telephone had hung. The stove and the fridge were puddles of white enamel.

Upstairs, only Bharati's study was saved. My study, over the kitchen, had lost its floor and through the floor had dropped five boxes of old manuscripts. In twists, ashes, and sodden piles, I could make out the old pictures, coats, ties, shoes, everything I'd preserved since high school and college—like a prop room for *American Graffiti*. A day before the fire, if I'd been asked to make a list of the things that I cared about most, I would have said my old writings, my plants, my books, our camping gear, the permanent things we'd started to accumulate in the past year or two—everything that proved to me I had overcome my false starts and had begun to accumulate a personal history. Suddenly I had no evidence of a personal history. It was a kind of freedom that depressed me profoundly.

We were paid the full insurance settlement; I took it to buy return tickets for four, Montreal-Calcutta via everywhere in between: $4,400. Insurance on all our luggage for eighteen months: $330. Shots to be taken. New rooms to be rented. Final papers to grade, packing, moving, storing, shipping, mailing. The car, the last object, to dispose of. It was now April. My birthday, the thirty-third, would come on the tenth ("You were in a fatal period between December and your birthday," Joshi-boa would say). We had a '72 Volvo in admirable condition. On the morning of April 5, I called in an ad to the *Star*, hoping for a quick $3,000. It was the last week of classes (we'd made it!), the snow was off the streets and the temperature was in the middle forties. A final drive to school, Bharati beside me, the colleague in the back, a block from home and—

An hour later, with Bharati still in the X-ray room, I slipped out of the Emergency to cancel the ad. And for the second time in little over a month, I was dazed and on the phone, speaking thickly to those institutional people you pay annual fees to in the hope of never collecting. All X rays were negative, but Bharati had cracked the windshield with her head, and her hand, chest, and knee would still be aching nine months later, in Calcutta. I came out of it with a bloody nose and lip. Two speeding cars had sideswiped just as I was pulling into the intersection, and the more negligent one, who had run a stop sign, had been tossed into our front end. Leaving for India in two weeks, beaten, I settled for the insurance offer of two thousand dollars, and used it to pay off all our creditors.

On April 20, minus house, furniture, car, debts, pets, books, art, a writing past, and winter clothes, I filled a new steamer trunk with dental floss, plastic plates, toilet paper, chocolate powder and pouches of Tang, Bart's schoolbooks for the year he'd miss, typing paper and a new machine, film, sheets, razor blades, and cosmetics enough for all the female relatives, and sent it off on *The State of Tamilnadu* from the Montreal docks. It was to arrive in Bombay sometime in late May. If I'm alive to collect it, I thought; there'd be fifteen separate plane trips between now and then. It seemed ridiculous to plan even an hour ahead. Would I be the same person there to meet this two hundred pounds of potential trash at the other end? (That too will be a joke. The *Tamilnadu* will dock six weeks late in Bombay because of the backlog of shipping in the Persian Gulf—the Shah is buying an air force, and civilian cargoes just have to wait—and we'll be there in the customs shed with the chief officer who'll order the coolies to take out every item and enter it on a list and there will be general hilarity and disbelief as he calls his brother officers over to inspect the tableful of things: "They come to India from Canada for a year and *this* is what they bring! What is this? For *between* the teeth? For the armpits?")

On the evening of April 23 we flew to Amsterdam on an uncrowded DC-10—before the whole world thought twice about DC-10s, before inflation, Watergate, oil embargoes—when life seemed painfully complicated, but hopeful. My light was on all night as I wrote a fourteen-page response to a set of questions an interviewer had mailed the week before, and I sent it back to Canada the next morning, from a mailbox on the Rembrandtsplein.

Europe bores me now.

We had budgeted time and money for a month in Europe before going on to India: the fresh, tourist-free, springtime Europe of cold drizzle in the north and acrylic blue in the south. Amsterdam to Paris to Geneva to Rome, then up to Hamburg where Bharati's married cousin lives. Another limbo for me; I yearned to get settled in India, and resented every traveler's check converted to francs or lire. A vision of India—or rather, of me *in* India—was ripening. I seemed to see myself learning Bengali stupendously fast and speaking it with friends; I saw myself at Satyajit Ray movies, at concerts and plays in a crisp white *dhoti*. I saw myself eating curry with my fingers. I was looking forward to heat (especially in frigid Paris wearing my Miracle Mart Korean cottons), and for the first time the art of Europe, even of Amsterdam, had been a bore. Back to the dreams of a flat we'd rent, of a worktable strewn with new stories, a novel, a play, this journal—why not? After fourteen pages on a simple plane journey, the whole world again seemed possible.

In Hamburg, the last stop, we checked into a hotel before calling Tulu-didi and Anil. Taking a hotel for a night in Hamburg would prove to be my first Calcutta mistake. It was time for me to start sorting out the multitudes of cousins and keeping their stories straight. Tulu-didi is the daughter of Bharati's father's oldest brother; Bharati and Tulu-didi had spent their first eight years together in the joint-family house on Rash Behari Avenue in Calcutta. Back then, they'd not gotten along very well. Their fathers are still quite distant. My father-in-law had pulled his family out of the joint

family and made them Westernized. Now Tulu-didi had her Ph.D.
in genetics (from British Columbia) and works on yeast mutations
for the university. She is the mother of two, and Anil, a Dr. Banerjee
in genetics, has a substantial and enviable position with the German
Government. Their courtship and marriage in Vancouver had been
the first irregularity in the joint family; the first love match in the
family's history. The night before we left they took us to Reeper-
bahn for a night of Wein, Wurst, and merriment. Our sets of children got along; Bart saved his impetuous little "cousin-brother" from
possible drowning in a lake. Their twelve-year-old daughter read my
book on the first afternoon and offered a sobering commentary. One
could see in their two children the making of genius: the fluent
triligualism, the expectation of spectacular results, the absolute intolerance of anything less than excellence. Dipali, the girl, having
exhausted all English-language facilities in Hamburg, was cramming
for entrance examinations to a British public school. Their six-year-
old son read and wrote Bengali, German, and English as well as
Bart did English. Dipali's cramming could have carried her into an
American university. By Bengali standards they were acknowledged
as "clever" children, though terribly uncultured and Westernized.
By unwelcome comparison, our children—and yours—are gentle,
whimsical analphabets.

They gave us the names and addresses of their closest friends in
Calcutta, a doctor-couple who had studied with them in Vancouver.
Added to relatives and Bharati's old schoolmates of fourteen years
before, they would be the only Calcutta contacts we had.

On Saturday evening we left for Bombay. We passed through
Athens just two days before a Palestinian group shot up the lounge,
by mistake, killing five and wounding twenty.

From the moment we landed, India conspired to write this journal. It was a bleached-out Sunday morning, May 13, 1973, in the
worst month of the year, when the monsoons have not yet "broken"
and the reserves of power, water, food, and the boundless tolerance
of the people are all nearly spent. It was nine in the morning, the
temperature already climbing into the hundreds, the sky cloudless
but not really blue: too much pollution, too much dust, too much
pitiless glare.

Santa Cruz Airport is a good place to start. The name is Portuguese, the reality Indian. It is served by most of the world's major carriers—Lufthansa, British Airways, Sabena, TWA, Iran Air, Swissair, Alitalia, KLM, Japan Air—and the runways gleam with 747s, Caravelles, and the various smaller Boeings. There is the requisite gallery for visitors, there are wide glass doors and buses to take you to the arrivals lobby. It is one of the modern, Western faces of Bombay. Of course, there will be more people on the ground than seem strictly necessary, and if you look out on the grass between the runways, instead of at the terminals, you might find whole families stooped in the grass, allegedly cutting, but really just squatting and watching. And if you had been watching intently just before you glided over the last roadway behind a high muddy wall topped with broken glass, you would have seen some of the most squalid *chawls* of suburban Bombay. Against the airport walls they prop two sides of whatever material will stand—tin, wood scraps, cans, old movie posters—and more of the same is piled on the top and weighted with stones. Waterless, drainless, lightless, in essence roomless, these are where the grass-cutters and "bearers" live. The several worlds of India, then: the borrowed West of the sideburned, aviator-goggled, Fu-Manchu-mustached ground crew, the 747s, the computers and telexes, and just outside, the ancient, unchanged spectacle of raw endurance.

And then one enters the Third World of India. Apart from technology and the eternal poverty, there is the bureaucracy. Passing through Indian customs can be a formidable operation, simply because so many people have particular roles to play. It is not a question of harassment, of opening the baggage and searching; Indian officialdom cares very little for people—only for paper. One passes through three or four separate rows of tables and each row either collects or distributes a new form. Before one can gather his baggage he will have been processed in several ways, all of them time-consuming and self-perpetuating; whatever is given out must be laboriously entered, stamped, and then collected. On that thermal Sunday of May 13 we selected a line in which we were third; nevertheless it took an hour to get past the desks to claim the bags. Each officer in white, with epaulettes and short pants, has a peon in khaki whose function it is, like an O.R. nurse, to hand him what he asks for or to anticipate it: to fill the ubiquitous fountain pen, to present the blotter, to lay out the proper papers in the designated order for the stamping and initialing, to scurry about to bring new batches of forms. All the while we are looking over the heads of hundreds of passengers for Bharati's parents frantically waving. They are out there, past a cluster of white-capped Muslim hajis, back from Mecca; the affectionate India waiting to receive us and make sense and comfort out of this mad first impression.

The white uniforms play their role carefully. They enjoy conversations with their peers, and show varying degrees of authority and affection with their old, unshaven peons ("*Pané deo, jaldi, jaldi*"— "Bring water, fast, fast"), during which time all work ceases. This is not meant to upset us, I am sure. It is serene. If it went any faster, the whole system would break down somewhere else.

Everything that a subtle analysis of India might reveal is present in this first encounter: contrasts, hierarchies, discomfort, and small abuses; dignity, abasement, protocol, theater, humor, affection. The uniforms: *white* that cannot be rushed or questioned; *blue* that guards, distributes, and collects; *khaki* that serves and carries. Fascinating, but in 105° with *Wurst, Bier,* and *gebratenes* Huhn and a sleepless night to churn it up, best contemplated under a fan, behind dark curtains.

When we finally got through, one bag was missing—mine. Fu Manchu filled in the tracer, assuring me it was still on the plane and was fated for a quick trip to Singapore before coming back. The children were already out beyond the barriers, smothered in the thick cool arms and sari folds of their Dodoo and Mommy-di, and Bharati joined them while I made my way upstairs to the Swissair offices— welcome blast of air conditioning—to describe the bag and its contents. All my clothes, my tapes, my film, all of Bart's clothes. Messrs. Mazmoudar, Fonseca, Gidwani, and Raman; the secretaries, Miss Chan and Miss Printer. I was alert enough to Indian names to know Gujarati, Goans, Sindhis, Keralans, and Parsis when I saw them, but also to wish an end to *too* much significance at once. I only wanted my suitcase. I promised to call that night; they promised to have my bag. Back down in the baggage area, I noticed an unclaimed bag like mine, same make, slightly smaller, but with Air-Kuwait insignia. I vaguely suspected something, but foolishly yielded to official assurances.

At that moment, my bag was with someone's illiterate servant, on his way to a train station en route to a village in Gujarat. In India, despite Fu Manchus and 747s, everything eventually proceeds at the rate of its slowest member.

It is Sunday, shortly after midday. The rest of the family has fallen asleep in the high, dark bedroom, under the fan that scatters lint. I couldn't sleep on the plane or in the house. I've had the first of two thousand cups of tea that I will have in the next year; I have read that morning's copy of the *Times of India* (its pages duller than on my first visit three years ago, almost preyellowed) and I think I have noticed creeping Americanisms from the last visit. "Truck" instead of "lorry," as well as the irreplaceable Indianisms: *Trucks Turn Turtle on Agra Road* and *Godowns Raided.* I have showered, and I have flushed away my last European meal.

I am standing outside of Dodoo's bungalow, part of a row on a high red hill overlooking a chemicals factory in a distant suburb of Bombay called Chembur. The air of Chembur is normally gray, even in these cloudless weeks before the monsoon, and the odors depend on prevailing winds from the chemical plants, fertilizer factory, and three major refineries. Something yeasty and slightly sour, other times cloying and toxic, like the clouds of DDT they used to spray in my childhood Florida, other times, and least offensive, an odor like burnt brown sugar.

The palm tree in the driveway makes a sharp dry rustle. With a single reptilian "caw" a long-tailed magpie drops from the tree, and for a second, under that black and white plumage, I sense an archaeopteryxian snakebird. The whole scene: brown, papery leaves, the blasted red clay hills that jut from the marshy shore with the jagged improbableness of a Japanese silk screen, the low gray "clouds" that are fumes of poisonous smoke, and the fiery smokestacks of the neighboring factories, combine with sleeplessness, to make me feel part explorer, part time-traveler.

Later that afternoon the boys, Dodoo, the driver, and I go to the nearest Bata store to buy some sandals. Sunday is another workday in the distant suburbs of Bombay; only in Christian areas and in the major offices are Sundays respected.

No trouble finding sandals for the kids, but for me there will be. Just being white and being in Sion brings families to our car, or causes them to stare into the Bata window as we shop. I slip out of my Hamburg loafers bought just yesterday and peel off the nylon socks that are already making wet footprints on the brown tiles. Is it awe, incredulity? The clerks gather to see feet that are albino white, toenails pink, foot rims red from so much heat, feet that suck and slurp, farting moistly as I walk. Each society has a way of shaming the fat; here, my girth is a virtue but it's my feet that make them smile.

I walk out sockless, with sandals, and by the time we reach the car I can feel blisters beginning on the sole. The kids have gone with Dodoo to buy a scooter, and I am left to stand with the bearded, khaki-clad driver, not yet knowing that he speaks English well enough to chat with. I want to understand it all; I am benevolently disposed toward everything.

We are standing in the parking lot in the middle of Sion Circle, a major node on the Bombay Road. There are no traffic lights, of course, cars and buses, scooters and handcarts all rumble, zip, whizz, and roll with a graceful recklessness. I see Bart and Bernie holding a bright red scooter, with the grinning bulk of Dodoo behind them, waiting to cross.

They can't see what I do. From the corner food store, two boys just their age come to the sidewalk with a limp jute sack, and from the sack they extract a long string of dead, puppy-sized rats, their tails entwined with rope, and one by one the rat bodies are extracted and thrown high over the traffic circle where they fall like volley balls, bouncing off the roofs and hoods of passing cars to the glee and laughter of the children, until they finally land, light as feathers, on the gummy asphalt.

I tell myself I don't care. That very morning I had opened the refrigerator and swept cockroaches off the bowls of food inside before I ate, and I had thought more of the problems of insulation and of ice trays so warm that roaches can nest.

We all piled into the car, happy in the heat, and I was pleased to keep it to myself. There was hope for me yet.

## 2

Bombay is built on a long, narrow peninsula, like the dangling neck of a mythic diving bird. To the west is the unbroken blue of the Arabian Sea; to the east, the deep narrow harbor. The head of that diving bird is downtown Bombay. Call the beak Nariman Point, Cuffe Parade, where the city and the state are reclaiming some acres at enormous cost from the sea. The neck is a good fifteen miles long, from Nariman Point where the land sells for over a thousand dollars a square foot, up to Chembur at the swampy head of Bombay Harbour, where the mud flats are deserted eight months of the year and underwater the other four. Bombay Harbour is deep and busy, in no danger of silting up, like Calcutta's, making Bombay the gate of India. And for Indians, making Bombay the window to the West.

Bombay is named for its harbor, the *bom baim* of the Portuguese sailors.

Along the ocean front, Marine Drive stretches five miles from Nariman Point in a wide sweep to Malabar Hill. Unbroken miles of five-story apartment buildings, sea-facing, pastel-painted (though often rusting and peeling) with enough palms in the skimpy yards to give a sense of a slightly seedy Cannes. But still a solid high-society address. The buildings all have names: Hindu deities mixed with Malibu Beach and a touch of Lisbon, a mélange of names that is typical of India. The apartments break occasionally for hotels and airlines offices, Western restaurants and milk bars, cricket fields, colleges, the aquarium.

It is possible to live in Nariman Point, Marine Drive, Pedder Road, Cumballa Hill, Malabar Hill, and to work in the newer office buildings where Air-India, Bank of America, and a number of other giant corporations are putting up creamy skyscrapers, and not have to contend with the "other" India. Displacement capital on the São Paulo model, that simply banishes the bustees, chawls, and street dwellers' bedrolls with twenty million dollars' worth of five-star luxury, as the new Sheraton-Oberoi is reported to have cost.

Perhaps the confidence it creates is also worth the social costs. One can sit for hours outside the Air-India Building and be free at last of the impoverished, infernally cluttered, endlessly demanding India. One can sit in astonishment of the moneyed young, the gleaming cars, the ever-present policemen enforcing the parking ban, and feel that, yes, India will pull through. A beggarwoman in tattered sari and matted hair would be as out of place here as she would be at a country club. This *is* a country club. You could pass your life in these apartments and offices, shopping for the latest clothes in the Air-India concourse, reading the London and New York papers flown in one day late, using only English, reading about yourself and your friends in the self-absorbed fashion and gossip magazines, and be living one Indian version of the Western good life, more comfortably and more compulsively than any American would dare to.

Compulsive, because Nariman Point and the people it creates are still a fragile structure. Not only is the land reclaimed, the new men who use it may also lack a bedrock. Bombay wealth is comparatively new, unlike Calcutta's. Nariman Point is an act of will, development from above, scattered almost symbolically over nothing but water. The *Times of India* "Annual," in commenting upon Bombay's urban development, argues that "an Asian city should have a low profile" allowing everyone access to the sky, simply because the costs of structural steel, concrete, electrical, and water services that go into a high rise push up the unit cost of rooms by astronomical factors. The capital-intensive investments of Nariman Point inflate land values so grossly and concentrate municipal services so intensely that the areas they touch remain forever closed to the poor and the middle class. In a purely socialist state they would have no place; in a Brazil there'd be no question. India, as always, must answer both sets of critics.

Inland a kilometer lies the old business heart of Bombay: Flora Fountain (which is dry), Fort, Colaba, Kolagura, where the old government offices and the British banks have their quarters and the buildings are Victorian-Indian: high-ceilinged, poorly lit, overstaffed, with rows of overhead fans maintaining a breeze that can almost be felt. The sidewalks around the fountain are wide, cracked, and teeming: The old six-story sandstone buildings of the last century accommodate themselves over the "footpath" resulting in endless arcades of one-man shops that line both sides of the shaded sidewalk. Belts, socks, shirts, ties, appliances, mechanical toys, fried and roasted

foods, sugar-cane presses, watermelon vendors, and all the various
Philips and Braun products lifted from ships and offered to the foreign sailors; ten feet of faded John Creasey, Alistair MacLean, and
Agatha Christie titles mixed with recondite strays from discarded
law, history, and stenographic libraries; American Express, department stores, food stores, druggists, specialty shops, sari shops, India
crafts, sandal makers, *pan-wallahs* offering their succulent cold betel
leaves, ill-lit restaurants not catering to Western trade, men's stores,
cinemas, camera stores, Khadi Industries, Handloom House, an art
gallery, a stationer's; people of every age and every community and
every social class all in a hurry, and the din from a thousand taxis
honking and a thousand vendors calling to every customer as he
walks. Yet in that crowded avenue of hawkers and walkers, people
still sleep. Others sit and beg. No one moves them, or complains.
One is rarely touched. Life is flow in India, everything moves,
though it moves at its own pace. In the true center of Bombay the
streets cannot be cleared.

This is where I began to love it. It was because I learned quickly
that in India commerce and community are the same thing, and
both are of the street. Where commerce disappears urban India becomes pale and hideous. India alerted me again to the basic social
value, buying and selling—knowing goods and providing goods—the
original reason that people came together.

If you continue across the diving bird's head to the harborside,
you come to the miles of docks, all enclosed by high gray walls. It is
an area of shipping offices, naval yards, of sturdy naval officers on
scooters in their crisp white uniforms, short pants, and knee socks.
Once again, the crowds thin out just as they do on the oceanside at
Nariman Point; there is no street commerce, the people here all have
a purpose, they all belong indoors.

All three parts of central Bombay were to become as familiar to
me as downtown Montreal, yet, as a cross section of Bombay, it was
no more typical of the city than a drive across Manhattan on Forty-
second Street would be. It is merely the tourist's Bombay, from the
Sheraton-Oberoi (so loving and vulgar a reconstruction of Miami
Beach as to be forgivable), to American Express with its horde of
black marketeers in front, to Cottage Industries Emporium on the

harborside, where the doorman shoos away the beggars and urchins who wait for the tourists as they descend from the taxis, chartered coaches, and chauffeured limousines.


### 3

What is the "real" Bombay, the real India, the real anything for a fiction writer? Digging deeper, you learn that Bombay's name is derived from *Mumbai*, in turn derived from the goddess Maha Amba. Doubtless, both origins are true. When my first book came out, I was asked the differences (as an American-raised Canadian) between Canada and the States, and all I could say was "texture." The textures of American and Canadian life are as proximate as separate societies can be, but if fiction has eyes and ears, attention to texture will disclose the difference. And if the writer cares enough, the "similarities" will be seen to have been as superficial as those between sugar and salt. To present texture and design without distortion was the job of fiction as I understood it. And it was the only way I had to present India. Between Canada and the United States you had to stand very close; you had to take in everything.

But India. Start at Nariman Point, where India comes as close in texture to America as it ever can. Listen again to young moneyed India in their latest Western clothes, flying off to London, New York, Kuwait, or the Gulf emirates, and watch them doing small things in public with their girl friends—rubbing their backs, patting bottoms, even holding hands—that would cause riots and bloodshed in a village. Listen to the men: *Hey, man, where you been keepin' yourself? All over, man,* and as a writer devoted to texture, you might notice that the faultless slang is spoiled just slightly by the men holding hands as they talk, by the girl pulling her sweater down and patting herself in the tummy, holding her cigarette out five minutes waiting for a light. The men's shoes gleam like molten glass. The girl looks unsteady on her elevated sandals. His shirt front is too tight, buckling around each button; these rounded Gujarati men aren't *that* suited to French and Italian styles. Under high enough power, watched long enough, all the uncertainties of middle-class Bombay could be reconstructed through such minute details.

At the other extreme, one could choose a village or an urban *chawl*. Suddenly the lens would have to be reversed. How far back can the writer stand before the differences make any sense? An old Muslim took me to his *chawl*. He pointed to a gray-haired woman in her fifties who brought him his lunch bag then shyly backed away. "That my number five daughter, *saab*," he said. A woman my age came closer to inspect me. "That my number three wife, *saab*." *Baas*, enough. Too much distortion, dizziness sets in. In the snake house of the Calcutta Zoo, I saw sixteen villagers. They walked like a herd of frightened animals, in a circle, each tied by finger to sari, or sari to sari, behind three male leaders. Their eyes were round, unblinking, deeply socketed, and profoundly wrinkled; it was like looking into the eyes of sad old apes. Their faces were terror-struck, some prayed. Some stumbled, for they were walking backward protecting the rear flank. Those coarse clothes, leathery breasts, naked babies clinging to the throats of mothers who could have been twenty but looked fifty-five, the guttural language that eluded everyone's understanding—that was the *real*, the landless, diseased, illiterate India that seems almost obscene to invade or interrupt. They moved through the snake-house crowds of Calcutta like a vast gray amoeba, three elders striking out like pseudopodia while the others filled in behind. One is always aware in India that *they*, that indefinable, unknowable, and unpredictable mass is out there, violent, suffering, simple, and passive, but no one in the cities really knows what can be done for them. They are from a different era. So nothing is done.

For a Westerner, there is enough unknown even on the steps of the Air-India Building, or with friends and family, and especially on the streets of any Indian city, to satisfy all his tastes for texture and design. To seek more is greed. *Bom baim, Mum bai*. Trust only texture.

4

Worli, Dadar, Mahtunga, Sion, Chembur: nodes along the north-south axis connecting the head and the neck of that ravenous diving bird to the suburbs and beyond, to India. Americans think of "suburb" as a refinement of the city: broader lawns, nicer homes, freckle-faced boys delivering the evening paper. When Vietnam news used to mention "fighting in the suburbs" or "bombing in the suburbs," I wonder what impression the audience had—men hiding on golf courses, alien soldiers tripping over tricycles? Nothing would surprise me.

Indian suburbs are self-contained markets surrounded by the full society that Indian commerce gathers: schools, bazaars, temples, churches, mosques, roads, shops, cinemas, rooms, and people, millions of people. Each "suburb" is a miniature of the main city itself, sometimes more ethnically or religiously concentrated, connected by train and municipal double-decker to the nominal center. Bombay's suburbs would be viable without a Bombay; like some low organism each suburb could survive alone and could eventually grow a new Bombay. My parents-in-law do not go into the city more than once a year from Chembur, some twenty miles out.

Most suburbs are links between the country and the city. When government statistics announce that "30 per cent of suburban women have heard of birth control," the implication is that an even higher percentage of urban women have, but that it is still practically unknown in the villages. When the filmmaker Satyajit Ray says that "I knew it would do well in Calcutta, but I worried about the *mofussils*," he is expressing the same idea. The suburb is quite literally *sub*-urban, in the process of dropping its village ways and becoming something new. Similarly, "suburban" education, "suburban" health care, "suburban" housing, all refer to the pebble-toss pattern of urbanization and social development that is India's way of dealing with a village culture embracing some 450 million souls that move like that mass in the Calcutta snake house, where they want, as they want, when they want.

Chembur at one time was synonymous with wealth, movie stars, a golf course, a movie studio, a prestigious national project like the Atomic Research Center (at neighboring Trombay), and a few large public and private industrial complexes such as the Fertilizer Corporation of India, Union Carbide, Esso, and the Burmah-Shell refineries.

In the words of the mayor of Bombay, Chembur today is a gas chamber. The air of Chembur is the most densely polluted in the

world. In the six months that I have lived in Chembur (in 1970 and
1973–74), I have never seen a blue sky, only a high white glaze, or
gray, depending on the season. The air smells permanently of incipi-
ent poisoning. The refineries and the chemical plants light up the
skies with twenty-four-hour flames; the air of Chembur is in permanent suspension with tons of debris. An Indian factory is like a semi-
trailer without a muffler, everything sacrificed for greater production
and hang the side effects. Blowing one's nose, changing one's clothes,
shampooing one's hair, even walking over a just-mopped floor, provide the evidence. I have seen it in shampooing Bernie's hair, the
gray rivulets streaking his back and shoulders; I have watched the
flakes of soot settle on my typing paper as I plan a sentence.

   But it all means employment. Calico Chemicals, where Dodoo is
director of Research and Development, employs two thousand
directly and probably another five thousand by deflection. Temples,
*pan* shops, tea and cigarette stalls, barbers and sandal repairers, tire
patchers, a gas station, a school, are all clustered within a few hundred yards of the gates, and the *chawls* of the workers stretch from
the factory gates to Chembur Bazaar, five miles away, growing ever
denser, more developed and diversified, the closer you get to the center (if anything in India has a "center") of Chembur Bazaar.

   No space in suburban India is wasted. The hard clay between the
road and the swamps supports the vertical stalls of dry-goods "shops"
that can hold little more than the shopkeeper himself, and a few
shelves of cigarettes, drugs, magazines, or whatever. Between the asphalt of the road and the rows of wooden stalls still more vendors
have spread jute mats to display bananas, dried fish, or religious calendars ("Daddy," Bart asked me that first week as we drove past, "is
that man selling flies?"). Children, dogs and donkeys, cows and pigs,
cyclists and thousands of pedestrians, thread their way around the
stalls and mats, squinting at the merchandise, assessing, listening to
prices, and moving on.

   It takes a couple of hours every day to shop for the day's several
meals, and even in the 100° heat and its unchanging rituals, shopping exercised an attraction for me. I could lose myself with Bharati
and Mommy-di, learning slowly to appreciate the shrewdness of
judgment, the elaborate seductiveness that must have been part of
all commerce, in the beginning.

On the roadside, rows of rusted metal carts are pushed every afternoon to the market site, and piled high with giant woven baskets (called *tokris*) of mangoes, beans, bananas, squash, okra, melon, and others I do not recognize. The name of the "merchant" is painted on the wheel rims—and he squats or stands beside it for as long as it takes him to sell everything; seven or eight hours at least. If he has no cart, he piles his produce like shiny green cannon balls on jute sacks or banana leaves, restacking them carefully after each sale. Orderliness within the jumble. Nothing is more appealing; the most appetizing sight in the marketing world is an Indian bazaar, with those lovingly tended mounds of vegetables, every texture and shade of green, knowing they were picked that morning and must be sold that day. I sandal my way gingerly around the leaves and mats, watch the naked children squatting as their fathers do, wetting the unsold vegetables from a pail of dusty water. Other kids with greasy rags begin polishing our car, meticulously rubbing all they can conveniently reach (since the car is dusted every morning and there has been no rain in six months, it is already shining brightly, and so the driver shoos them away). Frustrated as car polishers, they begin begging, reciting long verses in a croupy voice punctuated with *saab* and *babu* in a rhythm reminiscent of a Hail Mary. The driver flicks a rag at them and they back off.

Farther off the road are the permanent stalls with hand-painted signs in the inimitable Indian manner, mixing scripture and salesmanship in ways that seem exuberantly pious and scandalously blasphemous at once, like the "furniture ecclesiastiche" shops near the Vatican and the overworked grotto pictures in Quebec. Closer to the center the vegetable markets disappear, to be replaced by dry-goods wagons, and now the main road is paved and the roadside buildings are substantial enough to boast doors and barred windows (there is still no glass in Chembur Bazaar); on the upper floor there may be flats, a tailor shop, maybe a doctor's office. On the ground floor there may be a cinema, a pharmacy, or even a "cold storage" outlet specializing in sausages and frozen chickens (these would be Parsi or Christian stores; there are some well-to-do Goans in Chembur). The edge of the road will still be lined with handcarts piled high with lingerie, towels, old books on shorthand or constitutional law, old Phantom and Tarzan comic books. There is, as yet, no danger of a sudden rainstorm spoiling the displays in a Bombay May. There are carts heaped with sandals, tightly wound belts, fountain pens, girls' dresses, boys' socks, windup toys, in an unbridled display of faith in the failure of all birth control.

A perfect market situation exists in an Indian suburb. Everything must be bought fresh every day, since there is virtually no refrigeration. The same staple foods are cooked every day—there is plenty of spice to Indian cooking, without adding variety as well. The wife goes out at the same fixed hour every day. She must walk, and she will not walk any farther than necessary. Therefore, the same number of people buy the same amount of food every day from the same selection of vendors. The vendor knows how much to stock, how much defective merchandise he can unload on the poor and unwary, how much he can wheel around in the early morning to the homes of a choicer clientele and how much to keep for the heavy afternoon trade, and he knows how long in the night, under his naphtha lamp, he will have to stay before he sells it all. Then he will push his cart to his own *chawl* which can be several miles away (you see them on the main highways at night, returning to their beds, and if you rise early enough, you see them heading to the train stations and truck depots, picking up the merchandise before the sun is up). Physically it is animal work. Economically, perhaps only marginal. But it is the perfect market situation for everyone concerned, the envy of any American outlet. Commerce is community, community is commerce. Scratch an Indian and you find a businessman. Even Indian professors in the West sometimes offer to do a little import-export. It is not solely greed; it is a natural part of middle-class self-expression.

We turn at the high steel gates, the khakied guards salute us, we drive honking all the way through the factory and its twelve major buildings, and make the final turn up the steep, naked hillside to the row of directors' bungalows on top. We honk long and loud outside and Rajan, the house servant, comes running out to help the driver unload. Bart and Bernie run inside to grab a cold Coke. We enter Dodoo's house to have our showers, brew some tea, eat sweets and the crisp, spiced South Indian *muri* (puffed rice), and to read to the children. And to wait the endless hours for Dodoo to come up from the office bearing mail, if any, and for family life to begin, once the father is home.

5

He is my father-in-law, Bart and Bernie's Dodoo. He is in his middle
sixties, a fat, vigorous social mastodon of a man whose body is soft,
smooth, and luminous as buckwheat honey. The children love to
tumble over it. I think of him as a furnace of affection, stuck perpet-
ually on high. If it is possible to love too hard and too possessively,
he does. In India, to love is to control several destinies, even to dictate; love can be a tyranny. The cliché about the joint family, "in
times of trouble, a fortress; otherwise, a prison," is a saying of people
like ourselves who lead troubled lives and who could not trade their
troubles for imposed solutions. And so, respectful as I am of solutions and people who can impose them, I will never understand
Dodoo, respectful though I am of all that he stands for.

One night over the nightly round of domestic scotch and beer,
after his bath and two hours of prayer, as we sat in the living area of
the basement waiting for the nine o'clock English news and then the
enormous dinner, Dodoo (topless, in *pajama* bottoms, smoking in
the wheezing Indian manner while the ice cubes melted in his glass
and his grandchildren climbed on his shoulders and slithered over his
paunch to his lap, and while Mommy-di sat on the garden swing
that now serves as the living room sofa) told me the story of his life.
He knows it is a special life.

His *desh*, that all-important Bengali word that means more than
just birthplace, was in the district of Faridpur in what is now Bangla
Desh. He was born in 1909, the second son in a family of ten, two of
whom became premature statistics. His father was a policeman; his
older brother bought into lumber mills in Assam and did quite well.
His next-oldest brother was a radioman who went to sea, then returned about ten years ago, unwilling to leave again. He now stays in
his Calcutta flat with his wife and three daughters. The next pair of
brothers live by their wits in Calcutta as agents for just about anything. The youngest two manage their oldest brother's holdings in
Assam. The lone surviving sister is partially supported by Dodoo. He
alone received an education, and possessed the traditional Bengali
ambition to become a professional man.

In 1935 he received his Honour's Degrees (B.S. and M.S.) in chemistry. His arranged marriage to a seventeen-year-old Dacca girl named Bina Chatterjee then followed, and in 1936 a first daughter, Mira, was born. The three of them lived in a room in his father's house on Rash Behari Avenue in the south Calcutta section of Ballygunge. Bina's parents moved from Dacca about this time and rented a flat near the intersection of Rash Behari and Southern avenues, about a mile away by tram. Even today the remnants of both families—the oldest brother and his wife, Mommy-di's infirm mother and her two brothers—still rent at the same respective addresses.

In 1936 Calcutta was still the leading city of British India; the most sophisticated, and perhaps most world-minded city in Asia. Dodoo applied to the University of Heidelberg for additional research, was given a German scholarship, and then was granted the University of Calcutta's traveling scholarship for doctoral work at the University of London. His young family stayed back in his father's house, his wife serving her mother-in-law in the traditional way, and learning to despise it, in the traditional way. Dodoo, then slim, full-featured, and brilliant, sailed for Germany.

His father died about a week later. Perforated ulcer, premature Bengali death; in India the generations whirl with staggering rapidity. As the educated son, as a father and husband, it was Dodoo's traditional duty to return home immediately, accept whatever position his two Indian degrees would earn him, and contribute to the education and support of the rest of the family. His brother (now head of the family) and his mother wanted to wire him at Aden to turn around. According to Chatterjee family legend, Mommy-di and her father urged against it. Apparently their counsel was taken, and Dodoo was left to puzzle out his father's death for himself, from Germany.

It is hard to imagine an Indian chemistry student in Heidelberg in 1936; in blackest Nazi Germany, at the Nürnberg rallies, cheering the speeches of Hitler, involved with the student politics. Hard to imagine a Nazi scholarship. He studied, and thrilled to the nationalism of Nazi Germany. He begs me now to understand his feelings, and I can. He was a young Bengali weaned on the rhetoric of Indian nationalism and independence, and on a hopeless kind of love and hatred for the British. As a Brahmin Bengali he was never much taken with that form of pacifism preached by a *bania* Gujarati who ate with untouchables. He wanted *force*. Most Bengalis gave their allegiance to Subhas Chandra Bose, leader of the Indian National Army, a charismatic apostle of violence who finally perished in a plane crash with his Japanese allies in 1945. Depression-era Germany was a model of power, prosperity, and self-confidence. He would not be much disturbed by a racist police state (nor, in truth, would many Indians of his age and class) so long as he, personally, was not affected. Nazi rhetoric and prejudice were easily absorbed into prevailing Indian patterns, and what remained was a new and dazzling vision of a united people drunk on economic, political, and military success. The rise of Nazi Germany fired his own nationalism, as it did for millions of other Indians who had never left.

After a year in Heidelberg he went on to London to finish his doctorate, there to work in pharmaceutical chemistry. His work, apparently, was brilliant—I've been told by professors in Montreal that it is still considered classic. He returned to Calcutta in 1939. Bharati was born a year later, Ranu three years after that. They were still in the *jethoobari* (house of the oldest paternal uncle) on Rash Behari Avenue. He started a small pharmaceutical factory with a hustling immigrant business partner; they were too poor, the story goes, to afford stools for the research director, S. L. Mukherjee, Ph.D. Lon., to sit on. Life went on absolutely as usual, with Dodoo inventing the medicines, the young mother and the three little girls playing in the courtyard of the *jethoobari* with their cousins, and taking the tram down to the Southern Avenue *mamabari* (house of the maternal uncles) every Sunday.

In those years the *jethoobari* contained the families of the three elder brothers as well as the four unmarried younger brothers, the widowed grandmother, a mad sister, her husband and four children, servants and cooks (only Brahmin cooks can cook a Brahmin's food, and special cooks and kitchens had to be provided for the widowed *taku-ma* whose vegetarian food had to be kept separate from the rest of the family's), numerous hangers-on and vaguer relations who had followed the family from some remote part of East Bengal and earned their right to food and sleeping space. The house, like all things in India, is today precisely as it was forty years ago, though nearly empty. *Jethoo* is now seventy-three; he lives there with his wife and the families of his two sons, though the sons have chosen to live closer to their jobs. The daughters have moved much farther away; Tulu-di is in Hamburg. Another has married a communist lawyer and is rarely seen in the *jethoobari*. The Runyonesque brothers left the house years before and have returned only once—for the funeral services of their mother. As with all traditional structures in India—the country, the politics, the religion, the family—the house was elastic, capable of containing a small army of inhabitants, without appearing saturated. There were over forty in 1947. Now, at most, there are eleven. *Jethoo* and *jethi-ma* spend much of their time in prayer; the rows of gods and the shelves of pictures take up a wide corner of the ground floor.

By 1947, with Independence, the pharmaceutical factory was turning a profit. Dodoo was a famous man in that year of India's freedom—it must have been a great year to be young, rich, brilliant, and Indian—to feel the future laid out before you like an American Adam. He was to be one of the heroes of the new India. He wanted to build up his company, serve his country by eradicating TB, and win a Nobel Prize, all at the same time. It was the moment of the most intense confidence and idealism that the country would ever know. India would break free of its past and not make the mistakes of any other nation; it would take the best from every system.

Then came the first great change. Problems in the partnership. Dodoo resigned, moved his family out of the *jethoobari*, and out of India altogether.

He decided to settle in London to pursue research. The partner rushed to London to apologize. The crisis was averted, Dodoo returned to the company, to head up its London office. They moved into a flat on elegant Half Moon Street and the girls were placed in stiff little private schools where they first learned English, then carried off the prizes. They stayed three years; Bharati passed her eleven-plus exams and was pursued by a boy named Robert, the son of the Polish ambassador. Then came an offer to do research in Basel; again the family moved, the girls were placed in German schools, and for another year the life of exotics-abroad continued. Dodoo was continuing to publish papers (he had about twenty-five to his credit, as well as three dozen drug patents); the daughters were as brilliant as he, and the money was never a problem.

Perhaps he finally tired of feeling foreign. Perhaps he felt he had delayed his rewards too long; it was time to go home and start collecting. The partner wanted him in Calcutta.

They returned in 1951. By now the factory compound contained mansions, lakes, swimming pools, the world of Bharati's novel *The Tiger's Daughter*. The girls were placed in Loreto Convent School (strictly English-medium) on Theatre Road just off ultra-fashionable Park Street. Every day they were driven the twenty miles in and back in a monstrous black Dodge by two men—one a driver who could not leave the car, and the other a sidewalk escort who could not drive. Bharati remembers five years of drives in the hot black Dodge, seeing nothing of the life-swarms of Calcutta passing the rolled-up windows, her head throbbing with headaches that have not left her to this day. Five years of rising at five o'clock to study, playing roles in Gilbert and Sullivan, learning perfect elocution and waiting for graduation, then university, and finally an arranged marriage to a wealthy Bengali Brahmin professional man, named Banerjee, Chatterjee, Bhattacharya, Ganguli, or Chakravorty. It was all laid out, so simply.

They vacationed in Puri and Gopalpur-by-the-Sea; they went to Darjeeling in the Himalayas and rode ponies. Their house was a museum of heavy furniture left behind by fleeing Europeans. Dodoo enjoyed the good life: liquor and cigars, lavish parties, being respected by scientists and being admired as a conspicuous Bengali in a Calcutta business world dominated by hated, nonindigenous Marwaris. I can imagine him in this role, even tonight in 1973 with his grandchildren clinging to his neck, under a dusty fan in a Bombay bungalow. I can picture it because he is still the furnace, the heat source in any room: booming, proud, imperious, xenogenic. He has the gift of expressing affection, that exaggerated forcefulness of a powerful man in a fragile country.

Everything ended suddenly in 1958. The partnership dissolved; both sides sued, bands of workers loyal to Dr. Mukherjee or to the partner clashed on the factory grounds, and the army was forced to move in. A new partner took over the factory, and after years of litigation Dodoo was partially compensated. But everything was lost—

home, pools, furniture. He was fifty, out of work, in debt, with three daughters to marry off. Suddenly their marriage value had plummeted. He wandered to Benares, the holy city, to pray. A *sadhu* discovered him, told him an offer would soon come that he must accept. The *sadhu* warned him against despair and retirement from the world; it was not yet time. And an offer did come—to manage the pharmaceutical division of the Sarabhai chemical complex. In 1959 they left Calcutta for good, to settle in Baroda, in the western state of Gujarat.

Mira was already out of college and had applied to an early-childhood training institute in Detroit. Ranu, then sixteen, was accepted to Vassar on scholarship; she left but was back by Christmas, too homesick to continue. Bharati, always the docile and pliable middle child, stayed in Baroda (as a sophisticated Calcutta girl, she despised it), and took her M.A. in English at the university, getting the only "First Class First" ever awarded. But she wanted to be a writer, and from the chance remark of a visiting Ford Foundation lecturer heard that the University of Iowa had a famous "Writer's Workshop." How marvelously American, she must have thought: They can turn out anything. She received a scholarship for the following September, so in the fall of 1961 she and Ranu, trying again at Vassar, arrived in America; the two most protected women American colleges would ever see.

Ranu was again home by Christmas, but Bharati stayed. Ranu would complete her B.A. and then her M.A. (getting the second "First Class First" ever awarded), and finally her Ph.D. (on Faulkner), all from Baroda, and she would marry Vijay, a non-Brahmin, non-Bengali assistant sales manager with a degree in business administration, and she would become the third professor among Dodoo's daughters. All three daughters of S. L. Mukherjee have made headstrong love matches; all three are better educated than their husbands, and the two who live outside of India—cruel irony—earn more than their husbands.

In 1967 Dodoo was shifted to the Bombay (Chembur) complex of the same chemical company, and there he became the head of Research and Development for the Plastics Division. He earns a substantial salary, pays no rent, and spends nothing on entertainment or travel. The man who loved to party, who saw the world, who rode the crest of Indian idealism and lost it all, now prepares processes for clear plastic bottles, detergents, and Metrecal substitutes for the obese and affluent. His heart is still in research, in ending tuberculosis.

"Remember?" he says to Bharati, whom the family calls Mex. "Remember how you wanted me to win the Nobel Prize? Now I want *you* to get it. The Nobel Prize for Literature, Mex. You must think of nothing less."

## 6

A low overhang keeps away the sun and rain and protects the car. Sun and rain are the only meteorological facts of Bombay life. It is a spacious bungalow for just two people: two bathrooms, three bedrooms, a roomy downstairs that divides easily into a living-and-dining area, a kitchen, and a storage room. The downstairs opens onto an untamed thicket of banana plants, flowers, and stands of bamboo. Twice a day the house servant, Rajan, will stand in the middle of it and pour buckets of water over himself. Plastic cord is hung under the wide eaves, and the day's wash (augmented now by my shirts and underwear and the children's wardrobe) will flap ten minutes or ten hours, depending on the season, until it dries. The bungalow is provided free: one of the many "perquisites" built into the Indian business world as a way of getting around the impossibly high taxation.

The convenience is also an imprisonment. From the bungalow to the front gate of the factory is nearly a mile; the bazaar and fish market (a necessity to the Bengali palate) is a good five miles beyond that. And so, though they live on the factory grounds, a car must be kept to drive Dodoo down and up twice a day, and to drive Mommy-di to the various bazaars—fish, vegetables, fruits, liquor, eggs, cigarettes, sweets, medicines, laundry—four times a week. And since neither of them drives, a driver must be kept who will stay on duty ten hours a day, six days a week, for a maximum of two hours' "work" per day, and a likelihood of no more than twenty minutes'.

The driver wears khaki; it is a badge of professionalism. He is a tall, lean, black-skinned, white-bearded Muslim from Bangalore in the South; slow-moving, silent, generally cheerful, and when he carefully unfolds his gold-rimmed reading glasses (he has little to do all day but sit near the car reading his Urdu paper), one can imagine him scholarly. He is paid 250 rupees, (about $30) a month, good pay for a driver and phenomenal for the actual work he does. He has been working for the Mukherjees three years, but it is I who discover in the first week that his name is Bashir, and where he lives ("They stay somewhere near the bazaar," Mommy-di had told me when I asked, pointing to the dusty *chawl* behind the pens where the milk buffalo are kept). It was also up to me to discover that he speaks adequate English and seven Indian tongues (Urdu, Hindi, Marathi, Telugu, Kannada, Malayalam, Tamil) fluently. He enjoys teaching me Arabic script. He encourages us to take trips to Bombay, since he can pocket the two rupees' lunch money we give him. It is he who has the three wives and innumerable children, some of them younger than his own grandchildren, most of them living in the two rooms behind the buffalo pens. He has no clock, and of course no phone; nevertheless he arrives punctually from three miles away at whatever agreed-upon time is set the night before, even if it's four-thirty or five to catch a plane.

He has always been a driver. Back in his native Bangalore ("Beautiful city, *saab*. Climate very nice. Never too hot") he owned lorries. This was before the war; he worked under contract to the British cantonment. He drove all over the South: Madras, Hyderabad, Mangalore, Mysore, Bangalore, and up to Poona and Bombay. Then a new colonel came in. "One day, I drive to cantonment. He says, 'Show me your papers.' I give him papers. He tears papers up. 'There, you've been paid,' he says. I lost my lorries." Twenty-five years ago he came to Bombay to drive the city buses. After twenty-two years he retired and became a private driver. He says he is sixty-four years old.

One shouldn't ask the questions I ask; all the information I've elicited is vaguely useless. Dodoo had little interest in the driver's background. He knew only that he was a Muslim, which explained why he was a good driver, but also why he was given to occasional surliness and unexplained absences.

His job exists because Calico gives its executives a car allowance, and someone is needed to drive Dodoo to work and the *memsahib* to

the bazaar. Neither role is strictly necessary, however, since Calico
provides a daily bus to the bazaar, and Dodoo could get rides down
and up with any of his neighbors. It seems to me more an emblem:
If you have an important job, you must have a car, even if you never
go out. And if you have a car, you must have a driver. Driving, in
India, is for professionals.

The driving habits of a country are gauges of the collective personality. Certainly that's true of America—the lonely commuter pushing his two-ton investment over billion-dollar expressways devoted to
nothing but other investments trying to pass. Helicopters overhead
telling him what to avoid, radio shows, or crashes on the other side
of the highway his only distraction.

Plus the fact we are a country of law-abiders. We believe in red,
yellow, and green. Squeeze. Caution. Stop signs. Crosswalks. Double
lines. Dotted lines. Lanes. Everything in American traffic is strictly
regulated, and accidents are caused, invariably, by definable breaches
of law. We respect priority. My turn, then yours; I trust you to stop;
you move at my expense. In India there is no trust.

An American driver on Indian roads—or worse, an Indian transported to ours—would kill or be killed before coming to his first
corner. There are no stop signs in India. On the twenty-mile drive
from Chembur to the center of Bombay, there are four traffic
lights. American traffic runs on the system of priority; Indian traffic
recognizes only merge. Everything moves, simultaneously, at all
speeds. Since sidewalks, if they exist at all, are often used for selling,
most pedestrians prefer the outer fringes of both lanes. Cows, goats,
donkeys, pigs, are shooed into the road. The hand-drawn carts, the
bullock carts, the bicycles, must take the road. Buses, taxis, scooters,
pedicabs, cycle-rickshaws and (in Calcutta) human rickshaws, take
the road. Private cars and the lorries as well as the smaller vans take
the road. All motorized traffic, then, seeks the center, where congestion is most negotiable. One is always in the middle of the un-
marked road, or even in the other side; one is always confronting
traffic as a potential head-on dilemma. But because the driving pattern is infinitely elastic and the horn gives warning, last-minute
swerving avoids the inevitable. I witnessed many accidents in India,
but never did I see a head-on, or even a dramatic sideswipe.

Pedestrians know that to halt is suicidal, for cars are tracking in behind them. It is a continual sidelong progress, this business of making a turn or merely pulling over to stop and make a purchase. Cars start from the curb without looking; they bolt into the flow. Moving traffic warps around them, into the other lane if necessary. Cars entering from driveways and side streets keep "infiltrating left" without stopping. (Indian traffic, like British, is left-hand.) Actions that would earn assassination in America (honking needlessly, cutting in, tail-gating, U-turning, etc.) are all tolerated, not even remarked upon. The only "rule" seems to be that the car in front of you has every right to turn right or left from any lane, to stop, to U-turn, to swerve, to cut you off as though you do not exist, just as you have that right with the cars behind you.

*Texture, texture.* Compared with an Indian, we drive with one-tenth the awareness of everything around us. Policemen guard certain intersections, occasionally hauling a motorist to the curb—once hauling our driver to the curb—but all infractions are settled summarily with a one-rupee bribe.

Driving in India is a series of close calls, and the magical escapes wrought by drivers leave the Western passenger limp with respect, or with anger. Indian drivers are lucky geniuses—or incompetents. Then you realize it is something more interesting than that; you realize it is a revelation of how easily we apply the word "chaos" to situations that we cannot understand. One drives in India precisely the way one walks the streets, or shops, or prays, or survives the joint family—by keeping an inviolably private core, and cultivating an extraordinary peripheral alertness.

## 7

Rajan is a *chokra*, a Hindi word meaning "lad," quite often reinforced with the English, as in "*chokra*-boy." Chokra is his definition; he cleans, he cooks, he serves. He wears the clothes the Mukherjees give him, eats the food they buy him, sleeps on the floor they provide. Without the Mukherjees, he would be naked, sick, and starving. He was this way when he came to Calico; a scrawny, black, nominally Christian, illiterate Madrasi whose brother had starved to death, whose family could not keep him, and whose village provided no work. The only job he'd held, and perhaps it was not a job but a means of eating, was to scale the coconut trees and knock down fruit, and he remains, at twenty or so, the most agile, spider-quick, and silent man I have ever seen. He catches birds in his hands, lizards, snakes, and roaches; hangs lizards by strands of jute from the lichee tree, outruns soccer balls as they start rolling downhill, climbs to the roofs of houses, up telephone poles and palm trees, to retrieve kites. He is no longer scrawny. And though he speaks no English, he quickly learns the card games that Bart and Bernie play, complicated games like gin rummy and simpler ones like Fish and War, all with a fourteen-word English vocabulary composed of the ten numbers, plus "ace," "jack," "queen," and "king." He figures out the working of Bart's cassette tape recorder, and during the times that he's upstairs supposedly mopping floors, he's also slipping in blank cassettes and recording his own versions of Tamil film songs and a stranger, darker number that we later recognize as "Onward, Christian Soldiers." He learned Hindi within weeks after arriving in Bombay. By our standards he would have to have a genius IQ; by our standards nearly any child on the street would be a genius of anticipation and total recall. I think of it instead as the everyday currency of social survival.

Bombay, halfway up the opposite coast from Madras, is a magnet for South Indians. Rajan made his way here penniless and illiterate, nearly a thousand miles, using a network of "cousin-brothers" from his village or from his district who already had jobs or knew of places that could put him up. One of his village friends, also a Raj, was the *chokra* of another Bengali family in Calico; it was he (always knowing the entire social situation just by observing and talking to the servants) who brought Rajan to Dodoo's door. Without references and little Hindi, he was naturally turned away. Weeks later he returned, offering his services on approval. Finally he was taken in.

Age: twenty or so. Wages: fifty rupees a month (about seven dollars, with equivalent buying power in Bombay), plus clothes, food, and a place indoors. His hours are from 6 A.M., or slightly earlier when the milk is brought, till a little after midnight when the last plates are cleaned, seven days a week. He gets one month off, unpaid. He is treated fondly—the Mukherjees are affectionate employers—although, after a year, he is still not trusted alone in the house. It is he who will bear much of the burden of providing for us; there will be milk to take in early, there will be bland Western food to learn about, two kids to look after, two extra rooms to clean, and another Bengali in the house to cook for.

The Bengali palate is the least easily appeased in all of India. Twice a day there must be full four-course meals with fish and another meat, several kinds of curried vegetables, and elaborate fried desserts. The cooking is done by Mommy-di over a two-burner bottled-gas camp stove. The kitchen is stacked like a banquet hall with interlocking aluminum pots and stainless-steel serving plates with high sides, for Bengali food is wet (*jhol*, or gravy, being all important) and eaten with the fingers after being mixed with rice and squeezed into balls. Without steep sides, plates would spill a river of food over a Bengali table.

The floor of the kitchen is the true work space—traditional wives do not work standing up—there Mommy-di and Rajan will spend several hours of every day, peeling, cutting, and slicing the fish, chicken, fruits, and vegetables over a mounted blade called a *bonthi*. The fine operations of gutting fish, slicing tomatoes, or chopping onions and potatoes are accomplished by shearing the object against that wicked blade, while squatting on the floor in a catcher's crouch. Bent over a *bonthi* is a normal posture for an Indian wife and cook; the acts that we would stand to perform (mopping, chopping, etc.) are all done from that crouch. One often sees Indians resting in such a crouch; the "duck walk" is the natural way of wet-mopping an Indian floor.

Postures of wives and servants: stooped, floor-bound. Out in front, on the paved lane between the two rows of bungalows, the old women "sweepers" make their way, bent perpendicular at the waist, sweeping up dead leaves and dirt. One old sweeper, a strong-faced, almost autocratically gray-haired woman whose neck and midriff are beaded along their myriad cracks and wrinkles, is the mother of Mommy-di's part-time maid and washwoman (a job she does for half a dozen women in the colony). The washwoman is literate, a victim of ill fortune, and as such feels free to engage Mommy-di and Bharati in long conversations as she works. It is Indian soap opera. Her daughter, we learn, has taken up with the husband of one of the other sweepers. The girl, Diamond, is fourteen. Great care is exercised, on the days when she replaces her mother as laundress, to send Rajan far away on errands; even so, a liaison is suspected and much feared. The scandal of a *chokra* misbehaving would reflect badly on the house. The *chokra* is considered almost part of the family, not just a casual employee—no one knows, or cares, for example, what mischief the driver is causing. The *chokra* is a responsibility; he is treated almost like a son. Because he is trusted with so much, and because he is, for eighteen hours a day, an intimate member of the family never out of earshot, he can never be dismissed, or banished, in quite the way maids and drivers can. You have, in a literal sense, saved his life. He is totally dependent on you. He must act as one grateful for such treatment. He has no life outside of yours. The thought that a twenty-year-old "boy" might want privacy or might have lusts is contemptuously dismissed as Western immorality. If he manifests it, out he goes. "They," the laboring classes in general, are evil and lusty fellows, but not the *chokra*. And so, though he is twenty, he is treated as if he were ten, and worked as a man; the bond between master and *chokra* is a complicated one born of duty, affection, and callous indifference.

We can dream of having a 130-hour-a-week, twenty-three-cent-a-day servant as genial, intelligent, and affectionate as Rajan, but with our notions of secrecy and self-reliance we could never tolerate it. We would professionalize the relationship, which he wouldn't understand, or adopt him, which would drive us crazy. The porousness of an Indian house, in which servants are both ubiquitous and unseen, tolerated and abused, is part of a much larger social reality, one that will take me a full year to begin to accept. It is merely one of the first things one notices and one of the most unsettling.

How can you be with a man 130 hours a week and not know his full name, his village, his beliefs, ambitions, his character? The answer is simple: His character, beliefs, and ambitions are reflected in the quality of his work, his loyalty and efficiency. *Baas*. The relationship between master and *chokra* is a caste relation. Men are *not* born equal in the eye of God. Rajan was born to serve; he was born without personal ambitions. It is my duty to provide for him; his duty to serve me faithfully. And it is curiously like the roles within a family itself, for here, too, indulgence and authority, remoteness and proximity, strangely merge.

None of this was quite apparent on that first May Sunday. While the family was sleeping and I stood outside in the ovenlike sun where every object seemed to radiate its special heat, I was aware only of brute economics. The first questions I'd asked once we'd gotten inside were about the servants' hours and wages. I calculated Rajan was making a fraction over a penny an hour. And should he ever ask for more, no matter how loved and trusted he'd become, he'd be fired, for then he would cease to be a *chokra*. He may stay here forever on the terms dictated by Dodoo (marrying on one of his month's vacations home, and then sending his fifty rupees a month back to the village where his wife and the family that grows by one child a year will know how to make it last), but he may never change the relationship nor hope for improvement in wages and conditions. If changes come, they will come from Dodoo. He will share the fate of his master. Both sides know that should he ask for more, there are a hundred million more like him, *just* like him, waiting for a chance to eat like Brahmins, to see the city, and to be protected.

I thought again of Micheline, a girl we'd hired on referral from an agency. And I thought of a girl we'd hired before Micheline, who failed to show up one day and then called from a small-town jail fifty miles outside Montreal. They were holding her on "B & E" (as she delicately put it) and for receiving stolen property. A few days later, when she stopped by the house to turn in her keys, she told me she was a lesbian, a prostitute, and that she was on a maintenance program for heroin addiction.

Perhaps I am extraordinarily trusting; perhaps I am only pathetically innocent. I paid a near-ultimate price for my innocence; the same price, I think, that Indians pay for their extraordinary suspiciousness. There might be a dozen sets of keys to our burnt-down house circulating in Montreal's underworld, and still I laughed at Mommy-di's ring of keys, the twenty minutes' worth of unlocking of cabinets before I could get to anything of value.

8

Dodoo prays three hours every workday, and slightly longer on Sunday. He bathes twice, under that cold shower tap (the most welcome moment of the day is the gush of cool water on Chembur-inflamed skin; if strict water-control measures were not in force and the mosquitoes and roaches could be banished for just a day, I would spend my waking hours sitting on the slimy wooden stool under the stream of undrinkable water), and then retires to the prayer room, sits on a bed in front of the shelves of brass deities, hibiscus blooms, plates of sweets, and framed pictures of South Indian holy men and Bengali philosophers, clad in his *pajama* bottoms, his skin still cool, hair still moist and curled, his sacred Brahmin's thread over one shoulder and under the opposite arm, and places his hands to his forehead, closes his eyes, and begins the *pujah* with its Sanskrit chant, *Narayan, Narayan, na mostu* . . . swaying slightly, and utterly oblivious to my standing behind him. Bart and Bernie run through the house topless in their white *pajama* bottoms, cool after the bath Dodoo has given them, banging pots and pans to awaken the spirits, brandishing incense sticks and thrusting them into every dark corner, shouting, "We are the *pujah* men, we are the *pujah* men. . . ." They too wear *poyta*, the sacred Brahmin's string that Dodoo has tied and blessed and put over their necks, though they are not strictly Brahmins. Strictly speaking, because I am *mleccha*, outside the pale of brahminical civilization, they are untouchable. But that's all right. Hinduism is as flexible as it is rigid. They are honorary Brahmins.

And so our children sit beside Dodoo on the bed, one broad brown back and two frail white ones, all three with sacred strings, all with their hands cupped to their foreheads, two trying to repeat ancient prayers and Bernie content to pray with a phrase of his own, "Lufthansa, Lufthansa, let down your hair," and that too is all right. Dodoo will laugh and repeat, "*Lufthansa, Lufthansa, na mostu* . . ."; nowhere but here does one encounter such insistence on formal ritual, and such delight in diversion from it.

Hinduism does not interpret God, or His world. It does not guide or explain; it expropriates God's perspective rather than man's limited one. Hindu worship is transcendently individualistic; as he loses himself in prayer, Dodoo *is* God. He is participating in the wholeness of the universe. Presumably he then returns to his more limited self with greater harmony. But unlike Western religions, Hinduism does not exclude the worshiper for his unworthiness; it does

not ask him to confess or account for his sins, it does not compel
him to change, renounce, or improve, in order to participate in the
godly vision. To the Westerner, there is something tragic in seeing
starving, ill-clad, and ignorant people worshiping the created world
as though they themselves had created it. Our Western view is so
much more utilitarian: Tell me what I must do to be happy or successful. But in India there is no social message except to pursue one's
karma, making no sacrifices, demanding no changes. The social
world is satisfied by the Brahmin if he prays, by the warrior if he
kills, by the *chamar* if he serves, by the *bania* if he makes money.
Praying and serving and killing and hoarding; no universal injunc-
tions, all are the same in the end.

I once asked Dodoo, over the scotch after the prayers, how he—as
a man of science—could accept all this nonsense about matching
horoscopes and asking astrologers about auspicious days, and he simply told me (surprised that I saw a conflict), "As a man of science, I
put complete faith. Because I do not know *that* science, I cannot say
anything about it. A man of science must keep an open mind, that is
the first law of science. If I reject these things without knowing
them, I am not being true to science."

9

It wears you down, daily life that has a ritual sameness, when the ritual isn't yours. I am used to five or six separate *settings* a day—
home, office, stores, friends, school, and conversations with at least
twenty or so people; Mommy-di isn't. She has Rajan to give orders to
and she sees her husband for three meals but even then they don't
talk, not in our sense. She would not think of using his name; he is
always "he" or "my husband." Mrs. Chatterjee, fellow Bengali, lives
across the road and stops in for tea two or three times a week, and
has done so for six years, but she remains "Mrs. Chatterjee." It
seems to me that in Mommy-di's generation, deep attachment is reserved for family. She lives only for Bharati's visits every three sum-
mers and for Ranu's from Baroda twice a year, and for visits from
her younger brother, *chhoto-mamu*, a government official who fre-

quently visits from Calcutta. Bazaar-shopping is the only real escape from the house, an exhausting way to find distraction.

It is all faintly incredible. Except for accompanying us on our aimless trips downtown, Mommy-di would not see Bombay even once a year. No shopping, no dinners, no entertainment, no Sunday drives in the country, even though they have a car and driver. They subscribe to all the pillars of middle-class India: the *Illustrated Weekly of India*, the *Times of India, Reader's Digest, Eve's Weekly, Femina*; there is no television, and only the nine o'clock English news on the radio. Never have I devoured a paper more thoroughly than the morning *Times*. I'm so new and fresh to this country that everything about it, even its women's mags, municipal politics, Congress party infighting, and accounts of cricket matches, is a fresh delight. But I finish the *Times* by seven-thirty.

Then, nothing. The middle-class fears of going out alone make any trip an ordeal; taxi drivers are lecherous Sikhs who rape unescorted women and rob foreign men, buses are full of pickpockets, stores will all cheat. Child-beggars are professionals, maimed by underworld gangs; older beggars are lepers who spit on the coins in order to recirculate the disease. The sun will kill. Snakes might cross the road. Communal riots might break out at any minute. You'll get lost, and never be heard from. The children will be kidnaped. The middle-class imagination has been terrorized—which is not to say it is groundless—it prefers security to adventure. For a woman who never leaves her house, Mommy-di carries a ring of keys that would do credit to a medieval jailer. The Chatterjees across the road keep a padlocked metal band around their refrigerator, and then store the fridge in their son's room, since the kitchen has no door.

One day our children couldn't be found. The main guardhouse was alerted; the private army of Calico *durwans* were ordered to begin a search. Dodoo's and Mommy-di's blood pressures went up fifty points. Kidnaping was the only explanation—labor unrest is part of every factory, and the clashes between labor and management can become bloody, senseless, and brutal. Calico Chemicals was, in fact, just starting a strike, and it would go on for six months, and before it was over some female secretaries would be attacked with acid, and the marketing manager would be burned alive in his

car. Women met in clusters on the street, holding onto their children, grateful for having been spared. *Absurd, absurd,* I thought; I
the loving father not bothering to leave my writing. They'll turn up.
It was three in the afternoon; reluctantly I investigated the swings
and slides where Rajan took them after the sun relented: no sign.
No sign of Rajan either—open speculation that he'd decided to
strike back (in India, connections are made with lightning rapidity)
for a reprimand. He'd been acting strangely since "that bad girl" had
been working in the house. . . .

The point of all this is: There *is* no place for the children aside
from doing their drawings on the living room floor. Our children, accustomed in Montreal to taking their bikes in the morning and not
showing up till lunch or dinner, cannot leave the house without up-
setting an entire factory. They were not in the Ping-Pong room of
the guest house. They were not in the television room of another
house. Therefore they are lost, or kidnaped.

I remembered the most horrible story about India I had ever
heard. Mrs. Chatterjee had told us of a friend's friend in Calcutta
who had left her baby in the car when she dashed in to pick up her
ironing. The baby was gone when she got back. Police were notified.
No luck, no phone calls. Ransom was not the point. Children are always being sold or abducted into rings of beggars and prostitutes; deliberately maimed, blinded, acid-scarred, amputated, and muted.
This story was worse.

Three days later, a customs official grew suspicious of a Muslim
couple and baby trying to leave the country. Baby had no passport.
Baby answered general description. Muslim mother howled with outrage. Police were called, the putative mother alerted. She arrived at
the airport, took one look at the baby, and gleefully exclaimed,
"Dipika!" and plucked her sleeping daughter from the Muslim's
arms. Then screamed, and is mad to this day.

The Muslims were gold smugglers. The bundled-up baby was their
carrying case. Thirty kilos of gold bangles fell from the baby's
hollowed-out chest and tummy onto the waiting room floor.

In the form of its horror, it is purely Indian. I don't know if it
happened, but I am convinced that it could. Not that Indians are
crueler than we (quite the opposite), but that their cruelty is rarely
an end in itself as ours is; there is always in India a literal and utili-

tarian component to nearly any outrageous invention (rats at the feet of Ganesh), and we respond with horror or amusement to the literal, more than the invented.

Our children of course were safe. Rajan had taken them about ten feet away, to the basement of the next-door neighbor's, to play with their pet rabbits.

10

By late May the dust and heat were simply appalling; Bart had suffered all varieties of hay fever, asthma, and bronchitis ("I feel like an eggshell on a garbage heap," he said, collapsing in our bed); Bharati needed to get away from the domestic routine of squatting on the floor with her mother; Bernie had ceased eating; and I was going stir crazy for lack of stimulation. So we took off for four days of high living at the Sun 'n Sand Hotel on Juhu Beach, watering hole of the Hindi film stars and layover spa (in all senses) for pilots and flight attendants of the international airlines.

India offers many kinds of luxury, and in a year of liberal spending we were to experience them all. Sheraton-Oberoi in Nariman Point is America; Taj Mahal in the "Fort" area is old Raj. Sun 'n Sand is modern India, a Hindi film turned to concrete, pools, floor shows, sex, and booze.

While the hotel is directly on the beach, the management prefers its guests not to use it. One must walk down several steps from poolside and then be admitted to the beach by a *durwan* at the gate, who disapproves. The beach is as inviting as a freshly tarred road. The water is gray and matted, the beach is strewn with coconut fibers, garbage, seaweed, and paper as well as the human and cooking wastes of an urban bustee. Once at sea level you realize that no one swims in that ocean; the surf rolls in the color of old bath water, too much (as usual) is revealed in the underside of every wave. Then you realize—in my case for the first time—that you have strayed where you have no right, where you're not wanted, and where no one can help you. It is as though you had been swept to sea.

It is like an undertow, but it is an undertow of people: the beach dwellers, scavengers, and beggars, animal trainers and contortionists,

whose life is led under the poolside of the Sun 'n Sand, whose drift-
wood shacks are propped against the hotel's retaining wall, and who
live on the change tossed down by Lufthansa and TWA stewardesses in maddening bikinis, or by the bleary-eyed pilots, tipping it
over the side from the waiter's plastic tray. Those grinning freckle-
faced boys who can do twenty back flips as though they were attached to an invisible wheel aren't grinning when you see them up
close, and their freckles are the deep oval pits of smallpox scars, and
a creature on four legs, walking like a spider but with a very human
face, calls from the fringes of the crowd around me, "*saab*," his knees
and elbows and the hump on his back are higher than he can raise
his head.

I had wanted to walk the beach and pick up sea shells to bring
back for Bart but I couldn't get that close to the water because of
the smell from the rotting weeds and because within minutes I was
surrounded by a silent band of boys just old enough, one by one,
to challenge the strength of a grown man—and just surly enough, in
a group, to try it. Revolutionaries of the future, what better credentials than having been a beggar under the Sun 'n Sand pool, to have
lived on shit from the biggest spenders in the country? Undertow:
They moved around me as I moved, didn't smile when I smiled,
didn't move when I manfully chose to ignore them. Step by step I
fought against their pull. The group moved with me away from the
ocean and around a bend, out of view of the Sun 'n Sand. I started
pulling back, walking against their sullen flow, and gradually they
yielded. When I was directly in front of the hotel gate, I cut through
them decisively, mustering every drop of *pukka sahib*-ness ever denied me, and I was not challenged. It was the only time in India
that I felt that curious *This-is-125th-Street-but-I-must-be-in-Harlem*
terror of a New York tourist, about to go under. At no other time in
India, despite steep trails, dark nights, and devious alleys, did I feel
that unspoken danger.

One had the sense in that hotel that the "new money" and the
undeclared "black money" were at their ease. The staff was neither
professionally efficient (as at the Sheraton-Oberoi) nor obsequiously
attentive (as at the Taj). We found the waiters rude and inefficient,
unhappy in their role, accustomed (like workers everywhere in
India) to being bullied and abused before rendering indifferent serv-

ice. They were to go on a lengthy and rancorous strike in just a few weeks' time. The Sun 'n Sand was a playground for the rich Indian businessman without his family (better to stare at the German stewardesses), consular Europeans on short vacations, and the endless airline crews. German and American couples in St.-Tropez bikinis sat on the walls behind the diving board, lathering each other in oils every half hour; young Indian men stared at them from the pool, gawking at all that hardened female flesh. A few Indian families ate and drank at poolside—Parsis by the look of them, paunchy cigar-chomping men with fluffy white sideburns that looked at a distance like ear muffs, and women on whom a sari sat as uncomfortably as it would on Bella Abzug—and me, sitting by poolside too, admiring the girls, revolted by pilots' drinking so much, keeping four separate stacks of papers weighted down with saucers, glasses, and salt shakers as I tried to write and type a story about Montreal hockey fever of the early fifties called "I'm Dreaming of Rocket Richard." The world, for the moment, seemed thimble-small.

There was something coarse about that hotel. Perhaps it was a healthy coarseness; it could neither exclude India nor absorb it. Barefoot technicians hauled our furniture around to repair the airconditioner; their footprints were left everywhere on our tables, chairs, and linen. As usual, everything was replaced, but nothing repaired. Cats prowled the grounds, leaping up on the tables before the indifferent waiters could clear them. Out in the parking lot, I saw a pariah bitch lying under a tree, her mangy skin bleeding where the hair was gone, one puppy alertly watching me, six others sleeping, gorging, or maybe dead. Fertile India. Crows sat perched on chair backs, waiting to fight the cats for the left-over food, sometimes, in their anxiety, not waiting for the diners to leave. Stunning a large fly in the room, then lifting it out on the window ledge to blow away, I was horrified to return at Bernie's insistence. "Worms are coming out," he shouted. "Impossible," I snapped. But we watched her stagger about the ledge dropping pus-colored balls of maggots that the wind blew away. Later, I found a dead fly in my coleslaw: *texture, texture,* this goddamn fertile country, even killing creates more life.

We attended dinner and a floor show later that night. The kids were asleep upstairs; no one under eighteen was admitted to the dining room. I smiled indulgently; what could prudish India possibly serve up that even a child could find exciting?

It turned out, as usual, I was wrong. I had forgotten that the new god, "p'horen exchange," can dictate revolutionary changes if he wishes; in his name, all import restrictions are lifted, and all exotic corruptions are slavishly reproduced. The Sun 'n Sand earned a great deal of "foreign exchange" through its proximity to Santa Cruz Airport. The menu was well stocked with steaks and chops (my first steak in a month), and its imported wines began at 150 rupees ($22) a bottle. Champagne was going for $35, and bottles were popping. The Indian menu was the authentic stuff, Punjabi, and very hot; Bharati spent the rest of the night vomiting it up.

The Goan orchestra and singer did an impeccable medley of last year's hits; the songstress had a variety of voices—Streisand, Warwick, Flack, Fitzgerald (an improvement over the early sixties when Bharati had left India; then all the Goans had sounded like Doris Day). This one even made a few concessions she never would have five years earlier, by singing some popular Hindi film songs.

At a table below us (they had paid to be closer; we would have paid to sit farther away) two modish Englishmen were tearing into the steaks, washing it down with champagne. I'd talked to one at poolside (white man to white man, a bad habit) and found him brutal; a cotton importer with collaborators all over Asia, very much the new Common Market Englishman with no sentimentality about Commonwealth types like Indians, or Canadians. An Indian collaborator, all smiles and sideburns, now joined them for a drink. "What can I do for you, sirs?" he asked, confident that he had already done everything for them an alert exporter could devise. The textile man drew him closer, then pointed coldly at me and Bharati. He whispered something I couldn't hear, but had no need of hearing. Because I was white and she "Westernized" and beautiful, I knew he assumed that she, or someone just like her, was available. The Indian drew back, "Oh, that would be very good, sir," he laughed nervously, "very good indeed."

"Seriously," said the Englishman. "Do it. You know our room."

The nervous laughter gradually died out. "I will try, sirs. All I can do is try, no? Let us say after midnight."

"Let us say before," said the Englishman.

A drum roll. House lights dimmed, a corner spotlight was trained on the bandleader. "And now, ladies and gentlemen, the moment you have been waiting for. The Sun 'n Sand is proud to present, the one, the only, Yasmin in . . . 'The Harem'!"

"Oh, Christ," came a drunk American voice, "I came for 'The Seven Veils.'" The tableful of pilots started laughing.

The American flight-crew table was located far off the dance floor, up in a corner. I'd wondered why they'd reserved so far away—now I knew. They controlled the spotlight and its wheel of colored disks. And since they were here three nights a week, year in and year out, they knew the stripper's routine as well as they knew the runways at Santa Cruz. She begged the purples and reds for each new discard; the pilots gave her a glaring white. The maître d' kept grabbing for lights, Smiling Jack kept pushing him off. How many times had he seen her—a hundred, three hundred?—and what does it do to a stripper to know that half her audience knows her body like a husband? Give her credit: For a country that doesn't permit kissing in the movies and gossips about starlets smoking, Yasmin was as explicit, finally, in deep purple lighting, as a stripper can get.

New crews were in the next day. I finished "Rocket Richard." Yasmin did her "Seven Veils." Afterward we retired to our room, opened the windows, and watched a Goan wedding reception down by poolside. Alvarez married Pereira, with two hundred guests, an orchestra, and an emcee who told Sambo jokes and made up risqué stories ("I have just heard Mr. Alvarez say to Mr. Pereira, ladies and gentlemen, 'This wedding is costing me a fortune.' And do you know what Mr. Pereira said? He said, 'Don't worry, my son will start repaying your daughter as soon as they get upstairs.' So don't worry Bernice, Bertie will attend to you. Meanwhile . . .") and then came limbo dancers, and the hotel's songstress doing a special Warwick routine, then toasts to the priest brought all the way up from Goa who had married the Alvarez parents twenty-five years before . . . amazing, amazing, *texture*. Indian Christians, another form of the Western life; we closed the windows on them and on the Sun 'n Sand and returned to Chembur, back to the heat and dust, unrefreshed.

11

I had been writing five letters a day in hopes of receiving at least two or three. A few every week went to my editors in New York and Toronto, both women, and one day Bharati remarked to me that Dodoo was suspicious about so many letters going to, and coming from, women. I was furious.

Bored, hot, and self-righteous, I set out from the bungalow to mail my own letters. At least twice a week I had been driven to the post office next to the Needs of Life Co-operative Bank to pick up a dozen aerogrammes and to mail packages of books to myself at the Ramakrishna Mission in Calcutta, where we'd decided we would stay. I knew there was another substation a little closer, perhaps two miles away, and that the driver and the car were probably at the gas station next door to it. I told no one I was leaving; if my absence caused a panic—good.

It is absurd how small a gesture constitutes rebellion in India. A son smoking in his father's presence, a daughter exhibiting any will of her own. Here I was, a thirty-three-year-old father of two, published author, and tenured professor, denied the right to walk outside the factory; and now—if Bharati and Dodoo had their way—denied my last link with the publishing world. I walked down the unshaded hill, a giant of self-assertion and Western adventurism, and I was aware of myself committing some long-overdue, precipitous *fictional* act. I could see twenty miles ahead into Bombay Harbour; the ships looked like playthings. Premonsoon clouds—*clouds!*—lay on the hills behind. By the acid factory, on a tree limb scalded bare but kept permanently wet by a leaking steampipe, a cluster of wrinkly chameleons were enjoying a sauna. If I'd had my camera, it would have been a natural prize-winner. But I had bigger ambitions—to do something for myself, against my family's wishes. Nothing in India is bigger than that. *Durwans* saluted as I left the gates. I was in my blister-forming sandals, but no matter. I was walking an Indian roadside, in an obscure suburb that saw no white man, and I knew I was noticed and talked about in every stall I passed. Why is he walking, doesn't he know the sun is dangerous? What has hap-

pened to Mukherjee-saab's car? Where is his Indian wife? How bad
of her to let him go off alone. *Ha!*

Distances are prolonged in India, of course. The country is vast,
but vaster still is the time spent getting there. Distance in India is
time, not miles. Three miles along a single road is nothing for us,
but in the dust and heat, and fighting the crowds and slipping out of
the dust-smooth sandals with every three or four steps, getting a
blister and noticing that my shirt is soaking despite a slight breeze,
three miles becomes an absolute limit for a first day's walk.

The post office stood just next to the Indianoil station where the
driver had taken the car. Just as I turned in the post office, I felt a
rustling on my arm, a premonition of autumn in some northern climate. I looked up. It was as though the sky had parted in a vision;
the high glaze of summer had been rolled back like a planetarium
roof, revealing a primordial backdrop of purple fused with bolts of
lightning. It had all happened in only five minutes. The monsoon
(or officially, the first premonsoon shower) would shortly break, and
I'd gotten caught in it stupidly, giving them all a chance to tell me
so.

I ducked inside the post office where it was still high summer. The
lines for stamps, for registering, for weighing, for money orders, were
all equally long; I had one letter to weigh, which took twenty minutes, then I had to go to the end of the stamps line. The men
behind me all strained to read the addresses on my letter. The fans
inside were not working; the air must have hit 110° and 110% humidity; my thumb and forefinger had soaked the letters and when I
propped my elbows on the black plastic counter, I left pools of mois-
ture as wide as melted ice cubes.

The Indianoil station was next door. The sky had become a uniform purple and the street people were now scurrying; clothes that
had been drying flat on the dirt were being folded by waterside in
the *chawl* across the road.

I found the driver; the car was over the service pit in the back. The
Chembur station was run by a Mr. Banerjee, another displaced
Bengali Brahmin. Mr. Banerjee was famous throughout Bombay for
his hiring of the handicapped. He was not, however, an anonymous
benefactor. He was something of a showman-revolutionary among
gas station managers. The boys who pumped and checked the oil

wore little signs: *I am deaf and dumb. Please forgive me,* and the boy who made change spoke, but was blind. Mr. Banerjee knew all about me, and the book we were writing. "You should see what I have at night," he said, seeing my interest in his help. "Two polio boys."

### 12

There is still something terrifying in one's first tropical storm. It is as though the clouds contained some distillate of water that grew heavier and wetter as it fell. The parched, cracked earth could not contain such water. The sky was night-black and torn by lightning, the temperature dropped so suddenly that the gas station windows fogged over. The rain fell with the density of steam, and pushed itself through the locked windows onto the floors of the front office, which had to be abandoned. All traffic pulled over; work crews in the open flatbed trucks ran into the station to unwrap their turbans and squeeze them out, then to do the same with all their clothes.

Three hours later we drove home in a gray drizzle. The cracked mud flats at the head of the harbor had already disappeared. The roads inside the factory were already under several inches of reddish-brown water. The cars and trucks forged ahead like hydrofoils and the workers moved about gingerly, lifting their sari ends and *dhotis,* or rolling up their *pajama* bottoms, and carrying their sandals with their other hand as they walked. For the next four months that would be the style of public walking—or wading—all over India, swirling the legs carefully in front, holding the loose clothing ends high with one hand, and the sandals high in the other. No one remarked on my absence.

On the All-India Radio news a few evenings later we heard of an Indian Airlines pilot being fined for missing his flight. He had refused to wade from his company lodgings to the waiting bus, and no one had been assigned to carry him.

The monsoons are considered an unhealthy time by Indians; monsoons offer a name and focus to all the generalized complaints that have been gathering force during the long dry summer. Mommy-di's afternoon naps on the downstairs swing grew longer, her limbs grew heavier, headaches increased. "Monsoon diarrhea" was expected, and came, then the flu. Bernie fell ill with a severe gastroenteritis; he couldn't keep his antivomiting pills down, nor even the sips of water to guard against dehydration. Suddenly everyone in the house was ill, even Rajan, and the downstairs table that in happier days had held our drinks and spicy munchables now contained a graveyard of bottles and sticky spoons. I'd been seriously ill in India on my other trip; I wondered if I would see forty if I settled here permanently. Bart's bronchitis returned; he wheezed in our bed. The grandparents' blood pressure, Bernie's vomiting, Rajan's coughing and moaning from his bedroll in the storage room, became a monsoon serenade. Bharati and I were spared. The Calico doctor came twice a week, then daily. He was a gentle Gujarati, a competent doctor, but since he was attached to the factory and ran a dispensary in Chembur Bazaar, he was not considered a proper specialist. So a "Big Doctor" was called from downtown Bombay; he was Illinois-returned and showed up with a retinue of bag- and syringe-carrying *chokras*. He ordered the Calico doctor around like a first-year student, but ended by endorsing all his prescriptions. He charged one hundred rupees— about fifteen dollars.

It was not Dr. Vyas' gentle Gujarati ways that bothered me—it was rather that his visits were devoted more to discussions of his monthly retreats to worship the Great Mother, a saintly faith healer back in the mountains. Another man of science, undisturbed by simple contradictions. It had been Vyas who had diagnosed my fatigue and listlessness three years before as hepatitis, and who had confined me to the bedroom for two months of a three-month stay.

Our time in Bombay—the period of initiation, or inoculation, before Calcutta and coping on our own—was nearly over. The rains were constant now, the mosquitoes had disappeared to do their nefarious breeding, and the season of flies (clinging like raindrops to your arms and face and legs) had come. All the bugs of India were straggling indoors: mantises, and those mole-sized water bugs called *arshola* and those grape-bottomed black ants called *olah* that glistened like blackberries; the whole parade of insect life brings to mind something prehistoric, fossil flies trapped in amber, dragonflies with two-foot wing spans. Clusters of rain-hounded vipers were discovered in the corner of the Ping-Pong room; Raj and Rajan were called on to destroy them. India gathers into itself during the monsoon. We were unable to drive downtown due to flooding. Fresh fruits like the kingly mango start turning bad and are no longer sold; it is a time of bad fruits and vegetables, sickness, sluggishness, treacherous waters, closed resorts. Rajan had to be sent by foot to buy the medicines. For several weeks the random clutter of suburban India would disappear; street dwellers would settle in the shells of unfinished buildings; others took over the empty Ping-Pong room, or slept under the eaves of our bungalow next to the car. I could smell their *biri* smoke and hear them laughing, just under the bathroom window. One is more aware than ever, even pissing in the middle of the night, of never being alone.

Down near Sion Circle, where giant electric pylons had spanned the empty mud flats, fishermen were now at work, netting the waist-deep seasonal tidal flat for spawning fish. The overnight adaptability of the poor; India's two climates are as distinct as August and January in Montreal. With the coming of monsoons, Bombay fire departments are called on to answer "house collapses"; sometimes whole denuded hillsides slump into gullies, killing dozens. Roads are blocked by water and by mechanical failures; India more than usual resembles brain surgery by candlelight. Still, it all goes on. A good monsoon, on which the entire country depends for marginal survival, will mean hundreds drowning and millions losing their homes to flooding; a bad monsoon means that millions will be forced to abandon their homes and seek shelter in the cities, and thousands more will die of starvation or its close consequences. For us, insulated by family, shelter, money, it means only illness, anxiety, and irritability.

It has been seven weeks. We started in heat and dust, we are ending in the rains. We started healthy, but by now we've all been sick. I've lost fifteen unwanted pounds; Bharati has gained ten; the children have lost more than I wish to contemplate. The suitcase, after a world-wide tracer, turned up in a village in Gujarat—Gandhi's birthplace, as it turns out—and was later returned. A mix-up of customs men, pay-offs, mistakes. That Air-Kuwait bag that resembled mine had obviously been marked for special handling.

We had arrived in a very secure, orderly house, where nothing had changed in the three years between visits. Not a single new piece of furniture, nothing rearranged. The kids' 1970 wall scribblings and dirty-hand marks just as they were; my compulsive mosquito-squashing had not been washed. The only change is in the downstairs windows overlooking the garden. Two years before, in the "Bangla Desh War" against Pakistan, the government had ordered thick strips of PVC over all the windows as an air-raid defense. And two years later they are still up. They will never come down. What is, is right. What changes is for the best. Decorating, painting, spending on appearances, is futile. Everything reachable is obsessively cleaned; nothing else has ever been touched. We are leaving none too soon, with my in-laws suffering, the children ill, and Bharati and I unable to cope—for different reasons—with the oppressive routine of Dodoo's house.

A question was forming itself all during that Bombay stay; a Big Question, one that I had promised myself I would try to ask, in the *pukka* tradition of all well-intentioned Western visitors. The question didn't finally form itself until months later in Calcutta, but I see, setting this down a year later in Montreal, that all the components of the question were there from the beginning.

What we see in India—the Big Question goes—is it Hegel, or is it Marx? Is physical India the manifestation of an *idea* (Hinduism for want of a better word), from which the material world takes its evanescent shape; or is the solid material world best understood—and best altered—in terms of surplus labor and material scarcity? If I want to understand India, where do I look: to Dodoo in his office, or Dodoo at prayer? Which part of his life is the significant one? This is getting ahead of myself.

We were coming back from Bombay sometime after the monsoons had started (but had been "playing truant" for a week or so) and we were just beyond Sion Circle where those rats had been tossed in the air that first hot May Sunday. The highway is elevated over the flooded Thana Creek basin, and suddenly I thought of the word that described most of what I'd come to know of Dodoo, the hotels, the driving, the endless fertility, the clutter and suspiciousness. All was *swollen*. A general infection, septic and sensitive to even the slightest touch (or a bloated putrefaction, too late for reversal). People are in pain, obviously; everyone suffers from the swelling, even at the outer fringes. The pain is still within the threshold of tolerance, but not when it flares, and it flares somewhere in India every day.

<h2 style="text-align:center">13</h2>

Ranu, Vijay, and their baby son come down from Baroda for a vacation a week before we leave. We had seen them in Montreal the summer before, when Vijay had toured the States as a Rotary guest and Ranu had taken the time to work on her Faulkner thesis, and then to discuss it with a Faulkner scholar at Yale. It had all gone well; she is a brilliant woman, though very different in manner and appearance from Bharati. She is very much her father's daughter, and I suspect that her life, too, will follow some larger national destiny, just as his has.

Vijay is assistant sales manager of a giant electric pump corporation. If India is to survive agriculturally, electric pumps will be her salvation—Vijay is employed in a vital national enterprise. He is the modern Indian businessman, trained in the Management Institute at Ahmedabad (a direct creation of the Harvard Business School and the Ford Foundation); he could take his place as a Bright Young Man in any large corporation any place in the world. He is, as well, the only one of Dr. Mukherjee's three sons-in-law with bright financial prospects and the certainty of someday making a comfortable living. By background, he was nearly as foreign to the Mukherjees as I was. Their marriage had been a love match that Dodoo tried his damnedest to discourage. A man dies, Dodoo once told me, seeing his daughters throw their lives away on worthless chaps like the three of us. "Well, let them all go to hell, then, I say. They won't listen to me anyway."

"You gave them education," Mommy-di reminded. "They are good boys. What does it all matter?"

"It matters," said Dodoo. "Marrying wisely matters. I could have done better for them picking names from a hat." He laughed; he was teasing that night (he's more open with me than with the others; he wouldn't say such things to Vijay and Sudhir-dada, but he would show it). And of course by his standards, and by many of mine, he is right. Ranu was headstrong and married "beneath" her. Bharati was romantic and docile and married a *mleccha*, and now she wears miniskirts.

It was not merely to see us that they came. It was also to see Vijay's parents off from Santa Cruz Airport in a week—they were going to America for a four-month visit with their engineer-son in New Hampshire.

Vijay was twenty-nine that year, a handsome young man rising rapidly. His salary was fifteen hundred rupees a month; Ranu's was about nine hundred as a lecturer in English at the university, and since they lived in his family compound, in a wing of it that was legally his, and had free use of the various servants that had been attached to the family ever since his grandfather had built the compound in 1905, there were no housing or servants' costs. His parents lived in another wing—the two front doors faced each other under an entrance—but Vijay and his father had not spoken in over five years. As usual, it centered on marriage. They are Mahrattas, a proud warrior caste from Maharashtra. They are a famous family in the city, and Vijay was not forgiven for making a love match with something as exotic as an "overeducated" Bengali Brahmin. To his credit, Vijay ignored the provocation, affirmed his marriage to Ranu, and ignored the presence of his father just ten feet away. But with the birth of a son a few months earlier, the father relented. Now they speak, and so long as Ranu speaks Marathi to her father-in-law, she is accepted.

The year just passed has been a horror for both the Blaises and the Vanikars. They knew us in our Montreal prime; they can't imagine the charred relics; the crushed car that had driven them to New Haven to meet Cleanth Brooks. The Blaises lead dramatic lives; she's only had to contend with middle-class India.

Baroda has been heavily hit by power shortages; unlike the Calico facility (but like much of Chembur and Bombay), their electricity is off all night, and only on eight hours in the day. This makes useless the refrigerator that they saved two years to buy. And because of power cuts, the pump factory has been put on staggered hours. Vijay works nights and Sundays, Friday is his day off. But Sunday is

Ranu's only free day, and since she lectures eighteen hours a week in three different faculties, grades five thousand papers a term, is writing a dissertation, and has suffered a birth that nearly killed her, she tries to rest in the early evenings. And so they have not had a day off together, except for these vacations, in three years. He is either in after midnight or, on other shifts, out of the house by six. Water is turned on only twice a day, for two-hour shifts; all bathing and washing must be done then. He leaves on his scooter an hour before he's due—it's important to be first in the office ahead of his boss. The baby wakes at six-thirty and Ranu must change and dress him and get his food ready, and be in her first lecture by eight. She teaches three straight hours, six days a week.

In semiarid Baroda the summer temperatures reach a daily 100° or more, and since there is no electric power to drive the overhead fans, Ranu and Vijay lie awake all night on their griddlelike bed, catching their sleep only in the predawn hours. They try to do their shopping together on Friday afternoons or very early Sunday morning. This is the price they pay for having a Western marriage in provincial India; separate careers, marriage, a child, high income (a joint income of 2,500 rupees, for a couple not yet thirty, with no debts or household expenses, is extraordinary). He will be able to buy a car before he is thirty-five—usually a sign of inherited wealth or black money—and they could afford the finest of Indian vacations (Kashmir, Simla, or the South) but they are dutiful. They spend their three weeks in Chembur in Dodoo's house, sleeping in the smaller room (he is, after all, the youngest son-in-law); he will not be permitted our assumed access to the car (it will be pointed out to Vijay, who needs no reminding, that each tankful of petrol costs 130 rupees—nearly twenty dollars—and that to Bombay and back takes half a tankful). And Vijay, the aggressive man of business, will sit with us at night drinking the scotch and soda that he has mixed, watching "Daddy" alone smoking endless cigarettes. Every few minutes he'll be forced to ask, "Play some Ping-Pong, Clark?" Weather permitting we'll parade twice around the grounds while Vijay smokes two expertly cupped cigarettes. It would be disrespectful to smoke in the presence of an older male relative—even one who would tolerate it. Dodoo, at sixty-four, will not smoke in front of his older brother.

His parents arrived a few nights later—they stayed in Dadar with old friends. They came out to Chembur one evening for dinner. Vijay's mother was a strikingly handsome and strong-faced woman with iron-gray hair who looked like an aristocrat of the Independence movement. One could imagine her at the turn of the century leading a march or arguing a case at Lincoln's Inn. The father had also been a handsome man—Vijay came by his looks naturally.

And their departure precipitated the final domestic crisis. The gentle old Sanskritist they were staying with had no car. Their plane left at 4 A.M. and surely they couldn't trust a taxi driver at that hour. Vijay had assumed responsibility for taking them out in Dodoo's car, to which Dodoo agreed, but then Vijay demanded that Ranu accompany them, and to this Dodoo absolutely refused.

Battle lines were drawn. I joined Vijay's side; after all, Ranu was a wife and daughter-in-law more than just a daughter; her responsibility was to be with her husband. Bharati would also come with us. "No! I will not tolerate such idiocy in my house! You will all be murdered or worse and I will be responsible." To which Vijay responded, "Don't be silly, Daddy. We are two men." "Two morons, you mean. Don't speak to me about being men. Men don't expose their wives to danger needlessly. You and Clark go if you must. The girls stay back, *baas*." "How can I let my parents go, Daddy, without Ranu's blessing?" "She can give blessing right here." "No—she goes." "I will not permit it."

"Daddy," said Ranu, "I must go."


It's comedy and it's suffering, the demands of family, the power plays, the attempts to hold on to authority. In the end, all the young people went, leaving at two and not returning till a dawn-flecked five, and Dodoo would be standing at the door old and ill and forced into bed from an attack of high blood pressure. "He could have died because of your thoughtlessness," Mommy-di charged the daughters (the men were beyond reasoning with); she was disgusted with us all. The one thing that Dodoo could not tolerate—he who had seen all, been all, lost all—was disobedience in his own house. It was the lesson Vijay's father had tried to administer to his son, and he had lost Vijay in doing so. It was the right that old *jethoo* in Calcutta had assumed for himself—and had lost his daughters and his

younger brothers in doing so. In infinitely flexible, tolerant, elastic
India, obedience to the father was the brittle cord. Vijay had bent it
twice; he is a tough, lonely man.

The closet allegory is over. The Bengali Brahmin through whom
the twentieth century has flowed; his wife who has followed him everywhere but remained untouched; his daughters who will make con-
tributions to knowledge as important as his own, but who have
traded something in the bargain—their innocence, perhaps, their
*place* in some ongoing, creative flow. The daughters have lost their
place in the joint family that is India; they are inheritors of their father's double vision, but the sad fact is that the double vision cannot
be passed on. The daughters will suffer agonies their father never
knew—modern India is in for agonies the world has never known—
and it seems almost impossible to avoid or interfere.

## 14

Mommy-di's youngest brother (called in Bengali *chhoto-mamu*) arrived in Bombay two days before we were due to leave. He is short,
stout, brilliant and a bachelor, the family scholar, now fifty, and a director of one of the nationalized industries. He was in Bombay for a
directors' meeting, but nevertheless spent a Sunday in Chembur to
see the children. He would be returning to Calcutta in three days,
but we couldn't bear to wait for him. He would be the only person I
knew in the city.

The driver arrived at five o'clock Monday morning. We left
Chembur by six-thirty and arrived at the airport an hour later, in
time for the nine o'clock flight to Calcutta. The children were still
not fully recovered, but we couldn't take another day in Chembur. I
was thankful for all the inoculations, and I hoped the second shoe
had dropped. I was ready for Calcutta. I wrote to Ed in Montreal,
appointing him the guardian of our children in case Calcutta or Indian Airlines did us in.

Porters rushed to take our bags and typewriters; I struggled with a
tape recorder and camera bag, Bharati with all the smaller bags.

"Where, *saab?*" the porters asked, and I said with all my *pukka* confidence, "Calcutta."

They looked perplexed but brought the bags inside, then set them down in the middle of the waiting room, far from any ticket line. There were four long lines: Nagpur, Madras, Delhi, Jaipur.

"No Calcutta, *saab*."

Certain now that in all my confusion and anxiety I'd made a humiliating error (and already wondering how I could face Dodoo), I checked the tickets we'd bought three weeks before. What day is this? What month? Thank God, I was right. The airport was wrong. The country was wrong. I checked one last time: date, time, flight number.

"What seems to be the problem?" A stout, white-sideburned, white-suited officer had been summoned from his desk.

"I have tickets on the nine o'clock Calcutta flight," I said.

"Oh, that," he said, starting to turn away. "Calcutta flight is canceled."

From deep in my throat I felt a roar beginning to rise; it started as an expulsion of white man's guilt, then of my husband-love, then finally of all self-consciousness. "I have these tickets—" my lung power was rising, my good manners and provisional status were all swallowed back. He was ten feet away and getting farther. "Wait a goddamn minute." I shouted. "Are you trying to tell me the flight is canceled and you didn't call me? What the hell kind of airline is this—"

That at least brought him back, eyes still heavy-lidded, hand outstretched. "Show me tickets."

I slapped them in his hand. "It is as I thought. These tickets were issued before the new schedules. They are no good. All passengers on this flight have automatically been reserved on the evening flight via Nagpur."

"But-I-don't-want-to-go-on-any-goddamn-flight-to-Nagpur." *I want to be in Calcutta for lunch. A room is reserved. I'm an important person; I'm writing a book.* My teeth were so tightly clenched I could barely speak. "I've come twenty miles to meet this flight and I have people meeting me in Calcutta this morning—"

"I cannot very well fly you there myself, can I? You must make suitable arrangements."

"Why was I not informed?"

"Perhaps you were not in town. How am I to know why you were not informed? It was in all the papers."

"Hindi or English?"

"Both, I'm sure."

"And what if I don't read the goddamn papers?"

"Then you were called. Our people have instructions." He raised his hand, snapped his fingers, and waved a younger man over. "Raman will handle your reservations." He turned his back, a young man headed my way, and I found myself grabbing for the older man, shouting, "Look, here, you think you can ignore your responsibility in all this—*stop, goddammit*—but you owe me—"

He turned, seething. "What precisely do you want? Someone was supposed to call your contact number and maybe she didn't. Or maybe you didn't get the message. There is no longer a direct morning flight to Calcutta. I cannot make one." He waved the young man away. "Now instead of wasting your time standing here and getting nothing accomplished, you will please follow me into my office for discussion."

I was right; I was wrong. My position was essentially uncomfortable—guiltless, violent anger is not my style—the very force of my anger was directed more at having to return to Chembur and unpack the bags and go through the farewells to the kids, and to defend my error to Dodoo. He had, as always, in precaution-mad India, told me to call up the airport to reconfirm, even if it meant asking a neighbor to place the call for me, and in my new independence and trust, I had assured him it wouldn't be necessary. I couldn't whisper to the officer now, "Does this really mean I can't start writing my book today?" Everyone back in Chembur would interpret this as a bad omen, something inauspicious, and we'd be lucky if we could leave this week.

"Come," said the officer, and I stalked after him in a bad imitation of skepticism and self-righteousness. In his air-conditioned office he offered me a cigarette, then spoke of the understaffing (in *India*, understaffing!), the inefficiency, the indifference and disrespect for service. He was *truly* sorry. "I will telex your office in Calcutta, what is their telex number?" I could feel myself shrinking by the minute. The shame, to be a white man in India without a telex number. I confessed that I wasn't a businessman, that my reservations were not at a hotel, but at the Ramakrishna Mission, and *that* sounded like a Vedantic flophouse the moment I said it. I doubted they had a telex. I had the *mamabari* address, but no telephone. He would try to get a message through, he promised, to this place, this mission. I'm not a missionary, I wanted to plead, but settled for a Coke.

I suppose that was the final injection. We returned to Chembur, sullenly. Bernie came down with dysentery. Two evenings later, with Bharati deciding to stay back until Bernie recovered fully, and with *chhoto-mamu* now free to accompany me, we were driven again to the airport, this time to catch the Nagpur plane to Calcutta. I discovered too late that Rajan had forgotten to pack my briefcase with all its drafts of my book, and it was now too late to return for it. It would be put on the next evening's flight. And so with *chhoto-mamu* as my guide, on a tempestuous July evening, I left alone for Calcutta.

··ঃ‖ II

1

There was a baggage handlers' strike on the night *chhoto-mamu* and I arrived. Several wagons of suitcases stood uncovered for forty minutes next to the delivery chute, pelted by monsoon rains, while three planeloads of passengers milled around inside waiting for porters. Finally one businessman crawled the length of the chute, then out the narrow opening to the wagons and started unpiling the bags in order to get to his own. A second man, seeing his bags being roughly handled and dumped in a puddle, squeezed through the opening in order to teach the first one a lesson. Pushing and name-calling broke out. "Who you are calling a bastard? You have insulted my mother, you bastard." They feigned and lunged in the rain, with instant commentary offered by two young men squatting on the conveyor belt and peering out through the slot. "Now first gentleman lunges and misses. Second chap responds with tight slap. *Durwans* are disengaging the combatants." I had feared, being the largest and slowest-moving target, despite having *chhoto-mamu* at my side, that I'd somehow manage to be the lone victim of any violence. I was the only "European" in the entire airport; again, a melancholy sign of Calcutta's isolation. Finally we all climbed out to get our bags; mine were sprung open, oily and soaking. I was lucky I hadn't sent the briefcase. "Welcome to Calcutta," *chhoto-mamu* laughed. We had waited an hour, I had seen my first Calcutta distemper, how quickly it flared, how immediate are the irritants. And more importantly, had I known enough to consider it, I had seen the wit and improvisation that allows Calcutta to survive nearly anything.

After all the warnings about Calcutta, the drive into the city is almost a relief. Dum Dum itself is a placid village of orange-tiled roofs, ponds, and dazzling green banana trees. The traveler speeds along a divided, four-lane, open-country highway known locally as V.I.P. Road, and even as he passes the herdsmen with their grazing buffalo, or the hay wagons being pulled by sun-blackened old men, he might think: *They've lied to me.* They were right to censor Louis Malle's films. If this is the worst city in the world (actually, UNESCO statistics rank it second to Karachi in dirt, disease, and general destitution), then the world's not such a bad place after all.

The real Calcutta begins with a right-hand turn off C.I.T. (Calcutta Improvement Trust) Road onto Beliaghata Main Road. It begins suddenly at a stone Kali statue a few feet off the roadway, permanently lit and garlanded, and permanently worshiped by a small mob of kneeling women. It is tropically dark now, but not so late that the streets have emptied. It is the market hour all over Calcutta. The air is coarse with smoke and waste, blurring the street lamps, bare bulbs at best. *Chhoto-mamu's* company jeep follows the tram tracks in the middle of the road. Crowds surge, cows stray stupidly in our path, and human rickshaws clang their warnings, never breaking a jogging stride.

We are between monsoon showers and the bazaar crowds have choked off the road, moving from stall to stall. They must lift their saris and *dhotis* as they walk, for the road surface is half a tire underwater. A nameless dread sets in. The street is passable only in the center, over the tracks; rain and pedestrians have turned a wide avenue into a single rutted lane for trams and two-way traffic. Cars peel off, inches from collision: never slowing, honking, nudging themselves into the crowd. The pedestrians without looking behind them yield up the inches to allow the car to pass. We plunge into the crowd, shoppers shear off the jeep as though both body and bumper were positively charged. Their ranks seal behind us, like water.

This sudden unwanted equality with the pedestrian is part of the dread; you are hardly moving faster than he is walking, you are sitting while he stands above you, you hear the aimless tunes he hums walking past you, you pick up on a thousand scraps of conversation from couples brushing just past your cheek, your shoulder, the canvas flaps. In Calcutta the pedestrian is King. On the sidewalks (called "footpaths") the merchant is Prince, and in the gutters, cows are Queen. Cars are not part of the nobility, they are another addition to the elastic roadway, the latest addition. The human rickshaws with their *lungi*-clad Bihari pullers and their human cargo of fat women shoppers, or *babus* from the office, or stern old men in *dhotis* under an umbrella, have the true priority. They move around the crowds and cannot see behind them as they run (miss a step, stumble in that unlighted, potholed street, and they could easily crack a leg or run themselves over); cars must follow them and pedestrians must know how to look behind them when they hear the rap of the metal clapper against the iron frame of the "rick."

And one realizes, too, on that first dizzying arrival, that the cows which had never really materialized in Bombay are present in hordes everywhere in Calcutta. Cows are an ancient sign of holiness, and a sentimental sign of gentleness, but they are even more clearly an indication of urban collapse. Calcutta, among many other things, is the world's largest outdoor garbage heap, and the refuse of its streets supports hundreds of thousands of human scavengers, in precisely the way it supports millions more cows, dogs, and crows. Cows cannot survive where garbage is picked up, or where traffic flow demands priority. Things move by human muscle in Calcutta: the enormous racks of hay, the rickshaws, the handcarts. Even double beds and refrigerators can be seen perched on the heads of four men, running in step down the middle of a busy street. A stumble, a missed beat, and disaster. One merely adopts a new definition of garbage, or else he flees Calcutta in horror. For us, garbage is what we have no further use for, and our society permits the luxury of pinching off a resource chain at a fairly refined level. True garbage is what *no living creature* has further use for. And by that definition, Calcutta is a lot cleaner than Montreal.

Months later, alive to the streets, I would walk through such a district in the dark, carrying my tape recorder with the microphone open, just to catch these noises—horns, shouts, songs, snatches of transistor music, and the debased, guttural Hindi and Bengali of the beggars and country people thrown onto the city's streets, as well as the occasional, anonymous and ceremonially polite *"Good evening, saab!"* that would erupt from the dark. But that first night I wasn't charmed and I wasn't amused. I was sick and pale as soap, white-knuckled, in the belly of something I wished I hadn't started.

This is the most confined exterior in the world. The sidewalk braziers belch coal and cow dung fumes, and one feels there must be a fire ahead, a barrier, a sagging roof overhead, gases building up, a wall of people trying to escape. Police constables stand on platforms at the major intersections, permitting turns that would otherwise take all night. The constables are in white with white gloves, but they are guarded by three soldiers in khaki, with rifles. When they shout to us, and when *chhoto-mamu* answers, the language is Hindi. What alienation, I remark to myself, when the policemen don't even speak your language! When I ask about it, *chhoto-mamu* explains that no Bengali would be a simple constable. For that they get Biharis.

One begins choking on people. Such diversity seems ominous; even in their innocence they strike me as a mob. Each block driven without an incident seems a minor miracle; not to crush a child, not to sideswipe a rickshaw, not to be crushed by a tram. Or, not to be killed for having honked once too often and reminded the poorest, most politicized, and perhaps most excitable urban dwellers in the world that you happen to have a car, a driver, and an impatience with their presence. The streets are pumping people, the alleys and sidewalks are hemorrhaging. Beliaghata Main Road is like a puddled river bed, surged over by the evening crowds as from an unseen, broken dam. Our car, brushed casually by frail youths squeezing past, rocks just enough to tip my baggage. In an accident we could just as casually be plucked from the shell of the car and drowned underfoot.

Bengalis love to explain Calcutta; the identification with the city is so complete that the standard question put to an outsider—

"What do you think of Calcutta?"—is a shorthand way of asking, "What do you think of Bengalis? What do you think of me?" *What are you thinking, Clark? chhoto-mamu* asked on that first nighttime trip through Sealdah Bazaar, then finally down Chittaranjan Avenue to the center of the city. He must have known that of all the spectacles Calcutta can offer, the crowded streets in the evening are, finally, the most impressive. "What about the soldiers guarding the constables, *chhoto-mamu?*" I asked: What am *I* doing in a city where even the policemen need protection? "Why *three*, for heaven's sake?" "To protect," he answers. "They discovered that one guard, then two, then three, were not enough to protect the constable. Calcutta will always require three policemen to guard every traffic constable."

Calcutta on a summer night between monsoon showers: dark, smoky, loud, bewildering. We are passing the landmarks now: Dodoo's first factory, the Statesman Building, the Indian Airlines downtown terminal. Even here, on the busiest streets, the placid bulk of scavenging cows. The slow pace, the muscle pace of Calcutta life, is made up for with frantic activity. Buses hurtle by, packed with young men clinging to the outside of windows, to the hoods, tire mountings, and roof. It is we who confuse slowness with gentleness.

## 2

No amount of dedicated cramming can quite prepare a Westerner for sorting out an Indian family. Before leaving Chembur, I had dutifully memorized the names of Dodoo's Calcutta brothers, and of Mommy-di's brothers and sisters, as well as her many nieces. Bharati has fourteen girl cousins on the Chatterjee side ("cousin-sisters" in Indian-English), no males, a fact that will implicate even me several months later. Every aunt or uncle is given a special designation depending on the side of the family (*mashi* and *mamu* for maternal-side aunts and uncles; *pishi* and *kaku* for the paternal) and upon birth order within the family. Proper names are not used; thus *chhoto-mamu* means "mother's youngest brother." *Borro-mamu* would mean the eldest male from the mother's side—in her case, *borro-mamu* lives on handouts from his youngest brother and has been unemployed for nearly forty years. This has not deterred him from having fathered three daughters, all of whom are now in line for college and dowries, to be paid for by their lone employed uncle. *Mejo-mamu* is the middle. He runs a small import-export outlet from the *mamabari* on Southern Avenue. These are all relatives from Bharati's maternal side; none of them, therefore, have quite the authority of *jethoo*, who is her father's eldest brother, and therefore, the ritual head of her family.

On that first night in Calcutta, I was carrying a mental directory of about thirty names and a very incomplete grasp of the proper Bengali prefixes and suffixes, as well as a fainter recollection of which were kind and which were evil, which poor and which wealthy, who was mad, who was communist, who was a miser, who a lecher, who in the underworld, who in politics.

Husbands of mother's sisters are *meshos*—thus Dipu-mesho, a bald and witty engineer from Nagpur, husband of Bharati's aunt Kola-mashi, is the first to step from the waiting room of the Indian Airlines downtown terminal. "So, Clark." "So, Dipu," I mimick, which pleases him. He is a welcome sight; I had met him in Nagpur on a short visit three years earlier, gotten sick in Nagpur with hepatitis, and enjoyed a week's exposure to his sour and cynical disposition. He has cultivated a style to go along with his looks: understated, crafty, insinuating. In Bengali he is known as a malicious punster; in English the same wit comes out slightly ponderous. Though they have not lived in Calcutta for twenty years, they are in the city now because their only child, Jaya, will be getting married in five months and the arrangements for a marriage—gold shopping, sari buying, house renting—will take up the next two months. They are staying at the *mamabari*, and Dipu is using up ten years' accumulated leave. Jaya is a kind and well-behaved, though not attractive, girl; the match with a tall, fair airlines pilot is already the talk of the family.

"*Mejo-mamu* and I," says Dipu, indicating a tall slender man behind him, cheek bulging with *pan*, "were discussing the possibility that you and *chhoto-mamu* had decided to engage a rickshaw from the airport."

"Of course, not wishing to miss a single tourist attraction," I counter.

*Mejo-mamu* laughs again. He has an easy, a too-easy, laugh. He is tall and lean, with dark wavy hair, and is dressed in white *kurta* and *pajama*. All the Chatterjee women, plus *chhoto-mamu*, are short and plump and given to hypertension; *mejo-mamu* could have come from a different family. It is impossible to tell his age; his hair is still black. Though he is older than *chhoto-mamu*, he seems not to play a central role in the workings of the *mamabari*. He has a wife and two college-going daughters, and runs a small trading firm, specializing in the export of spices and handicrafts. It is a very small operation; the house is truly run on *chhoto-mamu*'s income, which is split among three separate families and a great many scattered, isolated individuals. The oldest brother, *borro-mamu*, was not there to greet me, nor would I ever meet him. He remained a spidery presence who sent one or another of his three daughters to the *mamabari* to pick up the weekly expense money. He was said to be the youngest-looking of all the brothers, and why not? With *chhoto-mamu* supporting him, his wife, and his daughters, with *chhoto-mamu* paying his bills, educating his daughters, and posting their dowries, he had little to do but interview the best possible grooms for each of his attractive girls. There is no question of his ever working; he is now retired, or unemployed, both of which are higher status than laborer. It costs him merely the indifference of his wife and daughters, a price that he finds within his means.

With the two *mamus* and Dipu I take off again, down Chowringhee, heading south to Ballygunge. The vast black *maidan* is to our right and the unbroken rows of darkened doorways and shuttered shops lay to our left. I can make out hotel entrances—Chowringhee is the Broadway of Calcutta—theaters, clothing stores, banks, office buildings; I could also see that the sheltered sidewalk is home to hundreds of men already stretched out asleep, or to groups of men and the occasional family clustered about a brazier, cooking their supper. As we stop at a light, men rush out to the car to sell us flower garlands. No one speaks to them, or takes a garland. "The Royal Asia Society," says *chhoto-mamu*, pointing to a substantial building behind the palm trees.

"And Park Street," says Dipu, "the justly famous Fifth Avenue of Calcutta."

We rattle on down Chowringhee; the *maidan* ends and the city

seems to start all over again. Chowringhee changes its name to
Asutosh Mukherji Road, and the district becomes Bhowanipur, still
aglow with movie marquees, jewelry stores, sari shops, and milling
with the crowds outside the cinemas. I know I'm in Bengal; three
posters two stories high of Bengal's matinee idol, Uttam Kumar.
"We live very close, now," says *chhoto-mamu*, but I could not imagine middle-class life going on so close to such noise and confusion.
But he points out the landmarks—where Babloo (Bharati's nick-
name) did this, and Babloo first did that. He knows every building,
every house; he has spent fifty years within five blocks of where we
are driving.

We stop briefly outside the *mamabari* so that *mejo-mamu* can get
down. We are at the edge of Ballygunge, where Asutosh Mukherji
changes names again, to Southern Avenue, near the intersection of
Rash Behari Avenue. There is an island in the middle of the intersection, a widening of the muddy embankments around the tram
tracks, a tree or two, some high billboards advertising cigarettes, and
on the grass, colonies of ragpickers who have set up shelter. They
have no roof, just bamboo stakes in the ground supporting some jute
sacks that serve as a wall. Naked children toddle to the edge of the
roadway, carrying pots to clean in the puddles, women cook over
braziers, others sit with their saris over their heads.

In the years I'd thought of Calcutta, in the tales I'd heard of the
*mamabari*, and in the generic term "Southern Avenue" that is
Bharati's way of evoking her entire childhood, I'd pictured something very different from that first night's glimpse. From the street
there is no "*mamabari*"; there are only shuttered shops, an entire
roadside of glass windows barred with iron grates. Beggars are already
sleeping in the doorways, naked babies are laid out three and four on
jute sacking, and a woman nearby is propped against the wall with
her hand listlessly out. Above this scene is a porch. The porch is off
the front bedroom of the *mamabari*.

The entrance is down an alley hardly wider than my shoulders,
through a locked door, into a dark storage room with puddles on the
floor, and up a concrete stair well. That first night I accompanied
*mejo-mamu* to the doorway but not beyond. I cannot come up; "the
women have let down their hair," and the lights are off. They will
expect me in the morning. The Ramakrishna Mission is just a mile

away, where Southern Avenue ends at Gol Park. My assault on Calcutta could begin the next morning.

After the major intersection with Rash Behari, Southern Avenue turns pitch-black; we are on the main road of an ancient suburb, in a part where parks and large houses still predominate. We can speed now, the breeze is refreshing, and I'm a little less tense. No people in sight, the first time in India that an Indian night has truly seemed empty, and orderly.

That is why *chhoto-mamu* surprises me when he says, "This stretch you must not walk at night. *Goondas* can attack you from the side and disappear."

"Even the police won't come here at night," adds Dipu-mesho.

"I'll take a taxi when I want to visit," I say.

"Try never to take a taxi at night," says Dipu. He warns me of taxi drivers, the worst *goondas* of all. I must never let Babloo get in the taxi first—those *goondas* are waiting for gallant gestures like that. They will speed off with her before I can get in. I promise to call Southern Avenue if I ever want a car sent.

I promise to obey. I am anxious, suddenly, to walk, take taxis, mail my letters.

We turn off Southern Avenue up a small alley behind an enormous gray building, then stop in a driveway with bolted gates. A *durwan* in khaki salutes, and opens up. We drive in, and there in the driveway, not moving, are two tall, white-haired gentlemen in starched *dhotis*, each with umbrellas and small boxes of sweets.

"Oh, my God," says *chhoto-mamu*, "Babloo's *jethoo* has been waiting here all this time."

"Oh, my God," I whisper. "And who's the other?"

"Shantu-kaku," he answers. Another of Dodoo's brothers.

They look like emissaries from a wizard's court. The Chatterjee side of Bharati's family is so relaxed, so at ease with me, that they make the complexities of Calcutta seem almost manageable. But not the Mukherjees. "What should I do?" I whisper again, for I had never intended to take on *jethoo* without Bharati to show the way. "Should I make a *pronam*?"

"Don't bother," Dipu whispers back. He and *chhoto-mamu* walk around the car to pocket the detachable wiper blades—a Calcutta precaution—then wait behind me as I step forward to greet the rest of the family.

I had practiced the *pronam* a few dozen times alone in Bombay; the quick jerk downward, flick of the arm, fingers brushing the would-be toes, touching my forehead with the fingertips ("taking the dust from an elder's feet"), then standing, filial or familial duties done. I'd seen Bharati do it dozens of times: the quick dive for a relative's feet, the jangling of her chains and bangles (for always, the context of a *pronam* is Bharati at her most traditional, in crisp sari, wearing her ancestral gold), and what I remembered most from those vivid scenes was not Bharati, but the recipient of the *pronam* standing above her, arms first extended in a halfhearted gesture to stop her, then tilting on his heels as she goes through with it, touching her lightly on the shoulders, or on the head, as a form of counter-recognition. It takes a determined democrat, such as *chhoto-mamu*, to nip a budding *pronam* by clapping the girl around the shoulders and giving a hug, or going for the young man's hand and giving it a mild, unpracticed squeeze before it can drop to his feet. No one had expected the *pronam* from me (no one knew what to expect from me), and I'd not yet been called on to perform. So, anticipating Calcutta, I had practiced on the legs of furniture in Chembur, gathering real dust from the floor in a single swipe, and I knew, once in Calcutta, that I'd be a hit if only I could put my practice into action.

And of course, I couldn't. *Jethoo* and Shantu-kaku, both tall and gaunt and white-haired (how could the black-haired, plush-upholstered Dodoo be their brother?), stand before me in their starched, formal *dhotis*, waiting—I feel—for something spectacular. I approach but can't bend. That terrible self-consciousness: *It's not my ritual; I'll look ridiculous.* And they can't extend their hands. A man like *jethoo*, a wheeler-dealer all his life, but exclusively in orthodox, middle-class Bengali society, has probably never had to shake a hand in his seventy-three years. Certainly it would not be a natural gesture with him—no more than it would have been with a King. He is tall, stiff, and unsmiling. He seems type-cast for sitting in a rickshaw above the crowd, urging some poor black fellow his own age to pull faster. And so I tent my hands in front of my eyes, and mutter my *namoshkar*, which seems to satisfy him. I take his proffered box of *rosha-golas*, and in we march, led by *jethoo* and the silent Shantu-kaku (he is an unemployed brother, I remember, with four daughters and a small rental income), followed by *chhoto-mamu* and Dipu-mesho, and brought up by two bearers struggling with my bags, to the office where I sign the registry (and explain that Mrs. Blaise, niece of all these gentlemen, would be a few days late), then to a self-service elevator (a sign of progressiveness in labor-cheap India), up three floors, then down a wide veranda to my door. All relatives enter to inspect my room.

At last, a pleasant surprise. The room is spacious, with two day beds, two desks, a built-in wardrobe, and an attached private bedroom. Even *jethoo* is complimentary. A bearer comes up with two trays. It is ten o'clock and the kitchen has been closed an hour, but Mr. and Mrs. Blaise's dinners have been saved. I'm alone, I protest, but the bearer smiles and uncovers two large platters of mutton stew, two large salads, two yellowish pudding desserts, two pots of tea. The *mamabari* relatives leave; the Mukherjees sit down to watch me eat. *Jethoo* starts asking questions.

He is upset that his famous niece is not here with me. I explain about Bernie's illness, then am asked why *I* had been able to come. Why has his younger brother permitted me, a *sahib*, to travel alone to Calcutta? Who will look after me here? Do I have an umbrella for the monsoon? Very well, he will be here at nine o'clock to begin shopping for an umbrella in Gariahat Market. I must not try these things myself; I'll be cheated. I get it postponed till five o'clock. What day, exactly, will Babloo be arriving? What flight? Very well, he will be here again. I mention how much we enjoyed ourselves with his daughter and son-in-law in Hamburg, how successful and hard-working they are, how bright his grandchildren are. He accepts the comments as a kind of tribute, to be weighed and stored. The grandchildren are not happy when they visit India, he says; it is the fault of their upbringing. Tulu had been raised "full-culture," in all the traditions, but she is falling away.

"And one more thing," he says, this time leaning forward, hands folded on his umbrella handle, "is it true that you and Babloo were forced to stay one night in a hotel when you visited Hamburg?"

"That was completely my idea, *jethoo*," I say, "my fault completely." I mention an Italian mail strike, the impossibility of warning them in time. "No warning is necessary; she did not invite you well enough in advance," he persists, cocking his head so as not to miss my answer. I knew this would be difficult; that is why I'd wanted Bharati with me. *Jethoo* wants me to confirm his daughter's inhospitality and rejection of family. I refuse. He goes on: His daughter and her husband are "full-culture" Bengali Brahmins; permanent settlement in the West has corrupted them. They have become rich—he can name their income in dollars and the cost of their apartment in deutsch marks—but what good is that if they deny their origins? Their children are European, eating beef and speaking an odd Bengali. They have become Westernized, and they visit only because they feel they have to. *No,* I say. They are very busy, her career and education are important to her. Her children are brilliant, what difference does the rest of it make? He goes on: She did not turn over her bed so that her cousin-sister and her husband could sleep. She made you stay in a hotel, and all Calcutta knows about it, and it is reflecting badly on me. Why have they done this to me?

And because the expectation of hospitality is absolute, there can be no excuses. The fault is mine because I had thought that a family of four landing on a doorstep unannounced might be considered precipitous. The fault is mine because I had wanted a hotel in order to control the situation from the beginning. I'd been wrong; I'd hurt their feelings and we'd spent two nights with them. It is family and it is tradition, and I had disturbed both with my simple notions of self-reliance. My God, no small gesture in the universe is ever lost—especially is it not lost among Bengalis.

I started reading Dom Moraes' *My Son's Father,* but without Bharati I had no sense of myself in this city. I stood at the opened window, staring down at a ruined mansion just across the alley, and at the families that darted across its roofless courtyards in the rain. They had no electricity. The women cooking with braziers under propped-up canvas had their lanterns set about them for light. Other lamps bobbed in and out of darkened rooms on the first two floors as children played, adults sought corners to urinate, and old women wrung out saris and hung them over the window ledges to dry. The rest of the night was thick as velvet, and the alley I had arrived in was ankle-deep in rising water. I walked back across the room to my bed and was suddenly struck still by the thick book over the second day bed. It said: CALCUTTA TELEPHONE DIRECTORY. It could have been a Gutenberg Bible. *Calcutta.* I am in Calcutta! The directory was the most familiar thing I'd seen that night, and the most moving. I started reading it, page by page. Two Satyajit Rays were there, and two dozen ways of spelling Mukherjee. I found Tulu's doctor friends, and the poet we'd once known in Iowa, even a Blaise. What kind of remnants still went by names like Lundquist and Ginsberg and others just as typically Italian and German and British? I often give "Blaises" a call when I find them listed in a strange city; in Calcutta I'd almost be afraid.

Late in the night, I was awakened by a crash of breaking china, followed by a metallic thud, a quick weight on my stomach, a scratching noise, then silence. The two full dinner plates had been knocked on the floor, I snapped on the light. The wastepaper basket was overturned, mutton-*jhol* was spreading across the floor. And worse: Whatever had done this was still in the room with me. Nothing in the wardrobe. The bathroom was also empty. I could not bring myself to try under the beds. I wondered if snakes could have gotten inside. After several minutes I looked up on the ceiling, then parted the curtains above my bed and the air conditioner. There at the top of the window, bright yellow against the stippled glass, rested a wrinkled, beady-eyed, rat-sized *tik-tiki*, a giant house lizard, its paper sides fluttering madly. But for breathing, it was absolutely still and unresponsive. I went outside and rapped the window under its white belly; it didn't flinch. Out on the veranda, under pale 3 A.M. lights that gathered clouds of insects, other *tik-tikis* were roaming about the floors, picking up moths and giant water bugs and heaving their eight-inch bulk around like miniature alligators.

Back inside, I swabbed the floor with a whole roll of toilet paper, set things right, and moved to the second bed. I pulled a sheet over my head and was out like a light.

At six-fifteen, came an insistent rap on the door. Quickly finding pajamas, I asked "*Ki?*" and heard from the other side, "*Cha.*" "Put it down," I said, then in Hindi, "*Udhar.*" From the other side came the grunt of compliance, the rattle of china as it was abruptly plunked. A shadow passed my window. The *tik-tiki*, unmoved from the night before, still dozed at the window top. On a tray outside the door rested an overturned cup on its saucer, a small bowl of coarse gray sugar, a spoon, and a sizable pot of tea under an oft-mended cozy. I wondered if this was a bizarre but touching gesture of welcome (and I was already wondering: *Whom do I thank? Whom do I pay?*) but then I looked out across the vast outfield of clipped grass and flower-lined walks to the other wing of the mission, and on each of those floors white-coated bearers were hustling down the verandas with trays in hand, setting them down, rapping on doors, and hurrying on. My floor had already been served; a tray was still outside my neighbor's door. A fine rain was falling, just enough to coat everything in a cooling slime. But for street-flooding, one could live with the Calcutta monsoon. The clouds were already white and almost fleecy. I had not seen blue sky in over two months.

After I dressed and poured the tea, there came another, more tentative knock. "Newspaper, *saab?*" An elderly paper boy had a jute sling stuffed with *Statesman, Amrita Bazar Patrika,* and a host of Bengali papers. He sized me up as a *Statesman* reader. One paid by the month, he explained. "Now?" I asked, and he seemed surprised; probably no one had ever offered to pay in advance. I took the paper, trusting to his accounts. Down on the ground floor across the lawn, a man was swinging a bell and shouting something I couldn't hear. Doors opened, men and women shuffled along their various verandas to the central stair well (they didn't have an elevator over there), then reappeared on the ground floor, papers folded under their arms, obviously heading for breakfast. Nearly all were Indian, but for a tall bearded young man, and a Japanese. A stout red-haired woman on my floor popped her head out to take the paper, looked directly at me, but didn't respond to my nod. I carried last night's dinner dishes out, including the two broken ones, and set them on the veranda, checked my still-sleeping *tik-tiki*, and joined the others for breakfast.

The Ramakrishna Mission stands like a triple-tiered stadium of battleship gray at the intersection of two main thoroughfares of Ballygunge, Gariahat Road and Southern Avenue. The roads radiate from a circular park (Gol Park) which gives its name to the entire neighborhood. Three other spokes branch from Gol Park, none nearly so broad and busy as the two major roads. Around the park are sweetshops, a gas station, shoe stores, a record shop, drugstore, and postal substation. After Gol Park, Gariahat becomes an even busier road, swelling with the intricacies of its famous market at the intersection with Rash Behari Avenue (Gariahat and Rash Behari being the Times Square of Ballygunge). Southern Avenue, which rises at Gol Park and ends a mile later at its own intersection with Rash Behari (where the *mamabari* stands, in its welter of tram tracks), remains a wide, grass-divided, residentially lined suburban boulevard. *Jethoo* lives on Rash Behari, not far from Gol Park. We were staying less than a mile from Bharati's two grandparental homes.

The mission, then, is wedged between smoky, noisy Gariahat and sleek, moneyed Southern Avenue, on the dizzying rotary of Gol Park. Like a giant on his knees, two long arms extend two city blocks along each major road; his backside is bunched along an alley that connects the two.

The building is a self-contained university—a solid three-story grandstand that entirely surrounds a carpetlike lawn with flower-bordered walkways. The lawn is mowed every day. Our room, one of thirty (ten on a floor) in the "International" wing, backs upon the quiet alleyway. These are the prestige rooms, generally favored by foreigners, or overseas Indians on scholarly projects. They are glassed-in and air-conditioned, intended for double occupancy, with two desks, beds, and closets, and the adjacent bathroom. The wing that is set against Gariahat contains even more rooms, suitable only for single occupancy, without air conditioning, with bars but no glass on the window. They are intended for students, but were occupied mainly by unmarried management trainees, executives on extended leave in Calcutta, central government functionaries on temporary loan to West Bengal, and by some foreigners—*chelas* of the many sitar and sarod teachers in the city seeking to live cheaply but not hazardously over a long stay in Calcutta. All residents take at least two meals a day at the mission. The monthly room and board, plus daily cleaning and room-tea, comes to approximately one hundred dollars a month —provided one stays at least two months. The "scholars" across the way pay even less, but suffer for it, in noise, crampedness, and, especially, mosquitoes. For the most part, the mission protects its guests from the more brutal confrontations with Calcutta life, while leaving most residents the illusion of still being in contact with the real India that rushes around that fortress like a river in flood. Occasionally, the mission exposes an institutional sordidness all its own.

The Ramakrishna Order takes its name from a Bengali seer—some would say madman—of the late nineteenth century, Ramakrishna, whose visions were publicized and poetized by a gifted disciple, Swami Vivekananda, and given to the world under the general heading of Vedantism. The Vedanta is the philosophy of the Vedas—in short, Hinduism itself, shorn of its shabbier elements. Sri Ramakrishna spent nearly all his adult life in a state of religious ecstasy. And due to the world-wide mission of his articulate disciple, Vivekananda, substantial amounts of money were raised in the West, and the funds established the Ramakrishna Order.

The order runs the mission as well as a chain of charitable hospitals, schools, and libraries across India, in addition to its well-known missions in Europe and the States. It is a shrewd order, mystical and practical in turns—a Bengali J. F. Powers could have fun with them —one that is, by now, only quasi-religious. While the headquarters in Gol Park still house monks in long saffron robes (monks from all over the world), the major emphasis of the order's teaching seems to be culture, education, and good works.

Sri Ramakrishna's central message, that all religion is one (he even apprenticed himself to a Muslim imam, and in later life could weep at the Bible and embrace statues of Mary and Christ as well as his beloved Kali), has now become a doctrine of world monoculturalism. *All Culture Is One* is an appealing article of faith that often becomes a stubborn piety. Toynbee and Jung, Einstein and Hammarskjöld, Tolstoy and Gandhi, Vivekananda and Whitman, can find themselves elevated into quirky syntheses. The essential mystical message of cosmic unity has become a vehicle for progressive reform, pan-culturalism, and charitableness. And so, as always, the extremes are fused. The saintly visionary has entered the pantheon of gods; throughout Bengal one finds his garlanded portrait hanging in shops or in shrines. His representation is as a gaunt, ill-shaven, short-haired ecstatic, in a trance, praying. Bengalis from orthodox Hindu backgrounds who scorned the major reformers of the nineteenth century, the more rationalistic "Brahmo Samaj," have embraced Ramakrishna, Vivekananda, and all that they speak for, ecstatically and uncritically.

In the first week of my stay, I was summoned to the main office, across that dazzling lawn, to meet with a nonrobed secretary of the order. Lapsed everything that I am, I feared an urgent invitation to attend prayers or lectures, but the request was entirely, and characteristically, different. He wondered if I would contribute to their journal, a pale blue quarterly of substantial size and eclectic contents, which circulated in nearly every library in the world. I pleaded that I was a fiction writer, that all I could attempt, short of giving them a story, was (laughably) an involved discussion of narrative technique in the short story. "I'm sure that is fascinating," he said. "It is all an aspect of something greater, is it not?" I suggested that I did not think it was, and so I never submitted, nor was I ever approached a second time.

3

After that first breakfast, I walked down Southern Avenue to the *mamabari*. The rains were over for the morning, and a warm breeze had dried the pavements. Ballygunge glistened under a brilliant sun. *Dhobis* had set out their washes to dry on the *maidan's* clean grass. Herdsmen had brought their buffalo to the same grass for grazing, and children were using the bubbling muddy fountains from broken hydrants to scrub the young buffalo. On all the available walls, on the occasional slabs of unbroken concrete, and on the metal light standards, the cow dung sellers had set their hamburger-sized patties out to dry: Each family seemed to have at least two hundred drying in the sun, and the children were constantly bringing baskets of the fresh manure to the mothers, scraped from the streets by hand as fast as the cows dropped it, to be mixed with straw and filler, before they headed out again.

I rang the *mamabari* bell and shouted up, "I'm here." A bowing servant showed me up the stairs.

*Chhoto-mamu* had already left for the office, leaving only the uncle from last night, *mejo-mamu*, his wife, *mami-ma*, a substantial woman my height but somewhat wider, and the two girls, Anju, age nineteen, and Pritu, twenty. Bharati's *dimma*, mother of the uncles and of her mother, is nearly blind and bedridden, and permanently in the back bedroom. Dipu-mesho, Kola-mashi, and their daughter, Jaya, were there, on the extended visit from Nagpur for the wedding. Both Anju and Pritu were tall and slim; Pritu was a beauty, though not adept in English. The younger was studying to be a lawyer. She was the clever one, perky, darker than her sister, and coarser-featured.

I had arrived during a teasing session between Anju and the witty Nagpur uncle. They switched to English for my benefit. He was making fun of her rough skin and saucy manner. It was like walking into a Victorian novel. The name-calling ("bundle of idiocy") was so dated as to seem innocent, and the young woman's turning to me for protection so trusting ("We will ask Clark if I am a bundle of idiocy. He will feel my cheeks and see if they are as smooth as ghee!") that I of course affirmed her charm and beauty. I was, in fact, charmed out of my mind. Her father, watching all this, explained to me that the traditional conduct between a brother-in-law (or cousin-in-law, in my case) and his younger sister-in-law is playful. Lots of nudging, pinching, and hugging to be encouraged. I did not pinch, but probably I nudged. I had never been so quickly accepted in my life. I could not tell if I was benefiting from tradition, a flirtatious girl, or if I had finally settled in the lone place that found my general looks irresistible. I was given the only chair in the open hall. The girls sat at my feet, and *mami-ma* brought tea. I *pronam*'d old *dimma* in her bed, tried out all the Bengali I had laboriously stored, and talked to them of India, myself, and my sincere and absolute pleasure at having finally arrived. I had a second cup of tea. I remarked on the blueness of the sky (now visible from the open hallway), like a summertime Canadian sky, something to feel homesick for, and Anju answered before quickly entering another room, "You need not feel homesick. You have only to look in the mirror to see such blue." "What?" I asked. "Your eyes," she giggled, and disappeared for the rest of the morning.

This flat has been the Chatterjees' home for nearly forty years. They have rented the entire time, and because of rent control they pay nearly the same rent now as they did in the 1930s.

Four rooms branch off a long hall. The hall binds the separate sol-
itudes of the various bedrooms; it is a living room, and when relatives stay for dinner (as we did, every Sunday), the women will all
gather here to eat, from the floor. One bedroom has a table for the
men to eat from, and a corner devoted to the shelves of gods. There
are three other bedrooms, one merely to store the heavy furniture
hauled from Dacca nearly fifty years before. There is a bathroom—a
traditional Indian bathroom of buckets and open drains—and a
dark, narrow alcove for cooking. Life centers in the open hall. All
that is typical of Calcutta, at least on one spectacular level, can be
seen from the front bedroom porch: naked refugees leading their private lives in public, beggars asleep on the sidewalk, bumper-to-
bumper traffic. The other end of the hall looks out over another
side of Calcutta, a tidy jungle of *batabi*, *devdar* and lemon trees,
banana plants and lush low shrubs. The barred windows contain no
glass; birds enter and leave every room at will. The day's wash is
strung along the hallway and over the stairs; pajamas, undershirts,
saris.

The flat holds three generations: one "nuclear" family and remnants of another. *Chhoto-mamu* is the only wage earner. Two ex-ser-
vants now hold jobs outside, but continue to work for the family in
return for food and sleeping space. *Chhoto-mamu*, then, provides a
direct livelihood for his oldest brother's family and for nearly all of
the *mamabari* expenses. After college, the various nieces will require
dowries, unless they succeed in falling in love, a vow to which they
have a solemn commitment.

Forty years ago, *borro-mamu*, who now lives in a flat in north-end
Calcutta, had a government job far away from Calcutta. It is said
that he refused to take a bribe, and was fired for it. His posture of
uncorruptibility has gone unchallenged ever since, as has his right
not to seek another job. Without his reputation for uprightness, he
might have encountered some objection to forty years of paternal,
and then fraternal, charity.

*Mejo-mamu* has dabbled in import-export for the past twenty
years, and can usually be found in his *pajama* and undershirt, sitting
in the hall, entering and erasing figures from his ledger books. The
front porch sometimes stores a jute sack of ginger or peppercorns. He
speaks to me of his suppliers in Assam and Orissa, his buyers in Can-

ada and the States. His "business partner" is also the house servant, a convenient subservience when it comes time to send him down to the docks or train station to pick up supplies. The family would not survive many weeks on his company's annual gross, but intimacy demands that the joint family tolerate a number of permanent grievances and illusions.

Things are simply not pushed to their limit, although everyone knows where the vulnerabilities are, and which knives do the most pitiless cutting. The joint family may well be "the fortress in distress" that traditional Indians feel it is; for me it came more to resemble a *No Exit*, a closet drama of resentment and dependence among people who, like cellmates, know each other too well to hide a thing.

Joint living is permanent theater. Passions run high, it is the instinctive topic of conversation, the inevitable subject of serious fiction, just as the escape from it into romantic love and personal freedom is the stuff of the Hindi popular movie. Family is all; it is impossible for the outsider to reconcile the centrality of the family in India with its fashionable marginality in the West. In India "identity" seems to me joint and collective, and one of the battles being fought in this generation—in Anju's and Pritu's even more than Bharati's—is to settle the demands of duty, as son, wife, or daughter, with the rising self-consciousness brought by education and Western influence.

For men like *chhoto-mamu* it has already been settled. To be educated, employed and productive, aware, enlightened and generous, means to renounce all personal aspirations and dreams of "selfish" fulfillment. From a Western perspective, it is difficult not to view the family as villainous, and *chhoto-mamu* as somehow supremely, if not pathetically, virtuous. Yet if one views the joint family as the indivisible social unit of India, then *chhoto-mamu* becomes symbol as well. A certain crude equation, an allegory, suggests itself. Family stands for village, unemployment, passivity, endless demands. The single wage earner stands for the city, activity, and the future, whatever it will bring. This particular family on Southern Avenue is a microcosm of the entire society.

The oldest member of the family, Bharati's seventy-six-year-old *dimma*—nearly blind and bedridden with diabetes and cardiac congestion—calls herself (in Anju's translation) "International Granny" because one of her granddaughters has married a Westerner, and two others have made love matches with non-Bengalis. Anju assures me that old *dimma* approves. She has been known to say, after the groans and complaints, the loud exclamations of disgust with life and her readiness to die, that one must move with the times. Caste no barrier. That old *dimma* should approve of the family spilling out of Calcutta, even out of India and out of orthodox Hinduism, is not believable. Old and infirm, she strikes me as a woman of unswerving opinion.

Yet, who can say? Indian women are astonishing blends of unbending orthodoxy and striking flexibility, as is India itself. I know only the bent old woman who *namoshkars* me from her bed, who receives my *pronam* with a toothless grin, who shuffles along the hallway to the bathroom at a ten-to-six posture thirty times a day. She seems to me merely a presence in the flat, like the old furniture lugged from Dacca, and cared for like a house plant. She has been preparing to die ever since her husband died twenty years before. She does not seem, in and of herself, to command respect. It seems to me that the warrant for life, for respect, does not reside in the individual soul; it resides more in having a role to play and in providing for the family. And what role is there for the mother of married daughters? So old *dimma* lies on a bed cursing the ingratitude of the family, cursing her fate, begging for death.

All of her ten children are either married, dead, or widowed, except for the most brilliant, *chhoto-mamu*, who supports them all. They in turn have not found him a bride because she might not tolerate such a flat, and anyway, where would they put her? An educated girl (he would doubtless demand a college graduate) would insist that he move away to Delhi to the luxury quarters that the government would provide. And then what would happen, with *chhoto-mamu* in Delhi, with a smart young wife whispering poison in his ear, to the daily dollops of movie money, sari money, and market expenses? Over the years a series of girls have been presented; in each case, *borro-mamu*, exercising his ritual role as head of the family, has declared each girl unworthy. And so now the breadwinner is fifty, an important man who has exercised his own role, the manliest role in the Hindu culture, that of *providing* for those who cannot. He could have a house in Delhi, servants; he could live like a rajah. Instead, he supervises one of India's largest public enterprises from his ancestral flat in Calcutta, eating at home, reading books every night borrowed from the Ballygunge library, and sleeping on his mother's bed. Old *dimma*, for the night, is put on a mattress on the floor. He was once a Sanskrit scholar, number one in university. He took an engineering degree when his father died, and he remains a witty, shy, encyclopedically well informed man, with no one to talk to. "I read," he tells me, "I keep company with the best minds. Like you. Like Babloo." In my eyes, in Western eyes, he is a tragic victim. But the longer I looked, the better I came to know him and to love him, I saw in that calm, pear-shaped little figure the shape of a hero; in the context of his world image, the shape of a god.

Middle-class interiors reflect an indifference to self-expression, or to improvement, that borders on the pathological. Furniture and utensils were either overused or never touched. In forty years the walls of the *mamabari* had never been scoured; certainly never painted. Everything remains as it always has been. No new furniture, new drapes, new pots—only new saris. *Why?* I kept asking myself. Nonattachment, indifference to appearance? Hinduism again, the working out of profound ideas on the simplest social level? Or is it Marx again? No one paints, because paint is too expensive, because plaster is too porous, the humidity too ruinous. The landlord wouldn't thank you—he'd try to raise the rent. Burglars would become interested. No one paints or scrubs because such labor is demeaning, and the servants wouldn't do it. No housewife, and especially no husband, would do that kind of labor.

Well-dressed men can be seen stepping down from taxis or from their own cars in order to urinate against any convenient wall. Do they do it because even public walls are more private, less offensive, and finally less unhealthy than what passes for a toilet in their homes? Why do anything in Calcutta when individual effort to beautify, to unpollute, to educate, to uplift, can only be mocked by inconceivable inertia? Is Calcutta the world's largest public urinal and garbage heap simply because ten million people are sharing the space and facilities that were outmoded a century ago by half a million? Does that explain it all—*is* it only Marx?

Or is it Hinduism. Deep down, is it the conflict with an older world image, the sort of thing that Jung and Zimmer tried to explain? Are all attempts at painting one's house absurd not because of paint quality and humidity, but because of maya, the doctrine of nonattachment, the inherited notion that attachment to material objects and to self-expression is all illusory? Calcuttans urinate against a wall and blow out long banners of snot onto the shoes of passers-by out of a uniquely Hindu standard of personal cleanliness. To carry a dirty handkerchief on one's own body would be disgusting. I would spend hours ridding my room of mosquitoes; I would squirm with anticipatory zeal as a mosquito circled, then settled, within swatting distance. One less mosquito in a room of fifty was a positive thing. Indians never bothered. Immunity? Stoicism? Reverence for life? Servants wet-ragged the floors twice a day; that 'alone passed for cleaning. The suitcases stored above the wardrobes were hidden by dust; the blades of the overhead fan were blanketed in lint. Didn't anyone notice anything above toe level? Should they? Who was pathological?

Is modern Calcutta the product of crowding, poor distribution, corruption, flight of capital, bad planning, and foreign exploitation? Or is all that irrelevant because it relates only *our* world image, and Calcutta still belongs to its citizens as a spiritual projection? Offering solutions for India sometimes seems as relevant as kibbutzing a chess game and saying, *If he moves his knight, he can protect his left flank and reverse the material loss,* and to have another onlooker reply, *No, that won't work. He's dead drunk, you see.* Bengalis loved Calcutta the way Florence, Paris, and London had once been loved—as inseparable from themselves, a wife. Marxists now speak lovingly of fire, famine, earthquake—any excuse to start over. But a poet of Calcutta, P. Lal, spoke to us in the voice of Hegel: Nothing will change that does not conform to the mythic patterns of the people. Marx or Hegel, Mao or Gandhi? It was another question I tried not to ask out loud.

## 4

Back at the Ramakrishna Mission that evening, the man sitting across from me introduced himself as Group Captain Basu, but allowed that perhaps I knew him by his writing name, "Kapu Das." I felt the question demanded an honest answer. As befits an air force officer (ret.), his English was clipped and *pukka*. He was now a steel executive by day, a poet by night; Mr. Basu in a business suit, Kapu Das in *dhoti*. "Do you smoke?" he asked. Ah, sensible fellow. "Do you drink?" Ah, very glad to hear it. Then leaning forward, dropping his voice to a whisper, "Do you love?" Ah, then you are a man. I had the feeling he was trying out some of his poetry.

The mission welcomes all visitors with scholarly projects; it is not always able, however, to distinguish between scholarship and dewy-eyed Vedantism. "Is your quest spiritual?" asked a white-saried, middle-aged American. She was a California librarian who spent one month every summer in Calcutta. Her diet was so strictly vegetarian (in fish-loving Bengal, fish are honorary vegetables, but not for her) that she even refused the gluey yellow pudding for fear it contained an egg. It was she, I learned later, who had dived so enthusiastically for the feet of the chief swami, in offering her first *pronam*, that to fend her off he had stepped backward, stumbled, and fallen across the flower bed.

I felt insubstantial in Calcutta without Bharati. Alone, I was fair game for the looser fringes of world culturism. Who was to know that my quest was nothing less than the retrieval of a buried self, the understanding of my marriage? Who was to know that I had a *jethoo* in Calcutta who'd just conducted me through the maze of Gariahat Market and that I now owned an authentic *babu* umbrella to hook on my arm as I strolled between monsoon showers, just like any office worker in any movie by Satyajit Ray?

After dinner I called *chhoto-mamu* about my briefcase. Voucher received, but no bag delivered. I despaired. I went back to Gariahat Market and bought paper, tried to write a story about the March on Washington, 1963, and found I couldn't visualize America at all. The next evening I accompanied *chhoto-mamu* to the Indian Airlines downtown terminal. We harassed the baggage clerks and finally got admitted to the warehouse. We discovered the briefcase in the desk of a junior officer, not because he'd wanted to steal it, but so that it wouldn't be transferred routinely without his knowledge. Perhaps he'd intended to ask me a favor—I was already getting requests, even from umbrella salesmen: *Saab, I have brother who wants a job*

... *wants to immigrate.* ... No one could release it for me that night, but I was not to worry. It would be delivered to the mission ("Ah, Gol Park, yes, very good") the next morning. And it was.

5

I had put myself on the trail of Rabindranath Tagore from the moment I could begin finding translations of his books. The influence of Tagore in Bengal is so profound it transcends "influence" itself— before Tagore there was very little to modify or influence. He virtually created it all: first saving the language from bastardization, making refined, precise, and lyrical discourse possible, and then he wrote the poems, novels, plays, songs, and essays that are still, for most Bengalis, the glory of their literature. I'd been making a pest of myself, asking every Bengali about the influence of Tagore, and since I couldn't read Bengali, a pest was all I was likely to remain. That is why, when a lecture advertised as "Tagore and Western Romantic Poetry (in English)" was held in the public lecture hall of the mission, just across the lawn from where we were staying, I was in the auditorium early enough to count the chairs (twenty-five rows of twenty chairs) and to sit, turned in my chair, to inspect the audience as they arrived.

Nearly the full five hundred showed up. The lecture was set for seven o'clock, predinner for most Bengalis. It was an audience exclusively male, but for a lone middle-aged woman with chopped-off hair and in a skirt—a self-conscious crusader, or perhaps merely a Christian. The only other "European" was about my age, in a *kurta* and East European by the look of his hair and gray trousers that clung tight where they should have flared, and vice versa. White like me, but carrying a Bengali book, he scurried far away. Those Romanians were a dutiful lot. The rest of the audience was composed of men over sixty, all in formal evening white *dhoti*. The old man one seat away seemed so enraptured with the prospect of the lecture that he didn't notice an oily ring spreading from a fresh bird dropping on his shoulder. Tagore, the universal genius of Bengal, had died in 1941, and most of the audience would have known him, loved him, and memorized his work when they themselves had gone to university.

On any given night in Calcutta, Tagore's plays, his songs, or his dances are sure to be performed; to call Tagore the Shakespeare of Bengal is to underestimate his importance, drastically. I had come to understand just a little of Tagore's great power from reading translations and trying to ask those who would answer, but I was still little more than a naïve believer in his genius. In wanting to know more, I was treading on the inexplicable.

Professor Banerjee wore a gray shawl embroidered with an edge of flowers, and he wore it theatrically loose about his shoulders. He was the third-youngest man in the hall, lean and tall, with more hair than any man has a right to expect at any age, oiled to a dull sheen and combed straight back. He was nervous and bony, with a long neck knotted by muscles, and the thin, expressive hands of a well-born Bengali. Two other men flanked him at the long head table, with pitchers of water and a precautionary pair of hurricane lamps. In Calcutta one never knows when the power will be cut, when "load-shedding" will occur, although Wednesday nights in Ballygunge were supposed to be safe.

He was a professor of Bengali and English at a large, poorly-thought-of university in a different state, and he was introduced to us as the son and grandson of Tagore scholars, himself an author of several books on Tagore, and a graduate of Tagore's own university at Santineketan—truly a man "with Tagore in his blood." The consanguinary audience applauded.

I had hoped that Professor Banerjee, as a younger man and as an academic, would be less dogmatic and slightly less Vedantic in his approaches—a little more the Leavisite or Empsonian. I wanted desperately to understand Tagore; it was the only literary way I had of understanding Bengal, and as a writer, I'd always come to the literatures of a new culture second, just after the museums. As for Tagore, I had read the three novels Gora, Home and the World, and The Wreck in Edwardian-sounding English translations and had found them to be works of genius, like discovered mythologies, the characters possessing the clarity and consistency of gods and demons. But the poetry, in the same translations (or worse, in Tagore's own), had never held up. Even with the best will in the world, I'd found it watery, trivially universal: the Vedantic stance personified. I'd come to accept the judgment of the West that Yeats, and Tagore's other early admirers—not to mention the Nobel Prize committee of 1913—had been more indulgent than rigorous in conferring the prize on him, perhaps sensing a spiritual vista through the haze of poor translation. So, hardened case that I was, I'd come one last time to learn about Tagore and why I should honor him.

"There are three reasons I love returning to Calcutta," the scholar began. "Foremost, of course, must be the *rosha-golas*." The audience roared its approval; he was among friends. He had begun on the properly British, properly modest note: *I come to Calcutta because I love Bengali sweets.* I too liked Bengali *mishti*, the best in India. From the Ramakrishna Mission it was only a five-minute walk over the drying cow patties flanking Gol Park to the nearest Ganguram sweetshop where we bought 250-gram clay pots of *lal doi*, the sweet, red, chilled yoghurt, for our daily lunch, and we would sit in the shade of the veranda spooning it out until the sides were scraped clean and flecks of clay began discoloring the residue, or until we had gotten too close to the dead ants that every now and then lay curled like surprises under the final curds (if ants lined the delicate 250-gram *vhar*, what more ravenous creature lay immolated in the one-kilo basket?). Bengalis, among many other less-complimentary things, are respected throughout India for their confections and collective sweet tooths; it is not merely fatuous for a returning Bengali to glorify the sweets of Bengal—he is asserting his kinship as surely as a Frenchman does by sipping red wine. "Secondly, of course, there are the theaters. Our incomparable Bengali stage." He fell for the moment from his stiffened strand of English into the pit of Bengali that yearned to receive him—it must have been a quote from Tagore on theater, judging from the sudden head-swivelings and applause. Even this I could accept: Not understanding a word, I had accompanied my wife's family to almost-nightly musicals and dramas in those seemingly ancient but merely dilapidated theaters in Calcutta's north end. While I found Calcutta itself a stage and all Bengalis at least partially conscious actors within it, the legitimate stage of Calcutta was an actor's delight; it is, I should imagine, the nearest thing extant to the Renaissance stage of England, where the whole society was entertained by plays immediately accessible to all its strata. Refined and coarse, subtle and broad, dry and mawkish, to audiences of the privileged upper classes, Maoist students, and

illiterate laborers, in steaming theaters where the exits are open
and the monsoon rains splash against the unamplified delivery.
Where babies cry, businessmen deal, old folks sleep: The universal
audience, a dead memory in the West, was still the reality in Bengal,
both a support and a curse (nothing in India is single-edged). While
it grants its artists an audience much larger and more knowledgeable than any comparable "general" audience in the West, it for-
bids them any departures or striking avant-garde innovations. In Calcutta there is no affluent, fashionably alienated, culturally articulate
audience to which self-consciously "difficult" art can be addressed.
Nor is there, in Calcutta at least, a newly arrived, freshly moneyed
class of Bengalis anxious to "get" culture. It is a loving, applauding
mass, and the art of Bengal must appeal, as it does, to all of them,
simultaneously.

"And of course," the professor went on, extending those simian
arms and snapping the fingers in our direction—one expected flecks
of water from such elegant fingers popping in our faces—"there is
my family and my friends. For truly as Rabindranath has written, of
all cities on the earth, Calcutta is the city of friendship."

Nodding agreeably, the charmed audience settled back.


Tagore, it turned out, had passed beyond all meaningful comparison with Western Romanticism by the age of nineteen, when, in the
poem "Chitra," he achieved what Wordsworth had despaired of ever
finding. Tagore had worked his way over tractless paths and arduous
journeys and had found where fled that visionary gleam. At nineteen! After that and for the next sixty-one years, his poetry was to
emanate from the top of the Romantic mountain, or from the other
side, and Wordsworth, even in the five years of his transcendence,
was to climb not halfway up its flanks. "Compared to Wordsworth,
Tagore is a giant to a dwarf. Tagore's eighty years of 'passing over
the arc' to Wordsworth's five. Nowhere in the West outside of
Shakespeare do you find 'the grand passion surging.'" He did not at
that moment pursue the limitations of Shakespeare. Wordsworth at
eighty, and such Western artists as Baudelaire, Kafka, and Beckett,
were still vainly seeking a flicker of the visionary gleam, but this
mere lad from Bengal had already bridged the gap between the
world of sordid reality and the world of pure vision. He quoted

Wordsworth at impressive length, then Keats and Shelley, then apposite lines in Bengali ("for truly at such times one must have recourse to one's mother tongue") and the *dhoti-wallahs* thumped their approval. "Surely," came the rejoinder, now back to English, "such profound sentiments is unknown in Western poetry, after perhaps the mighty bard." I too preferred it that way, for I like the style of Tagore recitation, the ever-rising inflection, reminiscent of Yevtushenko before a hundred thousand at Spartak Stadium.

And then, without a flicker of warning, the lights went out all over Ballygunge. The fans stopped. In the dark, the windows were opened. My shirt turned moist immediately, pools of sweat gathered on my thighs where I'd been resting my elbows.

The presiding officer rose to speak. Two bearers were called to light the hurricane lamps. "I believe, ladies and gentlemen, if our speaker is agreeable, there is nothing to do but go on."

"I cannot read my notes," the professor said. "All of this is useless to me. But," and now he addressed us, arms out, "a humble speaker can only beg patience when the gods have been so unsympathetic. I will go on without notes"—he crumpled them in his hands—"if you will but say yes." Now he seemed a giant, flames casting Audenesque crevices on his face and neck, and throwing his enormous shadow on the walls and ceiling.

The lecture did go on for another hour in gathering heat and mosquito infestation. It seemed, in the dark, that I could smell that squiggle of bird dropping a few inches away, and through the open windows, Calcutta itself was competing with Professor Banerjee. Or perhaps they weren't competing, for Professor Banerjee had long made his point and was now standing in front of the lanterns blocking all our light, arms akimbo and shawl hanging loose, celebrating Bengal, reciting Tagore, the brilliant, the sensuous, the romantic genius Tagore, in a voice so choked with awe, yet so practiced, that no Chautauqua ham would have dared to compete.

I was being brutalized. My precepts. My critical judgments, my reasons for having come, my respect for balanced judgment, for ambiguity, for the romantic agony of blurred vision and imperfect quest, my Leavis, my Eliot, my Brooks and Warren, all being brutalized by each new poem. Here was an audience that respected only success and responded only to love; Tagore was brilliant because he achieved what he had set out to do, not because he set out to do the impossible. And it made no difference that by now, in the dark, Professor Banerjee had shed all pretense of proving his point; he was now only reciting in the rotting humid night with flickering lights far behind him.

Then the lights came on. The fans dried me off in minutes. My eyes ached for the dark. "Ladies and gentlemen, I have departed from the text somewhat. I trust I am forgiven."

But he wasn't, not quite. He had demonstrated only one essential fact in his two-hour discourse in the light and in the dark: perhaps the important fact, that Tagore was in his blood and that he loved Tagore unreservedly. Now was the time for Bengal's other face. Why are Bengalis hated so, why were they feared by the British and every other conqueror? Not because of their physical ferocity certainly, but because of a daunting intelligence, an ability to learn the rules of any conqueror and to overcome them with their own mental sluggishness. Intellectual judo. The Bengali can be a disputatious bully, cocky, extravagant, and hopelessly committed to world culture and to his own central place within it. That is why Calcutta trams are burned in protest when André Malraux arrives in the city (for had he not suppressed Henri Langlois and the *cinémathèque fran-çaise?*), or when Third World governments topple with CIA intervention, or when South Africans tyrannize their majority.

The presiding officer had no intention of thanking the speaker and freeing him for his friends and *rosha-golas:* He began to dissect the professor's speech from his own copious notes. Twenty minutes later he had gone so far as to suggest that visionary Romantics differ from conceptual ones and that a comparison with Wordsworth was false and self-serving. Surely Tagore must stand with the two great visionaries, Whitman (right! I thought) and Victor Hugo (ah, *per-versité*). How can we compare Tagore with the great British Romantics when most of them died before their fortieth year? What might Keats have accomplished? The concept of beauty doesn't even exist in classical Indian thought—how can a poet to whom the concept of beauty is an imported affectation be compared to poets to whom it is a crowning obsession? And the modern masters—by what right are they termed Romantics? Read Jacques Barzun, my dear professor. Haven't they resolved the romantic tension between per-

manent beauty and sordid reality just as surely as Keats or Tagore—
but on the side of the latter? Consider Yates. Either we live without
escaping the sordid, or else we escape it poetically, almost at will,
like Tagore. Literature resolves nothing, he chided the professor.
Read Auden. And anyway, didn't Tagore write, at seventy-three, in a
tone much different from his youthful "Chitra," that man was a
beast?

The proud knots in the professor's neck began to sag. An aroused
audience was clawing the air for permission to speak. "Please," the
professor broke in, "allow a poor speaker to vindicate himself."

## 6

By the time Bharati arrived I had started to join a more boisterous
table of mixed Europeans and Indians. There was a young Australian sarodist, an American professor about my age, a studious Bengali
in starched *dhoti*, an outgoing Punjabi attached to the Bengal health
ministry, and a perky young Bengali girl who worked as a secretary
and wasn't afraid of living alone and mixing unabashedly. After a
few days, we were joined by a young London-resident Bengali professor; his place at the head of the table went unquestioned. He did
radiate a certain authority—his accent was rigidly upper-class British
—though it would take a day or two to find out why.

One night at dinner I was feeling particularly expansive, having
just returned from two hours in a sari shop, with Jaya, Dipu-mesho,
Bharati, and all the aunts and cousins. I started talking first to the
American and Australian, letting my specialized knowledge of
*namashkari* saris (those given in dowry) drip quietly into the conversation, and pausing only long enough to inquire what they had been
doing that day. I felt I was making progress, getting to know Calcutta.

Lenny, the American, mentioned he'd been interviewing Siddhartha Shankar Ray, the Chief Minister of Bengal that day, then
had been in the archives of the state government, researching the ag-
ricultural policies of the 1940–43 Bengal Common Front Government. 1943 had been the year of the historical famine in which millions of Bengalis had died; no Bengali alive in those years is without

stories of corpses in the gutters and beggars coming to the door. Satyajit Ray had just won the Berlin "Golden Bear" for his movie about the famine, *Ashani Sanket*, which had not yet opened in Calcutta. The scholarly, *dhoti*-clad Bengali contributed his own memories of the famine as a rural teen-ager, relating how he had come to Calcutta shortly after the war, as a *brahmacharya* in the Ramakrishna Order—a boy in saffron robes in this very religious order—then left the order to take up Sanskrit studies at the university, and finally left India to become a professor of Classical Indian Thought at the Sorbonne. And then the young Cambridge don contributed from a series of "rather interesting statistics" that he'd once seen that were only now coming to light. "Yes," said the American, "I read your article." The British policy of benign neglect had allowed upwards of three million Bengalis to starve rather than allow a fall in the price of food grains.

The Australian had been practicing sarod twelve hours a day for the past ten months as a *chela* of Ali Akbar Khan's son-in-law; the Sorbonne Sanskritist had published three books in French on the concept of Atman in Buddhist scripture. The American was Leonard Gordon, a professor at Columbia, author of two books on Bengal and now researching a third. And the Cambridge don was—as Bharati had guessed—Professor Amartya Sen, a legendary genius of her school years in Loreto, when superb intelligence (even in different faculties of different universities, in different languages) had held a riveting, almost sexual fascination over protected girls from good families, whose permissible fantasies lay only in the direction of tennis stars and movie actors. It had been as though his intelligence alone (his subsequent career in economics has borne it out) had made him an eligible match, in the eyes of wealthy, Westernized Brahmin girls for whom he was not otherwise (by caste, class, or profession) even remotely suited. His genius had made him an honorary marriage candidate in a class that—because he was a genius —he would have despised.

*Family, family, family.* In India all is finally family. If we in the West suffer the nausea of disconnectedness, alienation, anomy, the Indian suffers the oppression of kinship. If our concept of the hero implies isolation, risk, and such "manly" virtues as bravery, silence,

and fleshly mortification, the Indian concept of the hero is tied up
with social duty and an almost feminine form of solicitousness and
availability. We naturally link maturity with independence and self-
creation, the holiness of the quest for identity and self-assertion. We
consider a young man's break with his family (a ritual that grows
more violent with each generation) "an inevitable part of growing
up." *Still at home?* we might ask a twenty-year-old, implying, *What's
wrong with you?* Parents of such a child might even feel guilty.

In India, of course, identity never has to be sought; it is the lone
certainty, and one's identity determines nearly everything. The father decides his son's career as surely as he chooses his daughter's
husband. It is his duty to do so, and duty in India is discharged guiltlessly.

A few weeks after we were settled, two of Bharati's vaguer uncles
took us out to dinner. Both men were well-to-do, and each had a son.
The younger cousin, at ten, was already a complete little man: He
had the physique of a teen-ager and the bearing (voice, level gaze,
vocabulary, confidence) of an earnest young trainee in a prestigious
corporation. He spoke to me in English, to his parents in Bengali,
and ordered the waiters about in a Hindi that made them scurry.
"He is rather clever with words," his father explained. "That is why I
have placed him in an English-medium school. He will be a lawyer."
And the older uncle, father of a more childlike teen-ager who could
not speak to me and was too shy to speak to Bharati even in Bengali,
was going to a Bengali-medium school, because, his father explained,
he was good in math, and for an electrical engineer, a Bengali preparation is best. "Every year you check university results in the state
and you will see boys from Bengali schools are at the top."

Doubtless, both parents are right. The children probably will grow
up as lawyers and electrical engineers, and the lawyer is almost certain to play a role in the political life of India in the next half century. And with his dazzling command of English he will doubtless
earn scholarships to the West, and if he does not yield to tempta-
tions and marry a comparable starlet in the West (and break his parents' hearts), he will marry spectacularly well in Calcutta. She will
be rich, fair, convent-educated, and beautiful, and she will cement
his place in the Westernized upper-middle-class Calcutta high soci-

ety. His cousin, however, is destined for a different function and this is as clear at thirteen (and was, at six) as it will be at twenty-five.

The decision to start a child in an English-language nursery school must be taken at three, and it will be one of the most crucial decisions of the father's life. The competition to the best schools is so stiff, and the society so achievement-oriented, that five-year-olds are sent to special "cramming classes" so that at six, or again at seven, they may sit for their entrance exams at La Martinière or St. Xavier's. The results of those tests will determine nearly everything else about their careers: earnings, marriage, and social position. English mastery is essential, even more than it was before Hindi became the official language.

At the time we discussed it, I pitied the would-be engineer; it all seemed so arbitrary and iniquitous—"You be rich happy liberated lawyer" and "You be unemployed engineer"—but now, while I will never come to sanction such father-power, I also admire the older uncle for what he had *not* done to his son. Realizing his boy was of narrow gifts, he has equipped him with a servicable profession and brutally clear identity. Had he bribed his son's way into an English-medium school, he surely would have made him into one of the dispossessed, one of the balloons set adrift, not intelligent enough to master his advantages, but glib, a mimic Englishman, one of the *box-wallahs* (the employees of onetime British firms who have taken over the onetime British clubs and all the old British pursuits of horse races, booze, and social gamesmanship).

We were taken to the Ballygunge home of an old business friend of Dodoo's, now a managing director of a pharmaceutical factory. He is rich now, and enjoys his money immensely, a happy basher of corporate eggs. The house itself is huge, worthy of the larger fraternity houses of my college days, emphasized in fact by the contrast between the screened-in porch and decorated living room, all suitable for guests and entertainment, and the dingy, utilitarian bedrooms, kitchen, and basement dining area, equipped with plank tables and benches that could seat forty or more. And every night the family did seat thirty at least; for the managing director had three children going to college and one still in grade school, and his four brothers each with wives and four or more children also occupied the house, and each individual family had its own set of servants.

One of the sons, an M.A. student in physics, joined us for coffee on the porch. It was late at night, nearly midnight, but our host brought out his Grundig tape recorder and played us the tapes he'd made of the German Hit Parade of a year he'd spent in Germany, sometime in the fifties. We chatted for hours on the darkened porch in a smoky, silent winter night. Even in Ballygunge there were sidewalk sleepers—the rickshaw pullers who simply turned onto a quiet side street, joined their friends in the brewing of tea and a few hands of cards under a street light, and then a stretching out, bundling of the blanket, and sudden sleep. They were our company down below; we could hear their coughing and their moaning as they slept. On another balcony across the street I could see a man-shaped lump of white pajamas on a string bed, and I felt my usual well-mannered embarrassment over the blaring German singing (every time I recognized a song and hummed along, my host would turn up the volume a notch).

I remember all this because I was also trying to talk to the boy, and I was asking him all the wrong questions. "I guess you'll be sorry to leave such a nice place when you get married," I said, full of my easy compassion, and he shot his father a look that was clearly pained and puzzled (*What have you been saying to this sahib?*). He explained that *this* was his house. His sisters of course will move to their husband's houses, but he remains. His six male cousin-brothers will stay in the house, adding extra rooms if necessary, and they will bring their wives here, and raise their children here. Yes, of course, of course, I mumbled. Then, attempting to regain mastery of the situation, I asked if he was seeing girls at school and that was when his father answered for him. "He is only a boy of twenty-two—what does he know of girls? Let him finish his M.A. and get his Ph.D. at MIT and get a good sound job, then I will find him a bride." The son was smiling, and I was smiling, both of us, doubtless pitying the cultural constrictions of the other's society.

I am fascinated by patterns; how they reveal themselves, gradually connect, and flow together. Each new experience I thought of as an ink blot on a bright new blotter; I anticipated their spread, hoped for a final linking-up.

In that terrible panic of the first night's ride, I felt I could never make sense out of such vast confusion. I knew only one person, *chhoto-mamu*, and it would be an intolerable burden on any man, no matter how patient and knowledgeable, to guide another through his culture. Thanks to Jaya's wedding preparations, I was soon taken on shopping expeditions for gold and saris. I took photos in sari shops and learned the names for the various designs. It was slow and exhausting, like all shopping in India, because nothing in India is purely commercial; it is all family function, an opportunity for the women to be decorated, for the husband to exercise his knowledge and authority.

I had sent letters to a journalist, and to a Bengali novelist we'd known in Iowa. We had Tulu-didi's doctor friends to call on. There were dozens of old Loreto House schoolmates of Bharati's, now married into the business and professional world of Calcutta's upper middle class, as she would have been, had she stayed. There would be the surprise package; whatever turned up at the mission. There would be, I hoped, other novelists and poets, and with luck, the film director, Satyajit Ray. And that was it: a smattering of ink drops on a bright new blotter. How far the blots would spread, when they would touch, I couldn't guess.

Other than that, I had my books, my notes, and my husband's heart to say yes to anything my wife's city offered me. Not to hold back, not to judge, not to be shocked, never to say no. I was the *jamai*, the son-in-law, collecting all his wedding gifts ten years late. Though we'd been married ten years, it had been ten years of knowing Bharati on my terms and in my language. The only big adjustment in my life (accomplished with all the groans of a youthful identity crisis) had been a thirty-mile drive over the border to Montreal, the dropping of an accidental American passport and the reassertion of the Canadian. I was still a short-story writer, still an English professor, still a baseball fan, still at ease in my selective alienation, still reading and teaching and making friends among the same groups I would have had I stayed. But in Calcutta I couldn't choose, and I was on Bharati's turf, illiterate and deaf-mute in her tongue. My idea of hospitality while in Calcutta would be to give the largest number of people the greatest number of opportunities to entertain me.

7

Ink blots. Start one in Bhowanipur, the section of urban south Calcutta that lies between Ballygunge and the downtown. It is impacted, frenzied Calcutta, ceaseless commerce of every sort along its dark and smoky streets. It is my second night in Calcutta. I am still alone. I have gone out with everyone in the *mamabari* to have some of Jaya's old gold bangles weighed, credited, and then recast into different objects, for the wedding which is still five months off. New gold is prohibitively expensive in gold-mad India (smuggling being its only source) but gold-working is perhaps Bengal's greatest traditional art. By ancient Hindu custom, a wife can own nothing in her name but the gold she brings to her marriage—everything else is her husband's. There are horror stories in the literature and in the folk customs, of wealthy husbands' dying and the widows' receiving nothing. Also of clever husbands inducing their wives to sell their gold, and then throwing them out. Tagore's greatest novel, *Home and the World*, turns on that very device—of a wicked opportunist who convinces a weak but virtuous wife to sell her gold, in order for him to raise an army and defeat her noble and trusting husband. Cosmetically, the luster of gold seems almost invented to enhance a Bengali's flesh.

And so, true to the sacramental nature of the transactions, the gold store is permanently guarded outside, as well as locked from inside—one must be buzzed inside, after a proper scrutiny. The young men behind the counter move with the silken obsequiousness of assistant morticians. Bengalis can pass hours in the presence of gold. I took a seat and began reading an R. K. Narayan novel I had brought. A small boy, the store's *chokra*, was sent out to buy me a Coke.

As befitted the ritual solemnity of the store, there was a small private room in a rear corner, decorated like a stateroom, with paintings on the paneled walls, deep sofas, a carpet, a small private air conditioner, and velvet curtains over the window. I had passed it casually, noting an older man bent in consultation with a young Sikh couple. After half an hour, the older man came out, shook hands with Dipu and inquired of the wedding preparations, was introduced to the girls, then came over to me, shook my hand, and drew up another chair. He was a bald, myopic man in his late fifties, who spoke slowly, in the cadence of London.

He pointed out the framed pictures behind the counter. Did I notice something familiar? Indeed I did, they were calendar shots of Expo 67 in Montreal, which he had attended. He had a soft, moneyed way of talking; like a securities salesman, a lawyer, or a surgeon, he was accustomed to laying out expensive options. In this culture he was far more than a jeweler; in a society that withheld home ownership and cars from just about everyone, he oversaw the most rational and sentimental investments a couple was ever likely to make. He was not a trinket man. The *sardarji* couple left, thanking him; they would call again. Would I care to seat myself in his office?

"Montreal was very nice," he said, once we sat in privacy. "There was only one thing, very small actually. We had written well in advance and sent our earnest money, but when we arrived—"

I knew the drift all too well. "—It was a trailer thirty miles in the country?"

"No, I wouldn't say that. It was a rather nice place, actually, very close to the site. They simply had no record of us."

How earnestly I sympathized (the Good Canadian abroad); I hoped at least he'd gotten compensation, and yes, he had. He explained the purpose of the private office. "People want to talk with the owner before they purchase gold," he told me. "It is all a matter of trust. If my name and my family's name were not trustworthy, there would be no way I could stay in business." I told him I could see that; he did not need to advertise, and *trust*, I knew from Bombay, was in preciously short supply all over India. The high seriousness, the pompous, elaborate solemnity of the entire operation, seemed a properly Indian kind of accompaniment to the building of "trust," just as, for us, such sugary trappings would serve as a warning to possible fraud and dissimulation. He left me in the captain's chair, with the Montreal photo album and a second Coke.

I had the sense, alone in the soundproofed office with Montreal spread on my knees, that I'd been somehow dealt with. As a lone white man, I had commanded attention from the owner and a kind of deference that few Indians would get (in relative terms the unprepossessing Dipu was better off than I would ever be), but also that I'd been segregated. Excessive politeness was a tool used to keep me in my high and lonely place.

Out on the sidewalk after that first visit, an old man in *dhoti* and umbrella watched me waving frantically for a taxi. Even the empty ones on their way to tea stalls whizzed by with just a wave. "Hopeless, young sir," the old man said, like a voice out of the past. "Absolutely hopeless. Nobody cares for anybody."

The ink blots spread, ever so slightly.

We returned several weeks later on another rainy evening to pick up the finished earrings and tiara. Bharati was with us this time, and I was carrying a freshly unpacked copy of *A North American Education* which I had already inscribed for Anju. Bored by the first trip to Bose's Gold Store, I almost hadn't come this second time. I was reading my own book, and enjoying it immensely.

Again Mr. Bose came out, and lingered with Dipu *chhoto-mamu, mami-ma, mejo-mamu,* Bharati, and her cousins. He took a special interest in Bharati, whom he'd been told about, and then he came over to me. "Still with your nose in a book," he admonished, closing it for me and leading me into his office.

This time I started the conversation, suspecting that he'd perhaps forgotten our earlier one and might lead me back to Expo 67. I began by observing that he surely hadn't left his business in Calcutta just to see a World's Fair in Montreal. No, indeed, he said, and for the next hour he proceeded to tell me his life's story.

He was not himself to be a gold merchant—that was his older brother's profession. But his brother had died suddenly, and so he had taken over. It was a family business, and had been for generations. He was an economist by training—a Ph.D. from the London School—as well as a city planner. He was on the Municipal Planning Corporation for Greater Calcutta. Comparative urban planning was his special interest. The trip to Montreal had been incidental, part of a forty-four-city eighteen-month world tour. "In the world of urban planning," he said, "being from Calcutta opens many doors."

By this time I had questions of my own to put to a city planner. We'd suffered through the weeks of flooded streets, the power cuts that ended our workday at four o'clock and quite often didn't return our lights or fans till after nine; I'd kept daily clippings from *The Statesman* on the perilous food shortages, the hoarding, the smuggling into Bangla Desh, the adultering of all basic foodstuffs, the unimpeded flow of unemployable villagers into the city. Why couldn't the land tenancy acts in Bihar be enforced? He nodded, granting that it was a very serious problem. *Chhoto-mamu* had told me of river navigation problems brought on by the nightly theft of the copper lead-wires inside the river buoys—seven thousand dollars' worth of imported equipment invalidated for the sake of fifty cents' worth of copper. Couldn't the rivers be policed? Couldn't people be educated? I remembered the power lines outside Bombay, how the tops of the poles were wrapped in barbed wire to discourage the theft of transformers.

"You see," he began, in that velvet voice of the patient bureaucrat, "all of these problems you mention are interrelated." He spoke of development loans from the World Bank and the need for collateral, the slowness of the federal government and private industry to reinvest in Calcutta after the Maoist government of 1969–70. He spoke in analogies; I couldn't tell if he underestimated my familiarity with the problems, or if his own training as a world traveler and comparatist tended to blunt all his responses against the totality of interrelatedness that is Calcutta, and India. Of course Calcutta had staggering urban problems—but most of her urban problems have their origin in the villages. *That* is where the people came from.

He asked me where I was staying, and asked if I knew three or four of the permanent guests. I asked him if he knew the famous economist A. K. Sen, of Cambridge, now at the mission. "A *most* brilliant man, Amartya Sen," said Dr. Bose. "He will win the Nobel Prize." I asked him where he lived, assuming it must be Old Ballygunge or New Alipore. But he pointed upstairs. "I have a music and a prayer room here," he said. "I play sarod in the morning and three hours at night. I have been a *chela* of Mustaq Ali Khan for thirty-two years." I mentioned Charles at the mission, *chela* of Ali Akbar Khan's son-in-law. "He must come over," said Mr. Bose. "We will play together."

Outside, as our large group piled into two taxis, I mentioned (with a certain pride) that I had made some important discoveries about Mr. Bose. Starting from nowhere, I had extracted a number of facts—did they know, for example, what a multifaceted man he was? *Chela*, economist, Ph.D., city planner? No, they didn't. It was the first time I felt I had brought Bharati any news about Calcutta. Then she spoke briefly with Jaya in Bengali, and Jaya nodded, "Yes, I think so. I will ask *chhoto-mamu*." *Chhoto-mamu* only smiled, saying, "Yes, I think so," and then expanded on what I had learned. "Clark is right. Mr. Bose is a most learned individual."

Later in our room I found out that while he is all that he said, Dr. Bose was also the focus of a tragedy that had taken place some sixteen years before. He had been the brilliant professor home briefly from London, who had allegedly fired the fatal and accidental bullet that had killed his elder brother. It had been a famous trial in Bharati's high school years: brilliant boy, famous family, and it had inflamed speculation in gossip-mad Calcutta. He had been acquitted but not forgotten. The knowledge put a great many things in perspective. Was that why he'd been so anxious to isolate me? Why he'd been so insistent about trust, a good name? Even the smallest choice of going out to look at gold (I had nearly convinced myself that reading alone in my room would tell me more about India than going back to the gold store; egregiously friendly salesmen were the same all over the world) had yielded riches—earned and accidental. The pride of my discovery had lasted all of twenty minutes.

8

We were sitting in Trinca's, on Park Street, a onetime Swiss confectionery, now a glamorous restaurant on Calcutta's raciest street. I was having a furtive rare steak, and we were enjoying cocktails after a grueling tour of Loreto House with some of Bharati's old teachers. By now she had made contact with her married school friends who were taking her out nearly every afternoon. My links to Calcutta were still through the family.

Trinca's is a businessman's hangout. The other restaurant in the same half-block, Kwality's, attracts women and families. Trinca's has an orchestra and singer, Kwality's has none. Trinca's is convenient for businessmen—Punjabis and Europeans often—who have come to

Calcutta for a few days' stay at the nearby Park Hotel, and plan to get out as quickly as they can. The resident Bengali business establishment would prefer to lunch in the various downtown clubs, and Marwaris (the joke goes) would bring a few stale *rotis* and some *dal* from home. And so the atmosphere of Trinca's is definable: a little loose, a little tacky, dark and musty and moistly air-conditioned. "Jenny," the Goan singer, was liquefying a familiar medley into the mike: "I Never Promised You a Rose Garden," "Killing Me Softly," "Those Were the Days," some Flack, some Baez, some Fitzgerald, mixed with Hindi songs from the year's big hit movie, *Bobby*.

A young man with mutton chops and shoulder-length hair came out of the dark back room. "Excuse me, could you possibly be Clark Blaise?" he asked in a very British accent. "And are you Bharati Mukherjee?" We admitted we were. "No rush, then," he said, "but when you have finished your rare steak, would you care to come back to the bar and join Mr. Chattopadhaya and me for drinks?"

Bimal Chattopadhaya was the magazine editor I had written to from Bombay. I'd had several weeks to grow nervous about that letter; knowing that Chattopadhaya had been posted in a number of Western capitals, I'd affected my breeziest tone, and revealed myself, I now feared, callow and impudent. He hadn't answered, which could only mean he'd judged me an arrogant pup, best left to forage for myself. Thereafter, in letters, I'd been dignified and professional, an easier mask to assume.

The young man who fetched us was a copy writer, on his third quart of beer. Bimal was a gray-haired, well-tailored man in his mid-fifties, resplendent in an ascot and regimental mustache. The effect was of cultivated excessiveness, a man attuned to adventure, while doubting it would be worth his effort.

He had a position to maintain; he did it by not answering our questions too directly. "You went to Loreto House, I assume?" he asked Bharati. "You must have gone to school with, ah, Mira Sen? No? Her younger sister, then, what *was* her name, the one with the unfortunate set of eyebrows, you *know*, who married that chap from Indian Tobacco, the one whose father was convicted for fraud . . . yes, yes, *Gayatri*, of course, dear sad Gayatri Sen. Then you must have run with the British Council crowd, debating with that wretched little chap who later went to England and wrote those pathetic pornographies . . . no? You don't say? Which Mukherjee family *are* you from—Asutosh Mukherjee? Obviously not Sir Biren's family, they're all so bloody awful to look at. . . . Not Ajoy either? Now that *is* a puzzle, obviously rich and obviously Westernized. . . ." He rattled off half a dozen possible Mukherjee families which might have explained, logically, a product like Bharati. He could not have guessed the truth.

Bimal Chattopadhaya's protection lay in being just slightly outrageous, yielding points on accuracy (because it was a game, a competitive game) in order to draw out unguarded rebuttals and unintended confidences. Upper-class British irony, a game of high polish, whereby social occasions are an opportunity to expose your opponent as a fraud and hypocrite. Extra points are scored if your opponent doesn't realize—till later—that he had done it himself. In this he won. Our conversation that lunch hour, over beers, and then that night in his Ballygunge apartment revealed far more about me than about him.

As much as a liberal Westerner may fight it, he still makes the same mistakes; I began by making the V. S. Naipaul error. Because Chattopadhaya affected British ways, I assumed his life in Calcutta was unoriginal and imitative (that he was, in short, one of Naipaul's ex-colonial "mimic men"); I also assumed he must be alienated from Calcutta, still nostalgic for the West. He'd edited a popular rotogravure magazine in London, a fashion magazine in Paris, and an educational supplement in New York. When I asked him about racism in England, he answered simply that if one seeks racists and grants them their opportunities, he will suffer from it. On the other hand, if one has money, he simply buys a sound address and membership in a club ("Reform Liberal," he said, "not the Notting Hill Working Men's Recreational Lounge") that will remove him from the possibility of harassment. Bigots are everywhere, he added, though the pointedness of the remark escaped me till later.

Did I want him to admit some horrible degradation? Did I want him to say, "Yes, I was perfectly wretched in England." I think that was part of it; he played a drawing room smugness so perfectly that I rushed in to vandalize it. "I shouldn't accept being a displaced person anywhere," he said rather icily, indicating that like us, he didn't expose himself to any more squalor in the West or in Calcutta than he could comfortably bear, and indicating further that *we*—me in India, Bharati in Canada—were displaced persons without even acknowledging it. I asked him, again assuming that the various losses were too great to contemplate, what he missed most about the Continent. "Well," he began, appearing to consider it seriously, "with Gorgonzola at sixty-five rupees a kilo . . ." Just like us he missed the theater, wines, and cheeses, and *still*, I couldn't take his answers seriously. Surely he must miss the working conditions, the stimulation of big-time papers, the worldliness of London, Paris, and New York. I was not yet able to tolerate his satisfaction with Calcutta, his ironies with the West. Yet *here I was*, as Bharati would later remind me, a foreigner in Calcutta asking a native-born Calcuttan who had come back to his home in order to rise to the top of his profession, about his disappointment and dissatisfaction. (And for me to have snickered, during the ten years of our marriage, when visiting Bengalis would ask the same of Bharati in Montreal. "What have you given up? Is it worth it?" For the next year, I was to hear her answers, and it has shaken our marriage to its core.)

I wanted the dirt, the low-down, from a man I perceived as a journalist; what I got were evasions and flippancies. The Calcuttan has known for a hundred years how to parry an English question, how to turn a question around. I asked about the Bihar Tenancy Act, Punjab land grabs, the power cuts, the corruption—all items that had come from Calcutta papers. He nodded at each abuse, and then answered in just the tone of realpolitik that closes all discussion: "The peasants never had electricity and never knew they were supposed to have it until anxious little politicians anxious for their votes told them they had to have it. They don't have anything to plug in, but they have electricity. And because five thousand villages had to be electrified, industrialized Bengal—which means middle-class Calcutta—had to pay. You come here wondering why the peasants don't stir themselves and throw the rascals out? Wouldn't it be uncomfortable for all the lovely friends we have and all the gentle Loreto House girls we all know and appreciate, and for the nice life we have made for ourselves if they ever learned they weren't supposed to starve and suffer? What if they ever found out that it was stupid planning and corrupt politicians and manipulations of their ignorance that was the cause of their suffering? What would they do?

You're in the East, my good man, and don't ever forget it. What would happen to them—*what would happen to any of us*—if we didn't take it all passively? We'd die together. Don't make the mistake of writing that I don't recognize injustice and that I don't feel just as strongly as any high-minded Westerner on a two-week visit. But I thank God those people on the street and in the villages are as abysmally ignorant of their rights and of my privileges as they were at the dawn of history. The alternative is too horrible to contemplate."

We went out for dinner to his favorite restaurant. We were polite and witty. He pointed out the families at various tables, dealing out their biographies, entanglements, black money dealings, sex lives, directorships, pending court cases, attachment to one, or two, political parties, with all the authority of the classic, cynical journalist. All Calcutta is his city-room if he chooses. But he is a publisher, not merely a reporter; he is of two worlds and has chosen discretion over disclosure.

Like the young man he had been drinking with that afternoon, he was close enough himself to being a *box-wallah* to know that he could not belittle them as unthinkingly as Naipaul had. English had replaced Bengali as his natural literary expression; he even recognized a small absurdity, in certain eyes, in his position. But why demean him as a *box-wallah*, somehow less than his "pure culture" Bengali counterparts and certainly less fortunate than his Western colleagues? Such a man in the West, so brilliantly adept in an acquired tongue, and so attuned to a second culture, while being intimately involved in his own, would hardly be pitied, or patronized, especially not by people like me. How sophisticated he'd seem back in Montreal, for example. Perhaps he was not quite the noblest example of the Westernized Bengali intellectual (for that one should look to Nirad C. Chaudhuri, a resident of Oxford), but because of his self-awareness, his detailed knowledge of Calcutta, his personal taste and standards, his privileges, his scorn of hypocrisy, his position has become potentially tragic, should he choose not to yield to the new "Emergency Measures." Or, should he bow, he has become an emblem of the frailty of Westernization in contemporary India.

On the way back from the restaurant, turning to face me from the front seat of his sports car, he asked me—not for an answer, but as a speculative notion—how it was that all whites in India, like Ronald Segal (*The Crisis of India*), assumed an unassailable superiority. What was it, did I think, about their training that made them feel that their standards, their judgments, were all clearer, sharper, and more just than the local's?

For my part, I stayed up very late that night, writing an essay. Part of it I have used here, most of it was too defensive. I have no interest in playing his sport; it's too rough, the rules are far too complicated. I'll probably never fully recover from my anger ("Gorgonzola, indeed!") and my shame (I will always hear Bharati saying to me, "In the future you might ask yourself why it's so very strange to you that a Bengali journalist should be satisfied to be an editor of a Calcutta magazine"). It was my first encounter outside of the family. Aggressive journalist that he was, he had not waited for my second letter, my inevitable phone call. He had sized me up from Trinca's bar, plucked me from my rare steak, and he'd played me like a sportsman until he'd grown bored and decided to cut me free.

To see the truth clearly, to analyze fraud cogently and piteously, yet to be denied implementation or power—that was the role of the free press in India. Impotent truth or thwarted idealism is a prescription for cynicism, and cynicism is the style of the Indian intellectual. Cynicism is his protection against disappointment; it even allows a certain participation in the vices he abhors. It is to the intellectual's credit that he has retained an attachment to propriety and to truth as long as he has, for surely, in a country where the margin of security is narrow indeed, he is forced to suffer for the slightest miscalculation. But the idea of cynics ever uniting for reform is even more remote than the union of anarchists. And so the press of India published splendidly documented, insightful, and often passionate criticisms of personalities and policy failures, exposures that one would expect to see result in immediate rebuttals if not dismissals, but that, alas, was not the Congress party style.

Take for example, land reform. In July 1973 Mr. P. S. Appu wrote in *The Statesman:* "The widespread incidence of share-cropping, characterized by insecurity of tenure and extortionate rents, is perhaps the most formidable obstacle to the modernization of agriculture in certain regions." Mr. Appu went on to show that while the Bihar Tenancy Act entitles the landlord to no more than 25 per cent of the yield, any sharecropper not turning over at least 50 per cent would simply be evicted. *Baas.* At that level of nonincentive, no tenant farmer would add the necessary inputs, nor would he bother to plant a second crop. India is a vast land with more soil and water than it needs to feed its people and even to become a net exporter; it is the feudal structure of land ownership that underutilizes land and water, keeps the entire country on the brink of starvation, and floods the cities, especially Calcutta, with millions of illiterate, unhealthy, and unemployable beggars. Why, then, isn't the tenancy act enforced? The landowners, it goes without saying, have bought protection. The tenant farmers, who are little more than serfs, do not know their rights nor will they ever be told. Should they complain, they will be evicted, and in more extreme cases (of which a great many are documented), especially if they are tribal or untouchable, they could be murdered. Mr. Appu concludes, in that even, stilted prose that leaves the Westerner straining for its possible irony, humor, or outrage: "An outmoded agrarian structure, the main features of which are a land-owning gentry which takes no personal interest in cultivation, a preponderance of impecunious small holders with no access to inputs and a tenantry with no stake in the land, is to be blamed for tardy progress in the utilization of ground water."

Seven months after Mr. Appu's article, another appeared on the plight of the *bargadars* (tenant farmers) in West Bengal. A reporter in the *Times of India* pointed out that while there are 850,000 *bargadars* in the state eligible for new loans from the nationalized banks, only 25,000 had been registered. "The reason for the slow pace of progress is that most bargadars are afraid to register themselves; few of them are sure of government protection in case the landlords decide to evict them as a retaliatory measure. In some areas the police are said to be hand in glove with the landlords." Only the communists had been active in registering the farmers; Congress had not lifted a finger. On and on, daily exposures, daily accommodation, restrained but uncompromising accusation: cynicism. And now, after our departure, repression and censorship of all such "morale-sapping" articles, the destruction of an independent judiciary, and the end of what the Congress Party contemptuously refers to as "conceptual democracy."

An anonymous correspondent in *The Statesman* commenting on "The Greatest Corruptor of All" saw at least two years into the future when he wrote: "There is in public affairs nothing so pathetic, damaging and dishonest as an authoritarianism that does not come off." Foreseeing that the Congress leadership, in splitting the party two years earlier, had taken an irreversible step toward authoritarianism, he wrote: "Hence the identification of commitment with personal loyalty: and the intolerance of criticism that has become the dominant characteristic of post-split India. Increasingly there is a carelessness in distinguishing between the party and the nation; and if the Press, the judiciary and a politically neutral civil service have anything in common it is in asserting that this distinction is essential for the health of a free state."

It is worth quoting the last paragraphs of this essay, not merely for the deadly accuracy of its prophecy, but for the eloquence of its stoical fury.

> . . . Mr. Haksar's definition of the values appropriate to India cannot be bettered: "Secularism in thought and action, honesty, integrity and hard work as ethical compulsions, austerity and national pride, sustained by intellectual and spiritual self-reliance and some regard for the scientific temper. . . ."
>
> As individual qualities some of these are reconcilable with authoritarianism and some with democracy. Collectively they are consistent only with a system firmly based on the democratic liberties. . . . The decision that such freedom is a luxury which a developing nation cannot afford is legitimate; but it's not one which the Congress Party is entitled to take, or, indeed, is ever likely to take considering the enormous stake it has in the chaotic conditions to which it has so notably contributed.
>
> Lip service to a free press and an independent judiciary has long ceased to be taken very seriously; and the atmosphere which inhibits this independence and freedom is far more poisonous than the outright prohibitions on which

authoritarianism straightforwardly depends. It is this atmosphere, inhibiting, threatening, and unproductive that has settled on the country like a heavy pall; and in which the exhortation to commit and conform is all the more bewildering since nothing resembling Mr. Haksar's values can be seen, and the only possible commitment is to remain silent or actively endorse whatever conduces to the ruling party's comfort and convenience.

9

Popool, a second cousin by marriage of Bharati's, found me a sympathetic listener. He was a medicine salesman in his early thirties, whose routes often took him into Calcutta, permitting frequent visits to our room at the mission. Since Bharati was nearly always out with her friends in the afternoon, I had little choice but to become a silent hostage to Popool's opinions.

I had set the tone, on his first visit, by asking him what exactly were the reasons for the frequent "load-sheddings." His father was an electrical engineer, so the answer, I'd assumed, would be authoritative. And, I felt, if I could absorb all the social, political, and mechanical reasons behind a daily phenomenon like load-shedding, I would be well advanced in my understanding of Calcutta itself.

"You see, it is this Indira Gandhi," he said. "Her party wants country votes, so she promises them electricity. She has overextended the rural electrification program for purely political purposes."

I told him I had heard this before; was this the only reason?

"No, no, not at all. You see, the real problem is that the equipment is very old, fifty years most of it, and all of it from England. We cannot replace the parts except with new diesel generators, which only come from Eastern Europe. But the British still own the equipment [N.B.: Calcutta Electric Supply is, remarkably enough, still a private British corporation, though largely owned by overseas Indians], and they cannot extract sufficient profits from Calcutta to warrant new investment."

"Ah," I said, "now I understand. Colonialism, East versus West." I had little doubt where his sympathy lay.

"No, that is not the real reason. They could invest more if they wished. But they are afraid to modernize for fear of nationalization. The government is waiting for them to invest in new equipment, then it will nationalize. Calcutta Electrical Supply knows so long as their equipment is old, the government will not take it over. That is what happened to the coal, you see."

"What happened to the coal?"

"No coal is the most important reason for low electrical output," he said. Since most of the power stations were thermal, not hydro-electric, Calcutta power had nothing to do with water levels.

"But India is rich in coal," I said.

"Yes, India has abundant coal. But this Indira Gandhi, you see, is in with the coal-owners. She nationalized the private coal fields but she gave notice over a year in advance."

"That seems fair."

"But you see, that permitted all the owners to sell off their new equipment and put their profits in black money, and not repair any of the broken machinery. So government paid the price that was agreed to when all equipment was in the mines, and got the mines without any modern machinery."

"But surely they can sue."

"But that will not help, you see. Many have left the country. Many were foreign anyway. Just the lost equipment would not be so bad, but when the coal fields were privately owned, they used to bribe the railroads to keep extra trains in the coal fields. But when this Indira Gandhi took over, they would no longer pay bribes to other government men, so now only scheduled cars are running. Without extra coal cars to carry more coke, the generators cannot work to capacity. Only two and a half work out of four. It is not a question of too much demand for electricity, you see. It is un-derutilization of capacity."

"The same as the land."

"I tell you, Clark-da, it is all black money, all corruption. It costs fifty thousand rupees to electrify every village, where there is no need. Who is getting this money? What happens is the villagers steal the transformers to sell back on the black market and women drain off the light oil for cooking purposes."

Having established myself as receptive to tales of political mismanagement, I became the recipient, on succeeding visits, of great chunks of Popool's social and political philosophy. His politics were never quite consistent by Western standards; at turns Maoist and reactionary, altruistic and greedy, they seemed to me more rooted in passion and in cynicism than in anything systematic. "There is no end to black-marketeering," he told me on another visit. A doctor he'd been talking to had complained of the lack of cadavers in medical colleges. Could I imagine—in Calcutta, *of all places*, no bodies! Gangs were on the streets picking up bodies as soon as they died, or snatching them from the burning ghats, pulling them, still sleeping, from string beds on unprotected porches, and shipping them to medical schools in Japan and Europe.

Another day: "All these new buildings, how many you think are built with honest money? The contractors add to the bill. The promoter got his money dishonestly. The cement makers. The electrical engineers, every city inspector. Extra for wires, for pipes. Extra on labor charges, on transportation charges. I estimate it is sixty per cent black money, forty per cent sincere."

To make him feel better, I suggested that in terms of generalized corruption, political ruthlessness, extortion, bribery, political favoritism, preferential licensing, attempted or real subversion of the judiciary, manipulation of the media, and general brutalization of native idealism, India was less than a generation ahead of Nixon's America. And that with the Adjusted Rate of Corruption, when you consider that in America there was no real material *need* for any of it, India came off even better.

But he was in no mood for reassurance. "Only three things can save us. War, earthquake, or violent revolution. Then we could begin again. These days there is no honesty—everybody is dishonest. Making money is all they can think of, no matter how they make it. Everything is adulterated. The government, this Indira Gandhi, she pays money to the workers so they will be quiet. In the city you have money, positions are secure. But eighty per cent of our people live in the dirt, it is they and the city workers who must revolt. The middle classes in the city will never fight—why should they? They only want more money, less work, no matter how they are to get it. No one is safe any more. The boys who died in the Naxalite crackdown, they were our brightest boys, our best boys. They were murdered by the police in front of their fathers. But it will come back, it must. Only it must start and remain in the villages. That is where the misery is. That is where Indira Gandhi must go to pay bribery." Thirty thousand prisoners, he estimated, were still in West Bengal prisons from the police crackdown three years earlier. The government admitted to about a dozen. The spread is indicative of the amount of trust and openness that existed even before the "Emergency Measures" of a year later which eliminated the need to offer any explanations, or publicly raise any questions.

I often reported these conversations to Bharati after she came back to the room. She'd never been fond of Popool, and liked him even less now. While professing his sincerity and radicalism to me, I learned, he had suggested to Dodoo that since two of his daughters were settled in the West, he, Popool, should be included in Dodoo's estate. He also informed Bharati, in one of their encounters outside the door, that he'd used her name in an emigration application to Canada.

Twice in the six years prior to our arrival in Calcutta, Bengalis had elected radical "United Front" governments. Twice the poor had thrilled to the rhetoric and often the reality of revolution; the middle classes had cringed in terror and uncertainty, and the upper classes had fled, or sometimes paid in blood. Twice the coalitions had split, the economy had failed, and the central government had stepped in. Now, in 1973, three years after Bengal's latest flirtation with Marxist rule (as contended by fourteen configurations from mild socialists through native-bred "Naxalites"), the Congress party regime of Siddhartha Shankar Ray, a prominent Calcutta barrister and reported favorite of Indira Gandhi, was very firmly in power.

The Ray regime is not outwardly reactionary; by most Western standards, he is an honest, fairly progressive democratic politician burdened with an unholy skein of inherited and ever-evolving crises. Failed revolution had not, as yet, inspired the fascist repression that it had in Chile. Ray rules firmly, and his police inspector, Ranjit Gupta, exercises draconian power. Hundreds, and maybe thousands, of young leftists, it was rumored, were still in cells without hope of trial, or visitors. Occasionally some broke out; more often, some were killed attempting to break out.

But for all that, one could not term West Bengal of 1973 and 1974 a police state. (A Canadian, especially, should bear in mind that in his admirably democratic nation, *one* political murder in Montreal in 1970 placed the entire country under martial law.) Geoffrey Moorhouse, in his magnificent study *Calcutta*, estimates that in West Bengal in 1970, 147 "political murders" took place, with urban gangs murdering Europeans and middle-class Bengalis at will, and rural revolutionaries beheading *jotedars* (landlords) as well as their own fallen-away comrades with the same abandon. The United Front governments had deliberately withdrawn police protection in order only to monitor the class confrontation. Small wonder that when police service was restored, three armed guards were required to protect each constable, even three years later.

One would think, however, that after three years of fairly normal rule, the imprint of revolution would have faded. One might think it would pass like everything else in Calcutta, absorbed in the renaming of streets and the removal of offensive political statues. But Calcutta, as I have said, does not forget. The United Front governments of West Bengal (1967–68 and 1969–70; two separate regimes each lasting little more than a year) had moved on all fronts simultaneously: industrial wages, educational reform, and land redistribution, while at the same time settling old scores with political and financial antagonists in Calcutta. The result was economic chaos, as industries locked out employees and employees *gherao*'d management. But they also moved against real outrages and real grievances and moved with such rhetorical fervor that among some of the young cousins of Bharati (as a representative body), an instant revolutionary nostalgia had been created, composed of idealism, Marxist ardor, and Bengali chauvinism. The Naxals, at the cutting edge of the revolution, were "our best boys." Some unrepentant capitalists excepted, I did not find many middle-class people willing to condemn or totally disown them; on some deep level, I think, the revolutionaries spoke for the majority of Bengalis, and not just the most disadvantaged. There is a deep desire for honest, purposeful, and progressive government in middle-class India (which explains the acceptance of the Emergency Measures), and the Naxals were certainly all three. They were misled, perhaps, or betrayed. They were too impatient. The CIA destroyed them. Ranjit Gupta destroyed them; take your pick (I've heard them all).

The Naxals were not unlike, in rhetoric at least, similar youthful radicals in the West. But the American radicals were playing basically for media attention. Guerrilla theater required actors, roles, and directors; it didn't want theorists and especially not critics. In Calcutta the Naxals had no TV to play for. The targets were real people; as in Ireland and Israel the killings defied symbolic sense. It wasn't theater, it was only life; unbearable to watch. "The troubles" traumatized an entire population, and in that sense alone I felt that we were living in a time and place of political reaction.

We called on the Hamburg cousin's friends, a doctor-couple now well established in a double practice in downtown Calcutta. Dr. Vimla Sengupta was a gynecologist, as are nearly all women doctors in India. The number of women who would permit a male to examine them (or whose husbands would permit it) is limited to a minute segment of the urban upper middle class. And the number of men who would permit an examination (or trust an examination) by a woman must be correspondingly small. Vimla had met and married her husband in Vancouver, where they took their medical degrees. Dr. Asish Sengupta was a urologist. They maintained their own small clinic and surgery as well as a "Charitable Dispensary" in a poorer neighborhood.

The Senguptas' flat was just off Chowringhee, near the Tata Building, in that area of all great cities that seems to be reserved for the offices of the international airlines. On the ground floor was an art gallery, on the second a European consulate; the Senguptas alone occupied the entire third floor. As with most buildings in Calcutta, the exterior in no way hinted at the comforts within. The outside plaster was rusted and peeling. The lobby was dark and smelling of urine, the stair well unswept, and the walls had apparently never been painted. One bare bulb emphasized the dinginess while lessening the immediate danger of stumbling over a few discarded blocks and oddments of construction.

But the flat itself revealed Calcutta's other face. Order, peace, and calm; a cool and careful arrangement of chairs, low tables, paintings, records, and bookcases. Two porches overlooked the *maidan* and the

manicured grounds of the Bengal Club. Public squalor and private
splendor, one of the oldest clichés about India, confronts one everywhere.

We spoke pleasantly of Tulu and Anil in Hamburg. We went to
an English play in which their older son was performing. Asish Sengupta had written a number of poetry books; his wife sang in a number of native forms and languages. He was also a Sunday morning
habitué of the many coffeehouses of Calcutta where poetry and revolution mingle. The doctor-poet is not, after all, an unknown figure
in the West; nor is the doctor-revolutionary. In Calcutta, where
poetry-writing is in the blood, such triple fusions are to be expected.
Bright boys sought lucrative and socially respectable professions;
bright boys were first politicized by the anti-British feeling of their
school days and later grew disillusioned with the West. They sought
strength in an idealization of their own "pure culture." The same in-
fusion applies to our own corner of the Third World, black America;
in both cases the outsider is likely to feel as much abused as enlightened by contact with it.

"Outsider" is a term almost immediately applied. Bharati is of
course an outsider because of her marriage, her residence, and especially her choice of English as an artistic language. All Indians writing in English are outsiders; others are outsiders for the magazines
they publish in, the newspapers they work for, the critics who support them, and finally, I was to learn, the way they live, the tone and
style of their art. "Bengali culture" is a minutely subdivided abstrac-
tion; for those who still worship Tagore there were others, during the
United Front days, who destroyed his statues and defaced all references to him in libraries and universities. Many feel that Satyajit
Ray is the greatest living embodiment of Bengali culture, but there
are others who dismiss his work, abuse its alleged impurities, Western influences, and "Brahmo" contempt for the common culture. To
be a Bengali of the type I am describing is to consider yourself the
only reliable authority on what is pure and good in the culture.

We were in one of the clubs downtown after the play. We'd been
joined by a circle of the Senguptas' friends: a forceful right-wing
Bengali businessman and his wife, as well as a group of younger people, Sindhi and South Indian, all of them non-Bengali. I thought
back to our old Iowa friend, Sunil Gangopadhaya, who'd come to

Iowa as a poet, a friend of Allen Ginsberg's. He'd had trouble getting into the States due to his typically left-wing Calcutta politics.
He'd gone back to Calcutta after a year, then turned his energies to
fiction. In the ten years since we'd last seen him, he'd turned out
about forty novels. Two of them had been filmed by Ray, including
the celebrated success *Days and Nights in the Forest*. I began by asking Dr. Sengupta what he thought of Sunil Gangopadhaya. It was as
though I had said Richard Nixon.

"*That* writer," he fumed, "*that* writer is one of the most right-
wing writers in Bengal. He only writes of prostitutes and young people trying drugs and sex. All bedroom scenes, right-wing filth. You
must let me introduce you to *real* writers."

I mentioned that Sunil must have changed. Not the subject matter, perhaps, but the politics. For Iowa tastes, he had been a dangerous left-winger.

"He writes beautiful descriptions of sunlight on teacups and of
boys being out of work and just walking the streets. It leads to right-
wing despair and cheap sensation-seeking."

Who would be a "left-winger," I wanted to know. He named a
poet, now regrettably retired from poetry, who edited a political
magazine. "In his work there is always hope, never despair. He sees
beauty in everything around him, and the people, no matter how
poor they are, see beauty in living and in not despairing. His poetry
can make you weep."

"But how is that left-wing?"

"Because there is no hate in it. There is only love for common hu-
manity. It makes people aware of their brotherhood, it brings people
together. This right-wing pseudo-literature is always written in the
first person. The man can only write about himself. He has no story
to tell, only what happens to him in a wasted day. He starts with
nothing and he ends with nothing—it's all blankness, hopelessness,
useless. He is telling people to give up trying, just trust sensations of
the moment, like sex. It is immoral. When the United Front was in,
the students *gherao*'d his house, you know. They could see he was a
CIA agent."

I asked about Satyajit Ray, a man whose work I admired more
unreservedly than any filmmaker's in the world.

"Ray has done good work," said the doctor. "Every Bengali loves *Pather Panchali* and *The World of Apu.*"

"What of *Charulata*?" I asked.

"That, too, is very moving. He is in his element with Tagore stories. But when he tries modern themes and films set in the city with political meanings, then he is hopeless. Personally, I would rather watch a Hindi musical or something I *know* is not trying to do anything but entertain me, than watch an ambitious Bengali film that fails."

"Name one of Ray's that fails."

"There is one so bad that I vowed I would not see another, *Days and Nights in the Forest.* It was made with cheap sensational sex in it so it would make money for his backers in the West. He was one of our best filmmakers, I think, but he sold out for money."

"But that movie never *played* in the West, Dr. Sengupta! Only in university film series—his work is the hardest thing in the world to find in the West."

"We read that review in *The New Yorker*, it was in all our papers. *The New Yorker* said he is the greatest director in the world. He *was* one of our best filmmakers, I think, but he sold out for money."

I wanted to throttle him. "That review was of a limited showing in a small theater that specializes in off-beat films. Pauline Kael thinks the world should know more about Ray. And compared to real sex, there wasn't *anything* in it."

"Please, Mr. Blaise, I happened to have seen the movie. Ray showed tribal women prostituting themselves and useless Calcutta boys going out into the forest and trying to seduce unmarried girls and widows and then finally raping a village girl when they couldn't get their way. Even the widow was lusty. It was *all* sex. It made us sick."

I wanted to cry out weakly, *No, no, I'm* the Westerner here and *I've* seen *Last Tango in Paris* and *Deep Throat* and *I* know what sex in movies is like, and *I* know how chaste and obscure an item Ray is in the West! How can you say these things about the greatest artist in your culture? Mad Ireland, and now mad Calcutta; why must you grind your artists into exile?

His friend, the businessman, had been breaking in every few moments, usually in support of the doctor, though for a different purpose. His name was Guha, a Bengali and fiercely proud of it, though he was not attached to any part of the refined culture. So far as he was concerned, Ray was a third-rate director and he had proof of it. In one of his movies he had shown an older brother-in-law addressing a much-younger sister-in-law in the formal *apni* form. If a man doesn't know how people in his culture talk to one another, then what kind of director is he? And, in the same picture (the only one he'd seen, which had convinced him never to again), Ray had shown a *marketing* director of a fan company being held responsible when *production* was disrupted by a strike. The first rule of business is that marketing has nothing to do with production; if Ray weren't so "Brahmo" he'd know such things.

"Personally," said his wife, "I'm rather tired of strikers and the proletariat."

This untracked the conversation from culture and settled it on a related topic: business, and, inevitably, Marwaris. Mr. Guha, as managing director of a metal-casting foundry, was an expert on both business and Marwaris, and he held the floor as assuredly as had Dr. Sengupta a few minutes earlier. "The trouble with the Bengali is that he is lazy," he said. "No Bengali likes to work. Give him a white shirt and a desk and he's content. He has no initiative, but he's always ready to go on strike and make a fiery speech. Now the Marwari is a very silent chap who will work all day and all night to make more money. The Marwari is a perfectly lovable creature with his eye on only one thing." Everyone nodded; support for Mr. Guha came from all sides. I was surprised; Bengalis rarely had kind words for any other Indian, especially not the Marwaris, who controlled the economy of their city.

"The Bengali," he went on, "will never see that *he* is to blame for his own lack of power. He'll just go on complaining that nobody loves Calcutta and nobody will invest his money here."

This activated the Sindhi, who had been silently enduring the discourse on Bengali culture. Thinking perhaps he'd found an unexpected ally in Mr. Guha, he announced himself in full agreement. Bengalis were charming and intelligent chaps (was he himself not married to a Bengali girl?), but it was true: "They complained too much, felt too sorry for themselves, and tended to blame the city's

troubles on everyone but themselves. His wife was nodding enthusiastically.

"Ha!" cried Mr. Guha. "You earn *your* living here, but you'll re-
tire somewhere else, won't you? All the filth and squalor you see in
Calcutta—that is not caused by Bengalis. Those are all Biharis on
the street and they live like that because they send everything they
make back to Uttar Pradesh and Bihar. It is easier for them to sleep
on the pavements than to bring their families to Calcutta to live.
And we have to tolerate it because if we cleared the streets they'd
probably say we were fomenting communal revolution. The Bengali
is a very tolerant chap, he doesn't want other people to suffer, even if
it means that his city collapses all around him."

The Sindhi agreed that Bengalis were perhaps the most fair-
minded and tolerant people in India. And certainly they were the
most progressive and cultured, anyone could see that. Mr. Guha was
in high gear now, suggesting octrois at the borders of West Bengal
and shipping all the Biharis and Oriyas and Bangla Deshis and Uttar
Pradeshis back where they came from. Everyone agreed it would
be the only possible, but alas, not workable, solution to Calcutta's
agony.

Very late in that discussion, or in others that were to follow in
other settings, I came to realize that we weren't talking about politics at all. "Left wing" and "right wing" are modern versions of *cultural* terms going back over a century, distinguishing pure from impure art, native from foreign influence, Bengali from non-Bengali
backing. What we in the West might consider daring, expressive,
and fresh—in other words, *revolutionary*—they would term socially
irresponsible, subjectivist, and decadent.

The catchword for all good qualities in art, personality, politics,
and business is "sincere": One hears of "sincere money," "sincere
acting," and, of course, "sincere art." It means, I believe, a lack of
irony, that things be precisely what they appear to be. The highest
duty of the artist is to be sincere, to love his characters unreservedly.
That is why Satyajit Ray is universally respected for *Pather Panchali*
and condemned, faintly or harshly, for everything since. One aims to
*move* the audience, not to complicate their lives. And above all, one
must have Bengal in his blood, one must be writing of the "pure,"
the non-Westernized Bengalis. The ironical forms that love can take

are simply not respected. The "universal audience" that a Western author might at times pray for is an unforgiving mass, once any of its many sensitivities has been offended.

Tagore's novel *Gora* is on this theme: The aggressive "pure culture" is set against reform-minded "Brahmo" openness. Gora, the young man, feels compelled to passionately defend every segment of the secular and religious culture: suttee, untouchability, cow worship, consultations with astrologers, refusal to mingle with Europeans or speak in English. He even refuses to eat with his mother, since she had received her food from the hands of a Christian servant. In the end, of course, he must yield his stridencies (Tagore stacks the deck by making him the blond, blue-eyed orphaned son of Irish settlers) and accept the gentler path of vigilant eclecticism.

This conflict between the native culture and Western innovation is still at the core of India's internal debate. Marx or Hegel, again. How much "Westernization" can India bear, and still be India? In what ways can beneficial progress, in birth control, for example, be encouraged? Bribing men for vasectomies? Taxing the third child? Rewarding barrenness? Or is any such reduction in the birth rate possible so long as the *family* remains the basic unit of identity? I think there is probably no short cut. India must undergo the same long process that we did in the West, the gradual proletarianization of lumpen refugees off the land. *Then* the creation of proletarian personality that will be less class-conscious, less religious, less family-dependent, and thoroughly self-centered.

A Bengali historian by the name of Debraprasad Bhattacharya spoke at the mission one night on Arnold Toynbee. Part of what he said that night bears (as all things in India bear painfully on everything else) on the whole question of culture and politics: "Every civilization or way of life is an organic whole in which all the elements are intimately interdependent. It is impossible, therefore, to replace some single native element with some single foreign element. If we start by eliminating one single element in our native civilization, we must end by eliminating all the others. Similarly, if we start by introducing a single foreign element, we are driven, ultimately, to introduce a whole set of foreign elements. Our choice, in a word, is between all or nothing."

## 10

Anyone who knows contemporary Indian culture is likely to recognize three names, all from Calcutta: sarodist Ali Akbar Khan, sitarist Ravi Shankar, and the filmmaker Satyajit Ray. And of the three, Satyajit Ray has succeeded in a medium whose origins and fellow masters are far from India. What could be more inexplicable and miraculous, in Calcutta, than a master filmmaker?

The winter before, in Montreal, during those months between losing a house and losing a car, I had attended a Ray Festival, conducted by a Quebec Jesuit who was home on a year's leave from Calcutta where he'd been working in film for the past thirteen years. He was, in fact, the French subtitlist of Ray's films. He could have spoken for hours to that jammed hall of French, English, and Indians, but chose only to provide a cultural gloss and a summary of the critical reception each movie had received in India and abroad. The films, he assured us, despite their exotic settings, would speak for themselves.

I'd not seen any of Ray's work since an unappreciated undergraduate exposure to *Pather Panchali*. Now, fifteen years later, I'd come to value lucidity over brilliance and those ten films *gave* me Bengal, even before I left Montreal. The films of Satyajit Ray: still and lyrical, a Calcutta I could ache for those Wednesday nights in Montreal. *Days and Nights in the Forest* was realism of so high an order that it sustained all types of interpretation, and justified every excursion into violence, comedy, and improvisation. It seemed an effortless exposure of an entire social order, all the more remarkable for the casualness of its plot. Three carefree young men from the city go into the country for a weekend; one falls in love and is rejected; one flees from a widow who reveals her need; one rapes a tribal woman, is attacked and robbed by a villager. They return to Calcutta, seemingly unchanged. *Charulata*, a highly structured rendering of the Tagore story of a nineteenth-century Calcutta triangle so entangled with duty, respect, love, and repression that each touch of the would-be lovers (in this case, Charulata, the neglected wife of a newspaper publisher who is more attuned to the latest pronouncements from Disraeli's London than to his wife's isolation, and his younger, "poetical" brother who is brought to the house in order to tutor her) rippled through the audience like a shot. Unembarrassed weeping in the famous "Apu" trilogy; weeping of a different sort in the early (1958) study of an old zamindar's stubborn, ignorant, and finally mad decline in *Jalsaghar* (The Music Room). Pietism of the Kali worship, mixed with sexual repression, turning to mad violence in *Devi*; modern Anglo-Indian displacement in Calcutta in *Mahanagar*. Even a light treatment of filmmaking itself, using Bengal's enduring matinee idol, Uttam Kumar, in his only thoughtful performance in twenty years of nonstop romantic mugging.

I don't think a director has ever taken on so much of his culture and treated it all with such control, compassion, and honesty. Nearly everything I absorbed after arriving in Calcutta took me back to Ray's films, just as nearly any serious conversation we were to have in Calcutta would at some time include references to Ray's work, simply because, in his powers of representation, he had given us all a special intuitive vocabulary. Just before we left Montreal, *Days and Nights in the Forest* played briefly in New York, and Pauline Kael—long Ray's most astute and admiring critic in the West—declared him to be the supreme humanist of the world's directors. In our first week in Calcutta, his picture appeared on the front page of *The Statesman* for having won the Berlin Film Festival's "Golden Bear" for his latest film, *Ashani Sanket* (Distant Thunder), the story of the 1943 Bengal famine.

A well-educated Bengali, like Ray, is an instinctive synthesizer of cultures; it's part of his meticulous attention to detail and his alertness to serious events everywhere else in the world. The Bengali has lived with the English longer than any Indian, and he has absorbed him, while keeping his own soul, with astounding ease. The answer to Professor Bhattacharya's gloom about the inevitability of surrendering one's native culture if he adopts even a shred of a foreign civilization has to be, "Very well, I will become a *third* thing that is neither hybrid nor bastard, and that too will be unique." Pure culture is not possible for any of us in the contemporary world; it is only a question now of how well we can learn from each other. Ray plays Bach on the piano; he composes the sitar music for his films.

*Charulata* was paced with Mozart in mind; *Kanchenjunga* was structured as a rondo. When he speaks of influences, he cites Renoir,
Dovjenko, Lang, Lubitsch, Wellman, Raymond Bernard, Abel
Gance, Houston, Ford, Capra, and, of course, the postwar Italian
neorealists. And in this synthesis, mad, nightmarish Calcutta can be
an accomplice. Bengalis still assume that Calcutta is a world city,
that the world expects appropriate reactions from Bengali students
for any remote outrage perpetrated anywhere on the earth. I can't
imagine any other foreign city in which the death of the American
poet Conrad Aiken was a front-page event. But it was in Calcutta,
on August 19, 1973, along with a literary essay, in the *Amrita Bazar
Patrika*.

Articles about Ray and interviews with his associates and actors, as
gathered in a special 1966 issue of the Indian film magazine *Montage*, had stressed the balanced, essentially classical, side of his temperament. He often refused to shoot on days of extraordinary beauty
("a cameraman who can't curb his instincts to take a pretty shot is
often acting against the best interests of the film"); he would
sacrifice scenes in which a moment of unexpected purity had stood
out against a more mannered or inattentive performance. (The actor
Anil Chatterjee recounted just such a moment in the filming of
Tagore's *Postmaster*. The incident is not immortal in cinemagraphic
history, yet so full of the Bengali ambience that I will quote his recollection in full: "That child actress in *Postmaster*," recalled Chatterjee. "She is a born actress. She had never acted prior to that role—
and she hasn't acted since. There is a scene in which I brusquely ask
her questions like—'Why aren't you better cared for—doesn't your
mother wash your clothes?' She replies, 'No.' Well—this scene has to
be played with a lot of emotion, and in one of her lines there was
suddenly a delayed reaction. I assumed she had forgotten her lines
and looked up. To my utter surprise, her hesitation and the slow
smile with which she gave her reply was just . . . perfect. It was inspired! But it took the wind out of *my* sails. I fell completely flat in
my own responses. When the scene was over, Ray understood my
feelings and dissatisfaction with my own performance. I didn't even
have to tell him. He came to me and said we would reshoot. He
went over to the little girl and said, 'You were very good, but Anil-
dada was a little inattentive. So we'll take it again.' Another director

may have been so enamored by the perfect performance on one side
. . . he would have failed to regard the response to it as equally important. There you are!") Like the Italian masters, Ray deliberately
worked with mixed casts of amateurs and professionals in order to
maintain this freshness, balance, and reality. "Many stories never get
beyond the stage of contemplation," he said, "because they prove
uncastable."

Since he had been a commercial artist before making films, he first
sketches all his shots in extraordinary detail, then turns the sketches
over to his set designer. The shots are all so well planned that he
rarely requires more than one take, nor does he shoot longer (the so-
called "editing in the camera") than will prove absolutely necessary
—an inestimable advantage in film-short, power-short, money-short
Bengal. Most of his black-and-white feature films have been made
for under 300,000 rupees ($40–50,000); even the color feature
*Ashani Sanket* was made for only $85,000. And while he is forever
busy on new projects, it is obvious from reading the early interviews
with him that he carries projects in his head, and on paper, for several years before they ever get filmed. In 1965, in a conversation with
Georges Sadoul, he said, "It is still of Bengal that I am thinking for
another project, which will take place during the famine of 1943 that
killed my compatriots by the hundreds of thousands. The film that I
am planning is the adaptation of a novel by a new Bengali writer. It
takes place in a little village where provisions begin to run short. It
ends with the first death from hunger. But the villagers do not yet
know that the famine is going to kill them in very great numbers.
And then, I have in my head as well an idea from the time of
Tagore, about 1905, when the terrorists began their attempts against
the English colonials."

That first project was not released until 1973; and the second,
which would be Tagore's *Home and the World*, not only has not yet
been filmed, but creeps into Ray's plans as early as 1950, when he
had already scripted it and begun scouting the countryside for possible locations.

From my fastness in Montreal, I'd been tempted to think of Ray
in Calcutta as someone so much larger than life, so remote and
alienated, protected and self-protecting, that no mere one-shot novel-

ist and one-shot short-story writer from the backwaters of Canada
would be allowed to approach him. In my months of admiration, I
had apotheosized Ray into my own image of how a genius must survive in a ruined society; not as a Joyce, perhaps, because Ray was a
traditionalist who had stayed, but more a figure like Thomas Mann:
lofty, ironical, uncompromising, alienated by his refinement from the
clutter and sentimentality of Calcutta.

The Calcutta Telephone Directory in our room seemed to open
naturally to its pages of Rays—like all Bengali names, a common one
—as though every foreign scholar who had stayed there before us
had wanted to verify the same fact before proceeding. It seemed to
me extraordinary, that first day in Calcutta, that Ray should even be
in the phone book. I would not expect to find a listing for Fellini or
Godard; absence is natural—what explains a listing? There were, in
fact, two Satyajit Rays in the Calcutta directory. I made up a package of our two books, inscribed them, and enclosed a very proper
note, expressing a measured respect for his work, and the hope that
sometime in the next year we might get together. I picked up the
phone.

I held it a full five minutes, absolutely unable to place the call. I'd
wanted to verify the address, warn his servant, wife, agent, or secretary that books were coming. I knew no one in Calcutta but the
switchboard operator at the mission and the relatives at the *mamabari*. Whimsically, I called Anju, asking if she knew the address of
Satyajit Ray. "Bishop Lefroy Road," she said, which corresponded to
one of the listings. But I couldn't credit a mere teen-ager with such
obscure knowledge. I asked the operator downstairs. He told me, assuming I was going there in person, "Near Hindustan Hotel, sir.
Bishop Lefroy Road." I walked across Gol Park to the postal substation, and mailed our books away.

The next day I answered the phone. "Colin Blaise?" came a bari-
tone British voice over the echoing municipal connection. I was
about to correct him when he said, "This is Satyajit Ray."

"Thank you," I blurted.

"No, thank *you*. I've been very anxious to read *The Tiger's
Daughter*, you know. I was out of the country last week—"

"Yes, yes, I know. Congratulations—" I cut in again.

"—where I read that marvelous review of the book in *The New*

*Statesman.* You've seen it, no doubt, an absolute rave. Compares her with Thomas Mann and Lampedusa and all sorts of impressive company."

Bharati's first novel had just come out in its British edition. We hadn't seen any reviews. "No, we haven't heard a thing," I said.

"Well, marvelous, it's charming to be the bringer of such good news. I think I've even got an extra copy of it here someplace. Would you like to drop over tomorrow for tea, then, so that I can present you with it?" I said that would be fine with us.

Only after that first brief visit, and ones that followed, and after getting to know others who knew him well, did I stop to think how bizarre, yet how appropriate it was, that in Calcutta *he* should know *us,* and Bharati's book, and that he should be able to provide the impossible: a current, foreign periodical, even in surplus.


It is enough to say of Ray, the man, that he is a physical giant, and that his flat is scaled to his height, with chair arms that seem shoulder-high and bookcases so deep—intended more for art books and records—that our two books huddled among the *Whole Earth Catalogs* like fugitive paperbacks. Ray is a man of authority, the form of his intelligence is a rare one in our time: He sees life whole. He exercises more personal control over his films than any director in the world; besides writing the scripts and composing the music, operating the cameras and supervising sets and editing, he casts the nonprofessionals, designs the title-lettering, writes the publicity, and arranges the distribution. Besides the films, he writes mystery novels in Bengali and is the editor of a children's magazine for which he writes and does the art work. He has translated into English his father's classic Bengali nonsense songs and children's verse; he has even earned a dictionary citation as the inventor of "Ray Roman," an English type face. And he is, in that admirable Indian manner, always *available* to his friends and visitors. There are no secretaries and agents; there is merely the telephone which never rings twice. Over the next six months he arranged private showings at the surprisingly shabby Indrapuri Studios in Tollygunge of all the films that we hadn't managed to see in Montreal, just as he invited us, that first evening, for a screening of *Ashani Sanket,* just back from Berlin, before it was to open a few weeks later in Bhowanipur.

I had been wrong, obviously, trying to fit Ray into the whole sorry Western tradition of the artist-in-society. He is not at all socially removed (he is, on the contrary, almost avuncular), yet he is like Joyce in one important way. His subject matter, like Joyce's, is unfailingly local—village and city, past and present, of his people—and in no way does he relate to the tradition of the Indian cinema; like Joyce, he had to adapt foreign traditions to express a native reality. His importance for India is in that feat, in having found a way to *represent* Bengali life in a universal medium.

This is not always the way he is perceived in Calcutta. "God himself if He made a perfect film couldn't please a group of Bengali intellectuals," said Lenny Gordon one night at a party given by some poets we all knew. We were talking of *Ashani Sanket*. Their criticism of the film had been harsh, despite not having yet seen it. Ray, they charged, had "prettied up" the famine of 1943. There had been corpses in the gutters, children whose burst-open bellies were swarming with the flies—had he shown that? No? Ha! The explanation was very simple: "The West" could not have stood such images, so his "Marwari backers" had told him to make it pretty. "Sheer pornography," they sneered, for having cast Babita (the Bangla Desh actress he had used as heroine) as a Brahmin's wife. She is Muslim, how would she know the right way of serving her husband's food? They had seen pictures of her, and she is too beautiful; village women coarsen very early. She has plucked her eyebrows; she is wearing makeup; her sari is too urban and modern. Bengali literalism (which it serves), Bengali fanaticism (when it serves), was being directed that evening not against the film, not even against Ray, but against something more elusive for which the film and the director might even be sacrificed): against what they sensed was "impure culture." I had the feeling that the only way the poets might have been induced to praise the film would have been if we had sneered at it, calling it obscure and hysterical. What they could not forgive was that "the West" (meaning *The Manchester Guardian, The New Yorker,* and the Berlin Film Festival) was now finding universal values in work that had been "pure culture" Bengali.

Lenny, Bharati, and I tried to talk that night of impressionism, of *not* introducing brutal colonial administrators and *not* showing the stacks of corpses (which were obviously still to come), not out of a cowardly fear of alienating the *Guardian* or English-speaking Bengalis, or Marwari backers, or offending Western standards of good taste, but for the artistic purpose of showing what an Indian famine was like: starvation in shades of green. That was, to me, its enduring image; starvation not due to a lack of water or of vegetation, but rather a lack of money to buy rice on an inflated and mismanaged market. Poor planning, hoarding, smuggling; an indirect commentary on 1973 and a sensitive rendering of the tragedy thirty years earlier.

*If he means that, then why does he not say it?* they demanded; then he is doubly a coward. I could not communicate to those poets the *smallness* of Ray's audience in the West, nor could I convince them that a culture fed on *Last Tango in Paris* would hardly be shocked by a few stacks of baby corpses.

I am convinced that the problem with the reception of *Distant Thunder* in Calcutta (and by extension, any film or literature that lacks a political or emotional core) was that it did not *move* the audience to relive the literal horror, nor did it bring fresh charges of guilt and corruption. The camera stayed on the beautiful and serene face of Babita, and on the contented, then puzzled, then suffering face of Soumitra Chatterjee, and it sucked up that stabbingly green countryside, showing only one riot, one death, and only one very chaste rape ("He is obsessed with sex"). Oddly enough, when the film finally played two years later in New York, the general criticism was that it had overdrawn its villains, grown strident and propagandistic.

I had written to Ray and sent him our books because I had assumed there would be no one in the city to bring us together. I was wrong; nearly anyone could have taken us to him, because like an eighteenth-century man, Ray is a creature of his city, curious about the working of things, at home in every setting. Filmmaking is a profession as well as an art, as disciplined and responsible as surgery. I suppose it is his lack of pretension that draws so many people to him. One of Bharati's friends, a most unliterary woman, mentioned that because her pediatrician was a friend of Ray's (both as students of the sitar), Ray had asked him to keep an eye open for an English-speaking seven-year-old for the opening shots of *Simabaddho* (Company, Ltd.). As a result, she, her son, and husband had spent a week's shooting in Darjeeling. Any of the English or Bengali writers could have taken us to Ray. Lenny Gordon knew him well. Gaston Roberge, the Montreal Jesuit, was now back in town. The officers of the mission frequently showed his films—they were especially anxious to arrange an introduction. Ray was at the center of a great many worlds, an illustration that whatever rises must converge.

His "alienation" is, quite possibly, a reverse of ours; he has a vast audience but no artistic community, broad social contacts but little intellectual intimacy. His work is increasingly impressionistic, understated, and ironical, but his audience has never really valued, or perhaps even understood, such qualities. The mass audience of Calcutta must remain his first audience, the one which pays the costs, but for intelligent criticism he cannot depend upon it; it is doubtful, by now, that the general audience of Bhowanipur and New Market is even his primary target. He has become one of the handful of "world directors," like Truffaut and Bergman. Reference to his films alone will explain as much of the life of his time and place as any of us are likely to grasp. In some curious way, then, I too am Ray's producer, as are all cinema-goers in the West. In that way the Bengali poets were right, and their jealousy is understandable just as it is lamentable.

Working in Calcutta imposes special burdens, especially during frequent power cuts, but there are other frustrations to drive a serious artist to despair. Ray told us, that first afternoon, that he planned to begin work next on Tagore's *Home and the World*, the novel wherein a terrorist persuades an impressionable young wife to sell her gold. She does so, and he raises an army that kills her own husband. After twenty years, Ray at last had found a teen-age girl, an amateur, to play the role of Bimala, that most vulnerable of Tagore's characters. But on our next visit, he mentioned that the Tagore project was canceled; in the weeks between casting and arranging the first shooting, the girl's parents had married her off, and the young husband (or perhaps his parents) had absolutely refused permission for her to work, especially as an actress. And so a project that had been scripted for over twenty years was shelved again. I wondered, after reading in *Montage* that Ray himself had sold his wife's gold, and his mother's gold to raise the necessary money for shooting

*Pather Panchali*, if he did not have a special personal attachment to all three characters in that extraordinary book.

He went out to Rajasthan to film a children's movie based on one of his own short stories, and then he began filming his first Hindi feature, based on the allegorical Prem Chand short story "The Chess Players," set in decadent Lucknow during the last years of the Mogul Empire, as the British threaten to capture the hapless Mogul King. He shot two films and scripted a third, and wrote a novel and a number of stories, in the year we were in India. A culture is blessed to produce such genius once in a generation. Most, of course, never do.

"Shankar" (Manishankar Mukherjee), Bengal's most popular novelist, is a man in his late thirties, in charge of advertising for Dunlop Tire. He lives across the river in Howrah, far away from the lures of Westernization, where he is the head of a joint family of some forty people. Therefore, he apologized, he cannot be a very productive novelist. Sunil Gangopadhaya, in contrast, publishes four or five novels a year; Shankar is lucky to get out two, sometimes only one. He has published a mere sixteen, including *Simabaddho*, filmed by Ray. We suggested that sixteen novels by the age of thirty-eight, considering he could only write on Sunday mornings, was nothing to be ashamed of. He seemed dubious ("There are spiders, and there are spinners who must go to the shop for their cloth. I am only a spinner"). Shankar is a novelist of the Calcutta business world, a man who prides himself on his O'Hara-like knowledge of the world he commands. He is not part of the upper-class, Westernized business world we were coming to know; his novels are more likely to be about the young trainees we saw in the mission, still a generation away from acceptable, or damnable, Westernization. He, too, was upset when Ray had made his young marketing man responsible for a production delay. That mistake was not in his book.

No one's novels are edited, in the American sense; the author may remove a line or two in the proofs, and even his publisher doesn't read the books until they are set in galleys. His audience is, like Ray's, presold, an assured one hundred thousand per book, but that still does not permit the luxury of retiring from Dunlop and writing full-time. In fact, the "luxury" of full-time writing is surely a Western invention; it is we who dream of release from society and a moneyed dropping out of all responsibility. Such a man in Bengal would simply be unemployed, since no art is a profession. Far from gaining "luxury," he would probably lose all respectability.

"Art," in some profound and lost Western sense, is "amateur." Like Ray, like the great film actor Soumitra Chatterjee, who has starred in sixty films but still publishes a literary magazine, directs plays for workers in the suburbs, and is secretary of the Bengal Actor's Union, Shankar, too, functions very well in the "real" world. The writing is for love, and expression, and, of course, recognition.

He told us an illustrative story about the Bengali audience. He had received a letter from a Bengali architect who had just read one of his novels. While complimenting it in general, the architect was gravely disturbed by one fact. Shankar had described the area of the hero's apartment to be sixteen hundred square meters. But when the telephone rang, it required only three steps, from sofa to hallway, to answer it. A simple calculation thus revealed that the width of the room could not be less than so-many meters. Its length can be calculated by other internal references. *"Therefore, Mr. Shankar, I have calculated the area of the apartment as no less than nine hundred and not more than twelve hundred square meters."*

The story was told not in irony, and not to appall; it was told in chagrin, an illustration of the standards his readers demand. The Bengali can be savagely literal-minded, and the best Bengali artists are meticulous. This can be a fruitful union, as in the case of Ray, of the writer Nirad Chaudhuri, and many earlier masters of the Bengali Renaissance. Both qualities are ingredients of high culture and great art (a painter like Vermeer must have lived in such a time); but not in the proportions here described.

There is not much money left in Bengali culture. The film industry especially is dying. While we were in Calcutta, Soumitra Chatterjee donated a five-thousand-rupee prize to the union of Bengali cameramen and film technicians as a gesture of support for their demands for government subsidy.

The front room of Indrapuri Studios, where Ray's films are all composed, is a ten-by-ten room with one battered desk, four chipped and sticky chairs, and a wide bench. Two pietistic portraits of founders, a yellow surveyor's map of a coal field in Bihar (diversified holdings?), and a pharmaceutical house calendar are the only wall decorations. A fan throbs overhead, brickwork lies exposed from the dropping of ceiling plaster. Not the anteroom of the stars. Ray works for a director's fee—he does not even own prints of his films. The other serious Bengali filmmaker, Mrinal Sen, has deserted the mass audience and makes films of, and for, the radical intelligentsia. His films do not even pay back their publicity costs. Sunil Gangopadhaya, despite his forty-odd novels, films, and translations, still works full-time as a journalist. Through a series of workshops I conducted for the USIS, I met a dozen poets, short-story writers, and dramatists, all of them with extensive publications and performances. At the end of the series, they presented me with copies of their books—most had published far more than I. I doubt that any other "adult extension course" in the world could have counted among its dozen members at least ten with published books. And what were they on weekdays? Bank clerks, housewives, government workers, unemployed.

A *footnote:* Back in Montreal over a year later, the head of Montreal's Goethe Institute showed me a tableful of Bengali books— translations of Hölderlin, Rilke, and Kafka—and German books— translations from Tagore and the moderns—done by friends and members of an informal group that he taught during his six years in Calcutta. The Japanese and French in Calcutta, I'm sure, could show the same, and I have seen Bharati's cousins working on their Russian translations for that strange red-haired woman who lived next door to us at the mission.

I didn't believe that anyone, no matter what his language, could live in Calcutta for a year without discovering his own circle of young Bengalis, all passionately devoted to the future of Luso-Bengali, or Ugro-Bengali literature, all functionaires or unemployed by day, and scholar-poets by night. One returns from Calcutta with a sense that his own cultural credentials have suffered a disastrous de-valuation while he has been gone. That is why he sneers, remembering Soumitra Chatterjee, when certain American actors are called "intellectuals" and "politically committed" for supporting conservation and George McGovern; why he becomes less impressed with the broadsheet poets of his own city demanding greater attention for each new effort. Why he wonders where his own energy and commitment have gone.

11

Every few weeks the mission was invaded by touring groups: Japanese, Germans, Russians, and Indians from other parts. As I was getting into the elevator one wet August morning, I heard a whoop from the end of the veranda: "Hold it right there—I'm on my way!" My companion to the breakfast room was a theology professor from an Alabama university, in charge of a group of thirty temple-hopping students on a "Hinduism and Buddhism" field trip. They would be in Calcutta three days before hitting the South. While the two professors tended to eat by themselves, our table was selected by some of the more outgoing students.

We had not seen Americans—the loud, beefy Americans of Pepsi ads and surfer brochures—in nearly ten years. We'd not seen North Americans of any description, but for Lenny Gordon, in six months. And none of us, by now, were healthy. We were pulling out of the monsoons, when fevers, diarrhea, and a general murkiness of disposition afflict the entire population. Charles, the Australian, had lost fifty pounds in his year at the mission; I'd already lost thirty, and Bharati, significantly, had gained twenty-five. And so the vision of thirty blond Alabamans, all wearing sweat shirts with Greek lettering, cut-off jeans, and sandals, posed a random disruption that most of us considered intolerable.

All of us, I think, but Bharati. Of the kinds of Western behavior familiar to Indians, Alabama roughhouse and its innocent stupidity is not only inoffensive, it can be delightful. For many weeks she'd not been happy with our seating at dinner. She'd been forced, as dutiful spouse, to sit with the tight little knot of white men and their approved Indian guests. I think she wanted no part of us. She identified more with the earnest young trainees that we made fun of ("Shirt Ad," the preening young Johnson & Johnson marketing boy who dressed so impeccably that one longed to see him dribble poached eggs on his lap; "Super Slurp," who every morning pitted lung power against a bowl of corn flakes, and prehensile lips against the force of gravity in lifting two whole poached eggs from his buttered toast before they could slide to his plate). Meanwhile, our table attracted whatever whites and overseas Indians that came passing through. "Tree that Walks," an enormous American Airlines copilot who'd come all the way from California on a one-week vacation because someone at an airport had told him he had "a groovy karma." "Thought I'd check it out," he explained to us. In contrast, there was something heroic in maintaining an impeccable appearance on five hundred rupees a month, when you were probably only twenty-one years old and away from home for the first time in your life.

And so a teen-ager named Carleton joined us. I had forgotten just how unfurrowed the mind of an undergraduate can be, how undoubting; also how eager, innocent, and friendly. It was as though he'd been newly hatched from an egg. One could imagine him cheerfully digging holes for villagers' latrines; one could imagine him suffering heroic discomfort as part of a field trip. One could imagine him dropping bombs on a village from a B-52 and not thinking twice about it.

It was a *bandh*-day outside—meaning that the various unions and political oppositions had withdrawn all services and had flooded the streets with demonstrators (today's *bandh* was to protest cuts in the rice allotment to West Bengal); Congress leadership was calling for the maintenance of "a normal flow of life," an apt phrase in Calcutta. *Bandh* days are frequent; a kind of blunt Gallup poll that enables all contending parties to check their strength by a simple head count of demonstrators and effectiveness of the work ban. Knowledgeable Indians (and by this time we were knowledgeable) do not go out on *bandh* days; the possibility of random violence is high, as is the level of undirected hostility. Each episode releases some tension, but raises the expectation of eventual apocalypse.

All of us but Carleton had stayed in. Carleton, ignorant of *bandhs*, had left his group after breakfast, taken a minibus downtown, and discovered something that none of us had known. For seven rupees, a nonguest could swim in the pool of the Grand Hotel. "Very refreshing," he told us. "Then I had me a lunch in the Prince's Room. Real *kweezine par excellence*. And here—lookit here!" He passed around a Polaroid shot of himself pulling a rickshaw, as snapped by the rickshaw puller himself. "Christ, was he amazed! Y'all should have seen it. Bugged his eyes right out of his head. I let him pull out the flap and everything. Real cool, huh? They'll all get a bang out of it back home."

It would be pontificating to say that by putting a billion dollars' worth of technology in the hands of a Bihari rickshaw puller, and by inserting his own body into the puller's iron frame, Carleton had upset five thousand years of social evolution (which he had); and it would be melodramatic to say that what he had done so innocently could have just as well turned out, on a slightly different day, or with a different driver, or with a Muslim and not a Hindu, to have led to death and a riot. It is accurate to say that he had also revealed the rest of us as timid and untrusting, grim and self-satisfied.

The more-French-than-Bengali Sanskritist asked him, "What are you studying?" It was a European question, more demanding in its expectation than any question Carleton had ever been asked.

"H and B, off and on."

"H and B?" he blankly repeated.

"Hinduism and Buddhism. It's a course. Had Buddhism last year and pulled a B. We start Hinduism when we go back."

"I see. You are perhaps going into religious studies?"

"No, sir, I don't think so. Actually I only took it 'cause it's easy."

"And this trip to India—you think it will help you understand?"

"Yeah, sure it will, a little, you know. Like this afternoon we're all going out to . . . you know, *Dak* . . . God, I should look it up in my notes."

"Dakshineshwar?"

"*Right*—hey, very good."

"That is where Sri Ramakrishna stayed."

"Yeah, really? The guy this hotel's named after?" Carleton laughed. "Look, I'm no great scholar or anything like you guys."

"And whom have you studied with?" the Sanskritist pursued, again with European expectation.

"That guy over there," Carleton said, jerking his thumb in the direction of my elevator companion. "He's a real bright guy."

"A . . . bright . . . guy," the professor repeated, mouth shrinking, eyes dull.

"Yeah, knows a heck of a lot." He turned to Lenny. "And what do you do?"

"Write books."

"Yeah, really? What kind?"

"What do you mean what kind? History books."

"Yeah? I mean what level: high school, college, you know."

"What level? I would hope that the most sophisticated scholars in the world will find it a sophisticated book."

"Yeah? Well, I hope so too, for your sake. Well, off to the temples. Sure been nice."

Something just as funny—appalling and funny—had happened a year earlier in Montreal. When Bharati's first novel came out, we'd gone down to a bookstore at the foot of our street and shown the owner a copy of the book with an approving review and a glamorous shot of the author that was appearing in the current *Newsweek*. Perhaps one Montreal author per decade gets featured in the American weeklies. The owner flipped skeptically through the book, read the jacket blurb, then politely declined to stock it. "Houghton Mifflin," he said, reading the spine of the dust jacket. "I'm sorry, but there are so many little outfits like this that we just can't carry them all. But they did a nice job, didn't they? I'm sure you understand—if we carried every book from presses like this, we wouldn't have room for the commercial presses."

We went through the various permutations of civilized outrage: Houghton Mifflin was not a vanity press. He even had other Houghton Mifflin titles on his shelves. "Yes, well," he apologized, "maybe one or two." She asked for the magazine back. He complimented her on the nice write-up, and then added, "I couldn't help noticing that you're East Indian, too. Is she a relative of yours?"

It was a strained time between us. Days would pass without much talking; she wouldn't answer my questions. "You're very lucky you have your Canada," she said, "and that your Canada accepts you so nicely." I'd been getting letters from a newly launched Canadian Writer's Union, begging me to join. Bharati, predictably, had not been asked. Though her novel was unavailable in Calcutta, she was still a celebrity, thanks to that same *Newsweek* article of a year before. She'd been interviewed on the radio and featured in the Bengali and English press. *Desh*, a literary magazine that publishes a hundred thousand copies a week in culture-mad Bengal, did a photo-essay, and proclaimed her proudly as a "Calcuttar meye" (daughter of Calcutta). One night at a performance of Tagore's most famous play, *Dak-Ghar* (The Post Office), we found ourselves sitting three seats away from the actor Soumitra Chatterjee. We couldn't take our eyes off him, but during the intermission, it was Bharati who was approached by a row of teen-age girls for her autograph, and it was a friend of Soumitra's who turned to him and said, as we all filed back inside, "Bharati Mukherjee's in town."

Several months ago, in a moment of self-pity, I had written: "If I'd been asked to make a list of the things that I cared about most, I would have said my old writings, my plants, my books, our camping gear, the permanent things we'd started to accumulate in the past year or two—everything that proved to me I had overcome my false starts and had begun to accumulate a personal history." I think probably that was accurate, *then*, because I thought of loss in material terms, and I thought of growth as accumulation. I should have known better.

For people like me, literary types who went to college in the late fifties, India means, first of all, E. M. Forster's great novel, *A Passage to India*. It is the unknowable India of "the cave"; of Mrs. Moore's transformation into a god; of the Hindu banner GOD IS LOVE.

I was afraid of India on purely physical grounds, I knew firsthand of illness and secondhand of violence, and I knew now I was far more susceptible to accident and violence than on my first trip three years earlier. But I didn't mind that. I was, if anything, ripe for change, new settings, new images. I wanted to *acquire* India to replace all that I had lost or outgrown. I even planned to set a novel there; I've never spent a year any place without writing about it. But more than the physical, I feared India the way a good English student of my generation was trained to fear it (or better, *dread* it; since "dread" knows more than fear, dread knows the inevitability of the encounter, that it cannot be postponed). The fear is summed up in the subtitle of Frederic Crews' book on Forster: "the perils of humanism." India can soften the skepticism of a Christopher Isherwood, it can shrivel the compassion of a V. S. Naipaul; I thought I could avoid both sets of susceptibilities. And if something happened there to change me—and I fully expected that it would—so much the better.

Because that is the other side of Forster's legacy to good English students of the late fifties. When spinsterish Adela Quested enters that primordial cave in the company of Dr. Aziz, we know damn well that *something* happened. It wasn't an "advance"; it was the murdered sexual nature of Adela Quested rising to the surface. India had done it. By extension, *all* instincts (we think) are alive in India. We go to India to have our instincts roused. Marxists, Vedantists, Jungians, rock groups, suburban youth, California librarians, all the unmended victims of Western repression: We go to India to check on our groovy karmas, we go for nothing less than transcendence and transformation.

Back in the spring of 1973 (it is now the winter of 1975) I too had yearned for transformation in the year to come. I would shed my "learning," gather my humanism about me, trust my eyes and ears, and diligently search for caves to be reborn in. It would still have everything to do with *growth:* I would see more, read more, do more; therefore, I would be wiser, better. It would be a quantum leap in personal growth. It was time to test my capacity for sustained absorption. So much of Bharati was unknown to me because I had not been able to appreciate the texture of her first twenty-one years. I must have thought our marriage would deepen, grow even stronger.

What I should have said, back then, was that I valued my marriage most; what I feared most was divorce, and had I been wise, I would have known that going to India to understand my marriage might kill it. My voyage to understand India would stop ridiculously short of its goal. But what I *would* see clearly for the first time was that whole bloated, dropsical giant called the West, that I thought I knew profoundly.

From Canada came rumbles of anti-Indian demonstrations on the West Coast, the curtailing of liberal immigration, especially as it affected aspirants from the Third World. From friends and relatives in Calcutta came stories of harsh treatment, lost documents, insults by the Canadian High Commission staff in Delhi that could only be part of a deliberate policy of discouragement. Young Indians with

M.A.'s and job offers in Canada were being turned down; illiterate Punjabis who signed their papers with thumbprints were being admitted. It seemed as though Canada were determined to show that it could be as callous as the United States, only less efficient and courteous.

Naturally, I couldn't face all this at the time. The myth of one's essential decency dies hard among us Commonwealth types.

## 12

Let one upper-class executive stand for many: He is Bengali, of a good family but not exceptionally well educated. The family has been "Westernized" (which can mean many things) for a couple of generations. Perhaps the grandfather was a barrister in British times, the father an architect, even a politician. He is a man in his forties who started very young in the firm, perhaps twenty-five years ago, at the dawn of Independence when British companies were beginning to look for Indians. They thought they could hold on forever. The corporation is quite likely tea, which is considered more gentlemanly, but less crudely profitable, than jute. It is a gentleman's profession for a very good reason.

He probably started as a tea taster, a "spitter," a dapper young man who would go up to the laboratories every morning where perhaps five hundred cups of cold tea awaited him. He would loosen his tie and hang up his blazer, gather a bearer to follow him with a spittoon and a secretary to jot down his comments, and he would begin sipping, spitting, and quoting a price for each cup. The cups were each brewed from random samples of random chests from every tea estate represented by his company; the estate and the number of the chest were carefully recorded. The spitter's job—and for this, good breeding is the only attribute—is to place a value on every chest, from which the world's buyers will begin their bidding. When seventy-five thousand chests of tea are sent down to Calcutta every week from Darjeeling and Assam, and each chest weighs nearly one hundred pounds, and the value of the tea may vary from seven to fourteen rupees a kilo, and the specific price is dependent upon the impression gained on a swirl and gargle in a young man's mouth, and that young man could not hope to prove why, *exactly*, one chest was deemed a fraction of a rupee less valuable than another, one begins to appreciate why "gentlemanliness" is the only guarantee of integrity. Should the buyers from TOSH (the acronym of the Soviet consortium), Iran, Salada, Brooke Bond, and Lipton ever doubt his bonded palate, there would be anarchy on the tea exchange. Should a single estate succeed in bribing a taster (or be suspected of trying), chaos would ensue. It is still an innocent world; perhaps one of the last places in the world (and certainly in India) where the buyers must trust a broker's word. They are all gentlemen. A word, a handshake, are enough.

So our executive began in tea which certified his background and guaranteed his future. He was Westernized, but not crassly so. He was not yet well paid; entering "tea" for the money would not be a reassuring sign. Perhaps his family agreed to stake him for a few years. He was gradually promoted through the company ranks. He was now associating on equal terms with the English (though he would wait till long after Independence to be admitted to their most exclusive clubs); he was invited to tour the British and European teahouses, to become a consultant to the various tea councils. British interests, by now, were under increasing pressure to sell out; finally our young man bought a controlling interest, or a partnership, and became the managing director, the "Number One."

Socially, the Calcutta business world is horizontally fluid, vertically closed. Number Twos and Number Threes from a great many industries may know each other, even Number Ones will know the names of lesser men in other companies, but parties will be strictly for one's own rank. Complementary hierarchies of the British and the Hindus; it is a business pecking order as closed and codified as the vanishing caste structure, and just as unassailable.

In marriage the young man has been amply rewarded for his choice of profession. His wife will be called upon to host thousands of formal functions in her lifetime and to present herself daily in the clubs and charities of Calcutta. She will be from a "Westernized" but still proper family, not yet staggering down the gin-slick slope of over-Westernization. She is convent-trained, fluent and witty in English; she possesses all the talents and authority for running a large house and a staff of servants. In other words, she is a Loreto House girl with no intellectual pursuits. Her life's ambition has always been to be Number One's wife: Her beauty, breeding, and proficiency in English are her only relevant attributes. Should she be deficient in any category, she simply will not be chosen by the parents of the rising young executive. She would be married to a young man in a less-refined industry (jute or tobacco), or to a perfectly comfortable older man who will never rise above Number Three. Since marriage demands complete submersion in the role, superior intelligence is a most unwelcome affliction. Such deformities are dealt with like prominent teeth, to be corrected before the girl approaches eligibility.

Intelligence can be a blessing for unattractive girls from good families—they will be encouraged to become barristers or gynecologists, and eventually they will marry older men in the same profession—just as beauty might tip the scales for an aspiring girl from the middle classes. But at the upper levels, no admixtures are tolerable. Persistent ambition, knotty intelligence, a setimental disregard for self-advancement, despite the best efforts of a Loreto education, can carry tragic implications. Bharati and her two sisters should have married into precisely the class I am describing, and none of them did.

The margin for error is very narrow. A girl who has been raised in a genteel house, with the expectation of a genteel marriage, may find herself cheated for no better reason than a dark complexion, glasses, a flat chest, or an unquenchable curiosity about branches of knowledge outside the Loreto curriculum. She may end up—for she cannot refuse to marry—with a lout who will not tolerate the slightest deviation from expectancy, or the most pathetic gestures toward self-expression. Indian literature is full of such marriages; Narayan's *The Dark Room*, Nayantara Sahgel's *The Day in Shadow*. While we stayed at the mission, Bharati wrote a second novel, *Wife*, about such a girl, a Ballygunge girl from Rash Behari Avenue much further down the social ladder than any women I've been describing, whose only available outlet, suicide, is transformed in the madness of emigration to New York into murder.

But this is a happy story, and our young man has a host of brides to choose from, all from his own level of society, all with attractive (or malleable) personalities, all dying to marry him. The final choice will be the richest girl that his father can find, for the boy will need her dowry to buy control of the company, or to set himself up in the proper manner, once the British pass away. We met many such couples, because Bharati had gone to school with the wives and nearly all of them had married as they were supposed to. Some have succeeded spectacularly; others are the wives of junior executives, but obviously not discontented.

Arranged marriages may seem cold and calculating (and a great many are); they are usually the hardest thing in Indian society for a Westerner to accept. The traditional marriage arrangement is one part of the ancient society that has persisted, despite Western examples of self-determination, and ridicule from advanced thinkers both inside and outside the country.

We demand, "How can you marry someone you don't even know?" not stopping to think that if the fathers have done their homework, the boy and the girl *do* "know" each other. He knows her caste, family, and village, and in a traditional society, that tells him as much about a girl as psychoanalysis does in the West. Arranged marriages are of a piece with other traditions; they will pass only when a rootless, urban population has been created. Until then, it is a shrewd and unsentimental way of coping with the enormous odds against personal happiness. The traditional woman wants a man who earns, who gives many sons, who doesn't beat her: That is a good marriage. Indians simply cannot afford the risks that we take to be natural. The outlets do not exist. They perhaps have a less outrageous expectation of personal and unending satisfaction than we have (*Sex till 80!* read the brochures from Marboro Books that my university kept forwarding to Calcutta. *Where to go in Gay America for baths, boys, and beatings*). Indians look at our divorce rates (not our remarriage rates, for if divorce is a disgrace, remarriage is an obscenity) to draw a very logical set of conclusions. Something has gone haywire with our whole system; something occasionally goes wrong with individual parts of theirs.

We got to know many men in tea; some Number Ones, some Number Twos and Threes. A Number One would mingle socially with the governor of the state (Indira Gandhi's appointee, the ceremonial head); the commander of the Eastern (Calcutta-based)

Army; the inspector of police (Ranjit Gupta himself); other Number Ones from allied industries; consuls general from the more important Western countries; and the leading—only the leading—lawyers, bankers, and accountants in the city. Bharati and I became honorary Number Ones. I once tried to explain to a sympathetic Number One that in Montreal, as a simple English professor, I would never know the mayor, or any municipal, provincial, or national politician. I would never meet a police inspector or a general. I knew all the writers in Canada and a great many in the States; all my other friends were academics. In Calcutta we didn't meet a single professor outside of the mission. The Number Ones of our acquaintance preferred to think of us as "journalists" and not writers or professors. They preferred not to take in all I was saying, for they wanted to like us, and to admit me to a certain amount of parity.

One afternoon we were sitting in our room when Anjali, one of Bharati's old Loreto House friends, called to ask if we'd like to go to a charity première that night of Raj Kapoor's *Bobby. Bobby* was the biggest Hindi musical of the year, starring Kapoor's find of the Hindi millennium, sixteen-year-old Dimple Kapadia, in the title role. One can believe she is sixteen; she has the baby fat to prove it, and her uncanny resemblance to Jerry Lewis is emphasized by the dimpled chin. The movie magazines of the past six months had been full of nothing but stories of carryings-on behind the scenes, of Dimple's tantrums, of Dimple's sister ("Simple") trying to break into movies, of Dimple's hasty marriage and subsequent pregnancy with the faltering Number One male attraction, Rajesh Khanna, of his refusal to ever let her act again. We never went to Hindi movies, but we read the magazines; I had already decided I would see this movie even if I had to pay. "Yes," we said, as we always did.

The girl Bobby (it is not explained how she came by such a name, except that she is Christian) is the daughter of a lovable, rascally, drunken Christian fisherman. Supposedly they are very poor, although their beach-front cottage contains a large refrigerator stocked with several cases of Papa's beer. She is to be courted by Chintu (younger son of the all-time favorite leading man of Hindi film, Raj Kapoor, now strictly a producer-director with huge studios in Chembur). Chintu is a handsome boy, almost pretty, dimpled, pouty, and very fair. The Kapoor family hails originally from the area of the Khyber Pass, where Hindus were rare and tended to look like Persians, light-eyed and apple-cheeked. In the movie Chintu has returned home for school vacation and his parents have thrown a wild party in their Vegas-style mansion where seductively clad air-hostess types throw themselves shamelessly on him. Chintu sings, the girls sing, the parents dote. And then by accident Bobby and her aged grandmother (who had been Chintu's childhood *ayah*) stumble into the dance. She's wearing a school dress, her hair is in braids; she's Dorothy in Oz, Cinderella at the ball. The sophisticated girls giggle, but the prince is stunned. He must have her to marry, immediately, and only her. His parents are stunned (disgusted is a better word), for she is poor and her grandmother was a servant. A rich Hindu objecting to marriage with a poor Christian on grounds of money alone is like Archie Bunker objecting to Muhammad Ali because he's got a southern accent. They refuse, absolutely. The boy is hurt, resentful. The girl is in tears.

Now starts the real plot. Bobby somehow goes to Kashmir (the mountains of Kashmir, the skiing, romping in the snow, are the ultimate escapism for the Indian audience, stranger and more beautiful than a Kubrick set for us). Chintu follows her, disguised as a Muslim baggage porter, still singing of his love. Though her heart be aching she rejects his advances, for her parents would not approve. This goes on for the next three hours: songs, farewells, subterfuges, dances, suicide threats, murder threats, and final, last-minute forgiveness before permission comes down and "love" is allowed to conquer.

In form, then, *Bobby* is typical of the Hindi musical melodrama. "Love" is always the theme; the desire of a couple to marry and to surmount class, caste, community, or regional barriers. As in most fairy tales, the poor girl is often revealed to have been a rich girl all along (kidnaped as a baby, inheritor from anonymous relatives, or maybe just a "modern" girl testing her would-be lover); in other plots, the girl is about to be married off to a lout, a nonentity, a gangster, or some shady operator from overseas. The poor-but-honest, noble-hearted local boy must woo, or even steal and fight to get her back. It is as Nirad Chaudhuri has observed: No people in the world have more to say of romantic "love" than Indians, and less understanding of it. Inventiveness in the movie turns on the elaborateness of the barrier to true love, and the ingenuity spent in overcoming it. The largely illiterate audience throughout India would not tolerate any tampering with the formula, nor would it permit any deviation from reliable type-casting. Just as we bought tickets in the forties to Gable, Flynn, or Bogart with a sure sense of what we would see, so do the hundreds of millions in India and the Middle East support their various "heroes" with the same assurance. Feroz Khan will win the girl and overcome evil with acrobatic grace; Amitabh Bachhan with wit and sophistication; Shatrugan Sinha (who had started his career as a villain) with intimidating *macho*; Dev Anand, the Gregory Peck of India (though closer in age, it's rumored, to Cary Grant), with debonair charm; and Rajesh Khanna with man-of-the-people trustworthiness. The girl need only be innocent-looking and helpless; as in Western films there is very little scope for actresses unless they choose to play the obligatory "bad" girls.

Watching a Hindi movie, it must be stressed, is never as entertaining as talking about it afterward. The Pike's Peak footage of the normal film has to be endured foot by stupefying foot. A more lively exercise is to read about the films and their incredibly self-absorbed actors in any of the many film magazines, at least one of which, *Stardust*, is, quite simply, a great magazine that transcends the banality of its material. *Stardust* manages to be witty, intelligent, critical, and even compassionate about a world that is lacking in a single one of those qualities; half of its readership must be people who never attend the movies but who find the *world* of Hindi movies, and the actors, as absorbing as a great picaresque novel. Below *Stardust*, the level of reportage turns on interviews with "heroes," or on photo-features of "actress in hot pants," and insiders' tips such as, "We can't be sure if sweet little Dimple drinks or not . . . but smoke she certainly does."

On the stage of the charity première, Raj and Chintu Kapoor were on hand to auction off copies of the sound track. Raj gave a moving speech about the importance of cancer research, then dedicated the first week's receipts to the two cancer hospitals in the city. Marwari boys in the audience paid five thousand rupees cash from their pockets for the autographed sound tracks. And in dedicating the movie, Raj Kapoor let it be known that *Bobby* was his attempt to "project the teen-agers of today; their hopes and aspirations, their conflicts and their frustrations, and above all, their attitude to life and love." *Bobby* was the masterpiece of his middle age, his gesture to the rebelliousness of youth who all over the world were demanding justice and a voice in determining not only their personal futures, but the destinies of nations.

We met Anjali and her husband, a high-ranking executive named Nikhil, in the lobby at the intermission. Two hours had already ground by, and none of us could bear the thought of the second half. Fortunately, the reception at the Park Hotel was already starting. The Kapoors had left after half an hour. Poor Satyajit Ray was left in the guest box, grimly waiting for the intermission. On Chowringhee just outside the theater, several thousand street people and hundreds more curious middle-class youth had gathered. It was Hollywood on Oscar night, with giant portable searchlights crisscrossing the night sky, mounted policemen holding their *lathis* in case of a riot, and rounds of applause breaking out as each of us, celebrities in a way, came out.

Then suddenly we are again in the real Calcutta. It is eleven o'clock on dark Chowringhee. We are two well-dressed couples pursued by beggars; we walk till my pockets are empty. It is one of the last pleasures of the white man in India, distributing outrageous sums, by Indian standards, to beggars, more or less at random. When the beggars begin to cluster, Nikhil steps into the street, waves his hand, and his car miraculously appears. No matter how rich you are, how lost you are in the comforts of money or power, there's a potential *lathi*-charge not far away, and there's always that walk to your car down a street that is dark, smoky, and littered with sleeping bodies, and with the beggars who never sleep, groups of street children brewing tea around a fire, and the occasional mother propped against the wall, her babies sleeping on jute mats at her feet. Other babies sleeping, with no mother visible. The most chilling street in the world.

And then, seven hours after having said yes to an invitation, I'm talking to Chintu Kapoor and having my picture taken; talking to Raj and making arrangements to tour the Chembur studios, and I'm downing scotch with a tipsy lady who turns out to be the Chief

Minister's secretary, then with another lady, cousin of Raj Kapoor and wife of the commanding general of the eastern front. Two hours after that we've left with another couple, slightly younger and drunker than Nikhil, for whom the night is only beginning. We're in the back alleys behind New Market where the new couple, also Number Ones, Anil and Shaku, know a kabob hut that he always visits after parties. It is now 2 A.M.

What follows is not from a Hindi movie. It belongs perhaps in Mrinal Sen, or in Brecht, but good artistic sense would almost certainly rule it out. Terrifying, comic, sadistic; I am so far outside it in spirit and sympathy, yet so fascinated by its drama, that I want simultaneously to be ten thousand miles away, safe and, above all, *ignorant*, and to be there on the street with Anil, tape recorder going. It is almost 3 A.M. now, on a Calcutta winter night, in a Muslim neighborhood. The rickshaw pullers are asleep under their ricks. The street is quiet, but for coughing and babies' crying. There are beggar-women still making the rounds. Our red sports car is parked outside the kabob hut, we're all munching the spicy *shami kabobs* stuffed with shredded onions rolled inside *chapati*, and I'm dead drunk on Indian scotch and knowing it will not be kind to me in the morning. "Watch this, Clark," says Anil. "Oh, please, Anil, don't," says his wife.

He goes out on the street, one of the wealthiest men in the city, Hindu, and he begins shouting at the sleeping citizenry: in Hindi, in Bengali, in English. "Come over here. Right now, you. You heard me!" The rickshaw man comes close, face frightened. "Take out your permit, right away. *Jaldi, Jaldi.*" Anil holds the photo against the man's forehead, saying, "I doubt this is you." "*Saab*," the man is pleading, "*saab*, it is me. The picture came out darker, that is all." He makes the man count out all his change, all the while calling back to us in the car, "No. 3448, do you have that? False permit. Akbar Hussein, do we have anything on him?" An old crone with wild matted hair narrates to the wind as one of the street babies wakes and starts bawling. Anil starts talking to her, she goes on with her story, husband has left her, five children are without support, thinking perhaps this powerful man, if appealed to, will bring him back. "Five children, hear that?" he calls back to the car. He shouts back the kids' names, and I'm thinking: *Spanish Harlem*—what if this were Spanish Harlem? We all deserve to die because of this crazy stunt, right here, now. A beggar with an alms book comes up to the window of the car as Anil finishes his food. He looks it over, then up at the beaming face of the man. "Urdu? You're giving me a book in *Urdu*? Take it back. There is a country—why don't you step across the border? It's spelled P-A-K—"

"Shh, Anil, *please*."

The change from our kabobs is distributed to the rickshaw puller, who's laughing now at the joke he's been put through. "Ah, you no policeman, *saab*. *Ahchha*." He salaams and we speed away.

13

The monsoons had parted, it was October, the second summer; hot and dry with everything in the wildest bloom. The swamis' lawn required daily cutting; you could watch the vines unfurling. Tight, invisible buds became blossoms the width of my hand in the hour it took to eat my breakfast. And each of us, as we walked, wore a gray bouffant of mosquitoes over his head; random slaps of the hand would kill half a dozen anytime in the early evening.

In many ways it was the finest time of the year, a return to health and stability after the monsoons, a replenishing of waters, power, and a fresh harvest of fruits, fish, and vegetables in all the markets. The true summer, not nearly so desperate as the parched and searing months of April, May, and most of June.

Several of the mission residents would be out on the grounds just after dawn, gathering hibiscus blossoms and taking them back to their rooms for the morning *puja*. These were middle-aged men, upper-level executives with the large Indian corporations, whom we would see after breakfast in business suits waiting for company cars. But in the calm, postdawn hour, they would still be in *kurta* and *pajama*, gathering the crimson flowers.

For a Westerner, it is a soothing vision; gray-haired men gathering blossoms from gardens that could rival a Rose Bowl float. It is the great, benign, and enduring India, not the India of the half-men we have helped to create. Even if you didn't know that the purpose of their flower gathering is religious, you would sense something eternal in their preoccupation. These men are like *chhoto-mamu* and

Dodoo. *Chhoto-mamu* would take the four of us—Bart and Bernie had joined us now—around the countryside and to temples in other parts of the city, speaking to me of architecture, symbol and image, the shame of a *lingam* being bathed in milk when children were starving ("Hinduism was not always like you see it now," he would tell me, "there is much to be sorry for, but still much that is beautiful"), and he would find time, alone, to pray. Back in Chembur, Rajan would find hibiscus for *puja* long before Dodoo got up; and down in the office I had seen Dodoo call in his agile Christian secretary and send him scampering up a hillside to pluck an orchid from a tree, and I had seen that lilac orchid floating in a silver bowl of water in that evening's *puja*. Even without knowing Hinduism, you'd be left with gratitude for such a vision, the kind of eerie peacefulness that can hit you anywhere in India, especially when you least expect it.

These were, after all, middle-aged businessmen using the mission as a kind of hotel while they were on assignment in Calcutta. They were not here on retreat or for meditation; after gathering flowers they would return to their rooms (the cheap rooms with no protection from noise and mosquitoes), bathe, pray, change into suits, gather up their *Statesman*, and go off to breakfast. They would then look every inch the Western businessman, like Dodoo, like *chhoto-mamu*. They could talk with computers, make Rotary tours of the Middle West, and aside from a reluctance to take a drink, or a fondness for yoghurt and onions and a surprisingly firm demand that baths be permitted twice a day, we'd probably say of them (meaning it as a compliment), *They're just like us*. No, they're not, I thought that morning, they're not at all like us. Good for them.

One could choose a million examples: Sun 'n Sand, the social elite, Nariman Point, Johnson's baby oil at nine rupees a bottle, and ask, where does it end? An open society is a beautiful thing, vigilant eclecticism is surely a sensible aspiration. Yet how can these men on the lawn of the Ramakrishna Mission survive? Will we let them? One of those men took us down to his office in the Tata Building and spent a morning with us, showing the rooftop gardens, the magnificent view of Calcutta (the greenest city in the world from a hundred feet up), introduced us to other executives who in turn showed us their poetry, their paintings, talked by the hour of what we must do in Calcutta, whom we must meet, old friends offered introductions to Satyajit Ray, Utpal Dutt, Siddhartha Ray, Paritosh Sen. Had we seen Tagore's paintings, did we care to see Mr. Gupta's own collection of Kalighat paintings, the largest in the world outside the Victoria and Albert. *Yes;* always *Yes.* What of the old cook who took Bernie into the kitchen of the mission, because he'd seen him playing with a toy airplane at the breakfast table, and carved him a four-engine bomber from nothing but carrots?

There is also a truth in Professor Bhattacharya's disturbing quote: So long as India must compete with the world, it must import schools of management, telex, and computer, and then how long will it tolerate novelists and painters in the head office, cooks who carve airplanes, and men who pray and collect flowers instead of drink and chase women, like they're supposed to?

Living a year in India I understand the impulse to isolate yourself for at least two generations. With Western influence and Western models always in the people's eyes, how can they be patient with the discomforts of development? To be "Westernized" means, in a sense, to have a foreign mistress, one who distracts you from the only family you're ever likely to have. Americans laughed at the Russian attempt to Russify the universe, to substitute Russian inventors for good American ones. But when America evolved there were the oceans to keep the world away. We had time to believe we were the center of the universe, time to develop responsive institutions, a culture on its own terms. Those who didn't like it were free to leave or were driven out; foreign ideas got laughed off the stage. No need for censorship; patriotic ignorance took care of that. But we, who developed in solipsistic arrogance, with barely a memory of colonial tampering, who could not even tolerate foreign intervention in our hemisphere, exercise hypocritical outrage when poorer countries, with their very existence at stake, try the same.

Thoughts of a man on a veranda, in Calcutta. Given the chance, we will destroy everything that is good in this country.

## 14

What Zimmer, Campbell, and Erikson have stressed—that India still clings to an older "world image"—means that in isolated moments we may grasp it and escape ourselves in ways we never expected. All experience of India is a passage into myths that are still functional, rituals that still signify, art (like the classical dance) that is forever *in creation.* India seems, simultaneously, a remote past and a distant future. Calcutta is like a moon, a satellite torn from the same molten mass as earth, obeying the same universal laws, but otherwise so changed in all its textures as to be unknowable. Even the points of familiar contact, driving a car, mailing a letter, become infinitely rich and difficult. The clash of world image is, for me, the inspiration of all great art, it is the spectacle of history and the direct source of psychology. I felt engulfed by enough raw significance at every moment to drive me mad. Even V. S. Naipaul had noted (in one of his few favorable comments on India) that in Calcutta: "Nowhere were people so heightened, rounded and individualistic; nowhere did they offer themselves so fully and with such assurance. To know Indians was to take a delight in people as people; every encounter was an adventure." Everyone in Calcutta seems somehow purer, beyond analysis, more an epitome of his type. Everyone is out of Balzac.

In India, marriage, like death, is forever. The full Vedic rite, once endured, could not possibly be repeated. The girl (always "the girl" and "the boy") takes her whole identity from the two men in her life—her father and her husband—and marriage marks her transfer from one identity to the other. She leaves the private role of daughter and enters society, bearing all the gold that her father can give. She enters the state that is, quite literally, necessary for her salvation. And one wonders, in the perfectly balanced ritual life of the Hindus, if her entry into society does not signify her mother's new lack of function in it. Jaya's mother's tears for the three days of her wedding ceremony could not have been more bitter or copious if her daughter had died. And indeed, as daughter, she had.

Jaya was a plain girl in her middle twenties, an only child, a docile, devoted daughter. She was dark and gaunt in a culture where fullness and fairness are the only physical virtues. She was, unfortunately, her father's daughter; enormous eyes, mouth too wide, teeth too prominent. She was an outstandingly "good" girl—unassertive, compliant, cheerful, and patient. Her parents often boasted that she had no mind of her own. This perhaps told more of the parents than

of Jaya; she did indeed have a mind of her own, and for the past
two years it had been rebelling against her patience, her spinsterhood.

The period of waiting had grown far too long. She was not in
university, not in training for a career, not working, and since she
and her parents had settled in Nagpur, she was not even being exhib-
ited in the company of eligible Bengali boys. And in ritual society,
when the indicated rite is not performed on schedule, there is only
one possible interpretation: There is a flaw. In ritual society, there
can be, finally, no personal reason for missing a date with expectation. The culture provides four life stages and she had passed
through her daughtership and schooling on schedule, but then had
delayed the marriage. The *mamabari* back in Calcutta offered a few
tentative excuses, then gave up, for the joint family's heart is not in
making excuses.

Its heart is in gossip, in telling tales. And Jaya's situation did little
to dispel it. She had outgrown her ritual role: In her twenties, she
was still collecting dolls, still wearing her schoolgirl clothes, still
braiding her hair in a single schoolgirl plait, still piling up gold and
saris for that eventual marriage; still sleeping in the middle of her
parents' bed. And on that, the joint family built.

Since aversion in the joint family is impossible and psychology in
the Western sense nonexistent, what replaces it is its older world
image: tales. Women who would blush in shame at a rendition of
the commonest Western novels and movies will tell scandalous stories about people they hate within the family, of their infidelities,
witchcraft,    dishonesty,    embezzlement,    hoarding,    favoritism,
selfishness, impurity. Nothing is left out; husband's impotence, the
rape in childhood, promiscuousness of nieces, ingratitude of neph-
ews. How is an outsider to understand? Literally?—certainly not. A
defense against monotony? A symbolic reordering of the universe?
A Bengali has several ways of talking about himself, and one way is
to talk about his family, his job, his city; to create stories and retell
histories; Indian conversation consists of a world of tales, endlessly
intertwined, coy and squalid, symbolic and literal, told by women to
whom nothing, objectively, ever happens. They wash, they cook,
they go out only to the market, few people ever visit. What they
seem to be saying, in our terms, is: "I hate my mother-in-law and I

always will for having robbed me of my dignity when I came into this family at sixteen years of age, for having deprived me of my husband's love for as long as she lived," but what she might say is, "My mother-in-law carried on a lifetime affair with the landlord upstairs." A Balzac would envy these sheltered women the embroidered excess of their vision. And Céline the passion of their vindictiveness.

Yet everyone loved Jaya. I liked Jaya, she was, after all, Bharati's first cousin. She was a lot *nicer* than my wife. They had started out perfectly alike. Yet from that undifferentiated lowland of the joint family, Bharati had risen, mysteriously, like a monadnock. Since the culture dictated that growth could occur only in stages, to remain too long in any one stage was to admit being, for lack of individual differences, a freak. The Calcutta family kept muttering: She is not as bosomy as a film-star; she is too dark. She is not pretty. She is not educated. Her parents will fight all the time if she is gone. Her father is too cheap to find a good boy. All of this from her family, her closest friends—more than friends—parts of herself.

I heard these things in translation and wondered then if any institution more devilish than the joint family had ever been created. Later I would think they may not necessarily have been talking about Jaya at all.

It is December in Calcutta. Jaya and the family have been in the *mamabari* for seventy-eight days arranging nothing but the marriage. It is cold and rainy. The *biyebari*—where the ceremony will take place—has been rented. All the roles are portioned out; even *mejomamu* is allowed to handle the food. Because there are no male cousins on the *mamabari* side, and no husbands of cousins who can make it to Calcutta, the "second groom"—to be decorated in sandalwood paste and garlanded like a husband, to sit on the dais with the authentic groom—will be the only available related male, the *sahib* with a notebook, the skeptical Canadian. In the joint family everyone has a role to play.

About the boy, Arun, a great deal is already known. He is a Bengali, whose widowed mother and younger, retarded brother live down south in Bangalore. He is a pilot for Indian Airlines, living in

Bangalore with them. He is tall and fair ("Fair like Clark!"), polite and gentlemanly.

The boy *is* handsome. He came around just to introduce himself one evening in the summer when we were in Nagpur. He is tall and fair as a Punjabi, dimpled and reserved in an aw-shucks near-military manner. His mother is exacting all she can from having such a handsome high-salaried son. She keeps a list of the gold ornaments the bride will be wearing on the night the merchandise is to be transferred, and she keeps adding new demands in the way of saris for herself and various relatives. She has gotten a scooter for her son, furniture and a refrigerator for their flat (fortunately for Jaya, she will move into his Indian Airlines quarters and will not be "broken in" by her mother-in-law in the traditional joint-family fashion). All of this is accomplished with maximum unpleasantness. The boy stays far away from it—it is *meant* to be unpleasant, each side wants it known that they could have done better. It is ritual permanent theater.

There are several small irregularities in the whole arrangement, and one very large one. It is not really that Jaya is less pretty than Arun might have demanded. Nor is it that he has a retarded brother (who had, himself, been married the year before without the girl learning beforehand), nor even that it was not quite an arranged marriage in the strictest sense, since Jaya and her *mamabari* cousins had actually met him in Delhi Airport and had come to learn of their mutual readiness for marriage. Parts of the family speculated that he was really interested in Pritu, the elder of the Chatterjee girls (fair and pretty and only twenty), and not Jaya Bannerjee of Nagpur, but others defended Jaya by pointing out that Pritu was already a lost cause, set on a love match and ready to elope at any minute. As always, who knew? Everyone had a different story. But because they had seen each other and talked beforehand, it could never be a *proper* arranged marriage. It would be a *modern* arranged marriage, but even that was not the major problem.

It was worse. Arun's last name was Mitter. Bengali, but not a Mukherjee, Bannerjee, Chatterjee, Gangopadhaya, Bhattacharya, or Chakravorty. He was not a Brahmin. Double scandal. Jaya's father had either *allowed* his only daughter, the otherwise-virtuous Jaya, to make a love match, or, protecting her reputation but shaming his, he had *arranged* an intercaste marriage. To his credit, he boasted of the latter. It allowed him to appear secular and progressive (he is, in truth, an entertaining mixture of wit, cynicism, and frustrated worldliness); this is, after all, 1974. Move with the times, caste no bar. Arun is a good boy with a steady, guaranteed job. He is better than millions of Brahmin boys with nothing but their once-illustrious names to fall back on.

Such then is the responsiveness of the marriage market; depending on the quality of the goods, it is either a buyer's or a seller's market. Among the Hindus, everyone marries—"on earth there is only marriage," as D. H. Lawrence had said—an arrangement is waiting for the plain, the poor but beautiful, the brilliant but destitute, the thin, the fair, even the retarded.

Calcutta in December; for visitors, a perfect time. Temperatures range from the mid-seventies to the lower fifties. The street dwellers wrap themselves in double-thick scarves, in jute blankets, and sleep under whatever shelter they can afford. The middle class wear old suitcoats over their flowing *dhotis*, the women put on cardigans under their saris. The wealthier put woolen jackets on their dogs, and at the race track the super-rich can wear their imported tweeds and flannels. I still roamed the streets in a short-sleeved shirt, feeling really comfortable for the first time.

While the days are cool and generally cloudless (but for a freakish "cyclone" that struck during the wedding), the nights are dense with smoke from the millions of sidewalk braziers, the factories, the traffic, the general pollution. The nightly winter inversions, inadequate street lights, frequent power cuts, unlighted cars, street vendors with candles or kerosene lanterns set out around their mounds of fruit, popcorn, sweets, or flowers, all bring to mind a medieval village. One can walk the streets of Ballygunge on a December evening in a power cut and not be able to see his knees, the curbs and gutters, the outstretched arms, the cow patties, the broken slabs of pavement. At a quarter past five on a December evening the street lights —dim uncovered bulbs—are on, and the last orange glow of the sun is on the horizon. The toy merchants are out, the street fryers of the most tempting fritters and batterdrops in the world are shouting their prices. Popcorn is popping in battered metal pans, popped in the Indian method buried in blackened sand. Balloon vendors twist their wares, sending out a screech that attracts the children out with their parents for the nightly walk and shopping, and beggar children carrying yet-smaller babies on their hip or shoulder thread their way from open store front to open store front, hands out. Commerce, community, marriage, family; on the nights when I was feeling not Marxist but somehow Hegelian, I would drop five rupees—a good week's wages—into those hands, or others'. And I would think they were the same thing, somehow—commerce, community, marriage, family—all part of the Indian's identity, part of the world image that antedated my own.

On the side streets, any side street, the visitor would spot houses decked out in colored lights with canopies stretching to the gutter. Clusters of cows and beggars would have already assembled outside the walls, knowing that for the next few days mounds of edible garbage will be thrown out. These are the *biyebaris*, middle-class houses rented out for the ceremony, the feasting, the housing of dozens of relatives, and for enacting, for the untold billionth time, a rite handed down, intact, from antiquity.

We entered the *biyebari* at 10 A.M. The various rooms were occupied by teams of cooks, some trimming slabs of carp into bite-sized chunks, others packing betel nut into *pan* leaves, others frying *luchis*, still more making nothing but tea. Aunts and the female cousins busied themselves arranging saris that were to be shown to the groom's party on the night of the ceremony, when they came to inspect the merchandise. Jaya's *jethoo*, Dipu's oldest brother, had already arrived from his lumber mill in Madhya Pradesh. As befitted his importance in the ceremony, he was given a room of his own to receive the *pronam* of relatives, though he rose to shake the hand of the visiting Canadian. Four straw *tolas* were brought, filled with nothing but disposable clay cups and bowls, to be destroyed after each cup of tea and each small pot of sweet yoghurt. The rest of the eating for the three days would be on the cold floor, off banana leaves. The prospect of refuse from thirty meals, twice a day for three days, had swollen the small community of beggars on the street to about eighty, some carrying sleeping rolls and braziers, others merely their bowls. A herd of milling cows, sensing activity, had made the middle of the street impassable. In one corner of the entranceway, three hired *shanai* players—Professor Mustapha Ali and what purported to be his sons—were piping away distractedly, trying to attract the *sahib*'s attention for a free publicity shot. I obliged. Counting everyone imported for the work, but not counting the guests or family servants, there were about twenty cooks, carpenters, musicians, lampmen, teamakers, sweepers, and security guards.

In the next three days I suffered the full range of reactions to a ritual I could not understand: cruel, comic, absurd, moving, profound, unconscionable, scandalous. But I was to think first, in full sympathy with the tears and screaming of Jaya and her mother, that if the purpose of the ritual was to destroy the last remaining dignity of even a modestly independent girl, then it was a ceremony of genius. Bharati and I had gotten married, I couldn't help comparing, in a lawyer's office during a lunch break in Iowa City; a five-minute ceremony with a young couple who'd been having coffee at a nearby restaurant dragged in as witnesses. I'd never felt cheated or inauspiciously launched. But with this marriage ritual I was having another problem: Namely, if there had to be a fuss, I expected solemn fusses. If there had to be ritual, then I wanted it on a level of high seriousness, austerity, and simplicity. Danish modern. I couldn't cope with the impurities, as I saw them, that entered Hindu worship at nearly any level.

The mixture of ritual respect and gross banality, of ritual purity and low comedy, of ancient symbolism and modern commercialism —in short, the almost unconscious blending of the high and low, respectful and profane, symbolic and literal, left me confused. I placed myself back to a wedding I'd once best-manned. What would have happened in that Connecticut suburban church if the bride's aunt had burst into the ceremony bearing some freshly fried carp and exclaimed, "What a cheap priest they [the groom's side] found! This fellow is doing it all wrong!" And if the minister had retorted, "Let us hope the bride is less of a crow than her *mami-ma.*" Or if the *jethoo*—the oldest male in the ceremony and its central figure, if indeed Indian ritual has a center, but also an uneducated man who merely owns a sawmill—were to break off every few minutes of chanting with a "Huh? I didn't get that," only to have the priest fling a few more pinches of rice into the flames with a reassuring shrug, "That's all right. Just say anything." And what if an American bride couldn't repeat, "I, Mary Smith, do solemnly swear . . ." without bursting freshly into tears, and what if her cousins never stopped giggling? There I sat, second groom, in a cold damp corner in my Indian clothes, face made up in sandalwood paste, garlanded with white flowers that smelled of bubble gum, sneaking in an occasional shot at f/1.4 and 1/30, fearing that the slow lens noise was too prolonged and unholy, only to have the priest break the ritual and offer me a place in the center of the room between him and the bride, or next to her *jethoo*.

The weather had turned horrible, a constant drizzle and with the temperature in the mid-fifties, like a ruined summer outing in some mountain retreat. Toes numb, nose dripping, hands in pockets, Canadian turtle neck under my *kurta*, I looked forward only to tea. I drank thirty cups a day. Carpenters struggled with the giant canopy which was to stretch over the courtyard and provide shelter for two hundred diners on the night of the ceremony, as well as for the receiving line for the arrival of the groom and his party. Like erecting tents in a hurricane, like so much in India, a problem surmounted only by the employment of the cheapest resource, human hands. The physical discomfort—I was by now swallowing back those sulphurous belches that followed inevitably from more than one Indian meal a day—merely underlined a deeper, less precise upset. I was not witnessing a ritual, I was in one; I was somehow ritualizing. I sought my customary place on the back bench and found there were no benches, no stage. The marriage ceremony was happening in a room with a priest and her *jethoo*, where Sanskrit mantras were being chanted by the hour, with flower petals being thrown on oil fires, and it was being celebrated in another room where the bride was being anointed with oils and pastes, and where the cooks were frying carp and where the aunts and cousins were chopping vegetables and exchanging gossip, and in the hallway where an Important Political Personage was dispensing favors, and in the back room where her mother was still crying loudly, and out on the street where the beggars were setting up temporary residence, already scraping the piles of banana leaves of their *jhol* and heating it in their pots while cows munched the broad, waxen leaves. All of us were celebrating a marriage. And fifty miles away in Chandranagore, the groom was at the same time repeating his mantras in his uncle's house and bathing in colored waters, and soon his bath water would be sent with a servant by train down to Calcutta so that Jaya might also bathe in it the same day.

The purpose of the ritual was not to degrade or humiliate, of course; and the genius of the ritual was to emerge unchallenged. The purpose of *jethoo*'s mantras, and the cause of Jaya's tears, and the reason for her parents' sobbing in the back room was in the *meaning* of all the symbols. The purpose was to symbolize the family's relinquishment of Jaya (here symbolized as pots of fruit, rice, and flower petals) under the blessing of the marriage god, Narayan-Vishnu (the flame), and the consummation of the prayers and ceremonies was to coincide with the appearance of the groom, first through his bath water and other daily offerings sent down from his house, which were introduced into the ritual at precise moments, carried in by the bride's female relatives amid blood-curdling banshee wails (called *ooloos*), and touched to her forehead as she sat between the priest and *jethoo*. Of course there was order, even precision, to the ritual, but it was the order and precision of oriental carpetry, of intricate design endlessly repeated and varied, without a clear vanishing point or center of attention. It was a precision that demanded that the actual joining of the bridal couple could not be begun before 11:58 P.M. due to consultations with astrologers, based on the most dispassionate readings of the two horoscopes—despite the fact that a little juggling of the figures could have permitted an afternoon and not a midnight ceremony that would have permitted the two hundred guests to enjoy the feast and still get home for sleep at a decent hour. This way, fifty people had to be accommodated on various cold floors and the ceremony did not end until nearly four o'clock in the morning.

Jaya did not eat that day, and the decoration of the bride began in the early afternoon. She was powdered to a chalky grayness, her face was painted in yellow sandalwood designs. Honey was placed in her ears, so that she would hear only sweet things. On each ear she wore six sets of intertwined earrings—it being the only way of displaying all her gold at once. Her gold bangles extended nearly to her elbows, on each finger she wore three rings, on each toe, two; she wore a

tiara of gold, a nose clip of gold and pearls, concentric gold necklaces, gold chains about the waist, delicate gold chains about her an-
kles. She stared out passively from her chair through veils of gold,
while piles of silk and cotton saris lay folded at her feet. Cousins attended her sobbing with handkerchiefs, then returned to giggling
and gossip. The second groom sat in his corner, fully decked out
now, as isolated as the bride.

I thought of Jaya in Nagpur, the familiar little cousin who was so
good with "Bert and Barnie," who used to wear a loose top and ski
slacks and her hair in a braid. She was able to find cold Cokes in
those dusty alleys, lead the kids to snake charmers' huts, then take
them to the roof to fly paper kites. That girl had disappeared. The
woman on her throne was in chrysalis. She had been sitting without
moving for seven hours; her arms ached, she could not bend her
head, and when the groom's party finally arrived in a caravan of cars
and rented buses, she had to endure silently the inspection by his female relatives who lifted her arms to check their weight, who in-
spected the quality of saris, and who passed their judgments silently
but unmistakably that she must be a disappointment to a good boy
like Arun, so fair and handsome, but at least her father had met his
obligations. She must have been thankful for the dabs of honey.

I went out under the canopy to sit with Arun, to joke with him
about the hell of a fuss this whole thing was ("Ah, but it gives all
these people something to do for a few days, Clark," he said), and to
receive, for the first time, the *pronam* of his relatives.

The day after the ceremony, the *mamabari* relatives (but for Anju
and Pritu, who had gone on to Chandranagore with Jaya and Arun
the night before) packed up seven cars of relatives, filling the trunks
with more gifts, and headed up to Chandranagore for a reception
thrown by Arun's uncle. Chandranagore had been a French enclave,
along with Pondicherry in the South, until 1952, when a plebiscite
had returned both towns to India.

We arrived at night after a smoky run along fifty miles of Calcutta
sprawl. If any influence of the French remained, it was in the hint of
paint still on the upper porches overlooking the swirling crowds out
to shop along the main road; it was seven in the evening, marketing
time in Bengal. The town knew all about the marriage and of a pro-

cession from Calcutta; human signposts, spotting our strange cars, formed themselves in the middle of the road and conducted us down ever-darker alleys till a cordon of beggars raised their hands in front of a small door in a brick wall, topped with shards of glass. We parked, locked, and stepped into the garden of Arun's uncle, owner of several rice mills, *jethoo* of Arun, host, father-substitute.

Lanterns had been strung, the house was ablaze in lights, perhaps forty card tables had been set on the lawn, an orchestra was playing medleys of Hindi film, Beatles, calypso, and Doris Day songs. I found myself conversing in a corner with the uncle and other relatives; we were speaking French; it was still, after twenty years, a surer second language than English for some of the old people, and I felt for the first time, absurdly, that I had cracked an Indian language barrier. It was a different stratum of Bengal that Jaya had married into; aside from Arun, whose English was perhaps surer than his Bengali, very few spoke English at all, and those who did, didn't push it. Jaya introduced dozens of her new cousin-sisters and cousin-brothers, never faltering over a name or profession. Her eyes were as large, as happy, as I'd ever seen them.

So then, I thought: It works. Like some ponderous naturalistic novel that just happens to be unforgettable, the ritual with all its irregularities just happens to work. She knows that she will always belong to this man and to his family. All the joking and weeping, the tenderness and exploitation, the gluttony and deprivation, but mainly the moment-by-moment inventiveness *within* the rigidity, did something that no sanitized ritual ever could. It had brought me, for one thing, into the lives of Jaya and Arun and maybe three hundred others. It had brought me, of all people, fifty *pronams*. It had brought three hundred people into contact and that contact would not be severed for the rest of their lives. Jaya's remotest cousins in America will know of Arun, where he flies from, his income, his fairness and handsomeness and his retarded brother, and Arun's married sister in Madras and his copilot and his married brother in London, and the retarded one in Bangalore will know that some of Jaya's cousins have married non-Indians and non-Bengalis. All of them will know that Bharati Mukherjee, the famous novelist, who was reviewed in *Newsweek* and profiled in *Desh*, is a relative of theirs. I was beginning to understand why every Indian is so densely populated; how some of them can write five novels a year.

I ate silently, listened to music, and talked with the retarded brother, who spoke the most perfect English of his family, and who asked me more questions about Canada than I could answer. And I talked to myself as though I were my own small son: *You're seeing something incredible, kid. Remember it.*

"Everyone seems very happy," I said, after the dessert, remembering the recriminations of the week before.

The brother walked with me, his head thrust forward in the way of the feeble, but his face a more complicated and troubled version of his brother's smooth perfection. I could not help feeling that he was a proper companion for me that evening. We were walking behind the orchestra, by the wings of the house where servants were already scrubbing the giant pots.

"I wish someone had died when I was getting married," he said, "but they didn't." He entered the kitchen, dropping the empty pan of sweets in the water. I walked on alone.

There was a large garage at the end of the servants' wing. A side door was open and I went in. It was a cluttered garage, of course, more a storage room for devices I'd never seen and couldn't imagine in use. But there in the middle was a dusty reminder of Chandranagore's colonial past, and a kind of symbol of something I'd been thinking about ever since arriving in that rusting Fort-de-France of a town: a gray, classic, 1937 Citroën with boxes stored on its hood, a sagging canvas for a roof, its windows rolled down, and sudden activity from inside. From the front seat, one dark servant's head shot up, stared hard, then popped down; from the back seat two more and a woman's guttural retort.

I was back in the yard seconds later, ready to join my retarded friend who asked me where I'd gone. Through the looking glass, I thought, saying nothing. It seemed to me just then that I was standing at the end of an era, of something that went back unbroken for five thousand years but couldn't go forward even another day. I joined the two families in the main house for tea, unable to speak.

We left the *boubhat* after midnight when the town was as silent as sleep under the ubiquitous winter smoke. The cars traveled again as a caravan, for Indian highways are not safe at night—a sudden ambush by *goondas* crouched in the smog-laden gullies, a quick shoot-out, mass murder—the stuff of the daily papers. Indian roads are empty at night but for the Sikh-driven lorries carrying produce and at least two guards. In parts of central India, traffic is not safe even by day.

But I was glad to be on the road in *chhoto-mamu*'s car with its borrowed driver, and with a good assortment of the *mamabari* relatives. I was next to Anju, my favorite among the cousins, who was spinning tales about Arun's family and the goings-on in the *boubhat* after the ceremony; how rich the uncle was, how nice Arun was, how happy they would be, and yes, she suspected that despite all the practical jokes and padlocks and bells outside and hidden alarms inside, the tapping on the bedroom windows, she suspected that the marriage had actually gotten consummated on the very first night.

We pulled over sharply. "Flat tire, sir," said the borrowed chauffeur. Everyone got out. "*Chhoto-mamu*," asked Anju, "do you know this fellow? Is he reliable?" Always the fear; an unknown servant is in cahoots, his cousins are waiting in the smoke. The stuff of the papers, of Hindi films. It was the most deserted part of the road, swamps on one side, a darkened old estate behind slogan-plastered walls on the other. If he wasn't honest, we would soon find out. I remembered that first night in Calcutta; Bengalis feel unsafe in open spaces.

*Chhoto-mamu* assured everyone the driver was reliable. The car was unloaded. Twenty women, overdressed in Benarasi saris and gold jewelry and a like number of well-to-do urban gentlemen in their best suits stood in the middle of the Grand Trunk Highway eying the banks of smog like a herd of wary musk-oxen. It was a cold night, a breeze drifted over the water that felt like a drafty air conditioner. In what seemed the distance, one could hear the tinkle of bicycle bells, as empty cycle-rickshaws emerged from the smog, passed without looking, then disappeared again in the haze.

"Did a movie called *The Garden of the Finzi-Continis* ever come to Calcutta?" I asked Anju, who of course said it hadn't.

I could sense the sleepers coughing in the dark, and others walking on the gravel as they made their way to the nearby water. The night was crammed with people, all just outside our twenty feet of visibility. I kept talking of a movie Anju would never see, of a social order at the outer edge of refinement, that shatters like crystal when the mood turns suddenly brutal. I could feel brutality coming to India as surely as we heard bells and footsteps in the smoke. I mentioned the old Citroën, the servants who used it, the strange, retarded guide to the ruins.

"He makes me so sad," she said.

"Something he said to me was almost sinister," I said, aching to explain it to her.

"You know what he told me?" she asked. "He told me he wished someone had died when he was getting married. Can you imagine!"

"Yes!" I could barely contain myself now; I *could* imagine it, just as Faulkner had. A desire to start over. But Anju was still talking and I held a momentary, uncharacteristic silence.

"I don't know if you know, Clark, but if someone dies during a wedding, then the whole thing is canceled. Then there wouldn't have been a wedding, you see."

I admitted that I hadn't known.

The driver stood up, smiling, and nodded at us all.

"The flat is mended," said *chhoto-mamu*. "*Chalo*, let us go."

*PART TWO*

# ·᠊᠊ᠵᡅ I

# EMBLEMS

## *Isolation*

It was not yet a time for emergency measures. It was a year of protest marches and labor strikes and of heartbreaking letters in local
newspapers. It was a year for predicting horrendous famine and economic collapse. Street people knifed each other over minor irrita-
tions. Housewives complained of food shortages and adulteration;
neurasthenic women spread newfangled ideas about dust pollution
and nervous tension. Students rebelled against irrelevant syllabi and
poorly devised examinations; in some examination halls, they
stabbed to death defenseless proctors. Cities changed their characters: placid Ahmedabad, where Gandhi was still revered, staged a
memorable riot, while unruly Calcutta preserved a fragile calm. In
Bombay some literate young ex-untouchables read *Soul on Ice*,
formed an America-inspired militant group called the Dalit [Op-
pressed] Panthers, wrote angry poems, and battled with the police,
who, they claimed, were recruited from higher castes. In Kera
women members of a volunteer defense force wore men's uniforms
and undertook night patrols. In Orissa one million people were

devastated by floods. The Guru Maharaj-ji was said to have been harassed by skeptical customs officials at an Indian airport. Rich young Indians drinking cappucino at the Sheraton-Oberoi in Bombay were heard to concede that the American Hare Krishna chaps might have some spiritual insight to offer India, after all. The Prime Minister, Mrs. Gandhi, went on an official trip to Canada and saw snow on mountaintops in Banff National Park. No, it was not yet the time for excessive measures. It was still a time for gossip and innuendo.

It is, of course, America that I love. Where history occurs with the dramatic swiftness and interest of half-hour television shows. America is sheer luxury, being touched more by the presentation of tragedy than by tragedy itself. History can be dealt with in thirty-second episodes; I need not suffer its drabness and continuum. If I give him thirty minutes, John Chancellor will provide neat beginnings, ends, and middles; he will guide me to my catharsis. When he bids me good night, I have been ennobled. There is so much less confusion in America.

In India, history is full of uninterpreted episodes; there is no one to create heroes and define our sense of loss, of right and wrong, tragedy and buffoonery. Events have no necessary causes; behavior no inevitable motive. Things simply *are*, because that is their nature.

Going to India was Clark's idea. I was surprised by his enthusiasm. Prior to this, India had been a place to send the family on summer vacations so that he could have undisturbed time for writing. He had shown little curiosity to learn Bengali; he had, in fact, seemed bored by my endless stories of a tribal childhood. In cynical moments I had joked that going to India was for him a bizarre death wish. Then, in the space of three months, he had broken his hand, we had lost our house in a fire and our car in a three-vehicle crash on a quiet street. Suddenly, Calcutta seemed less terrifying. India, I warned, would be the fourth and fatal accident.

For my part, going to India was simpler than going anywhere else, simpler even than staying in Montreal. I knew the rules in India (I hoped I still remembered them); there, I felt, it would be possible to control my destiny better. In Canada I was helpless and self-absorbed. Ours was the only house on the block to suffer the embarrassment of a major fire. Fires occurred to poor, or to careless, people. I was personally not to blame (I was anxious for my neighbors to understand that, at least); I had been at the department meeting; the baby-sitter, cooking french fries for my five-year-old, Bernard, had permitted the fire to start and spread. But we cannot escape the consequences of our most banal ambitions, and so there we were, homeless, petless, and plantless, though, thank God, not childless, on a subzero February afternoon. I was going to India, then, because I was tired and irritable and because I thought of myself as a careless person on a callous continent. In India I would relearn the precautions taken by a people fluent in self-protection.

Of course I had other reasons for going to India. I was going because I had discovered that while changing citizenships is easy, swapping cultures is not.

For a Commonwealth citizen like me, becoming Canadian took no more than five minutes in an unpretentious office. A maternal French-Canadian official insisted over my protests that Indian citizens were British subjects. In the end I undid the work of generations of martyred freedom fighters, pledged loyalty to the British Queen, and became a Canadian citizen. But in Canada I feel isolated, separate in the vastness of this underpopulated country. I cannot bring myself to snowshoe or ski. Unspoiled nature terrifies me. I have not yet learned the words to the national anthem. I tell myself I shall never make friends here, though, in truth, I am lying; I am unlikely to make friends in any country. In Canada I am both too visible and too invisible. I am brown; I cannot disappear in a rush-hour Montreal crowd. The media had made me self-conscious about racism. I detect arrogance in the slow-footedness of salesclerks. At lunch, in the Faculty Club, I am not charmed when colleagues compliment me for not having a "singsong" accent. I am tired of being exotic, being complimented for qualities of voice, education, bearing, appearance, that are not extraordinary.

But if as a citizen I am painfully visible, I cannot make myself visible at all as a Canadian writer. The literary world in Canada is nascent, aggressively nationalistic, and self-engrossed. Reviewers claim that my material deals with Indians usually in India, and because my publisher is American, my work is of no interest to Canadian writers and readers. In Canada I am the wife of a well-known Canadian writer who "also writes," though people often assume it is in Bengali. In order to be recognized as an India-born Canadian writer, I would have to convert myself into a token figure, write abusively about local racism and make Brown Power fashionable. But I find I cannot yet write about Montreal. It does not engage my passions. It is caught up in passion all its own, it renders the Asian immigrant whose mother tongue is neither French nor English more or less irrelevant. Montreal merely fatigues and disappoints. And so I am a late-blooming colonial who writes in a borrowed language (English), lives permanently in an alien country (Canada), and publishes in and is read, when read at all, in another alien country, the United States. My Indianness is fragile; it has to be professed and fought for, even though I look so unmistakably Indian. Language transforms our ways of apprehending the world; I fear that my decades-long use of English as a first language has cut me off from my *desh*.

In those weeks of preparation, of applying for American Express cards and of packing an enormous shipping trunk with typing paper, color film, two-ply toilet paper, deodorant, dental floss—all the exotica of North America—I realized that though my usurpation of English had forced me to act as if I were rational and analytic, it had not destroyed completely my susceptibility to magic. To be a Hindu is to believe in magic; it is to see madmen as visionaries and prophets. The trip seemed to have detonated an energy which I had spent years restraining and disguising. Perhaps the broken hand, the fire, and the collision were the result of this unleashed mental energy. Perhaps I was a fool to think that the trip to India was to be simply a fourth event in a chain of disastrous events. In any case, in those weeks, while friends talked to us of modern India with its tiresome problems of overpopulation and hunger, I thought of the India of derelict temple friezes, embodying in plaster or stone derelict wisdom.

I thought particularly of a temple relief from Deoghar, Bihar (an area crowded with skeletons in maps of global starvation). I had not seen the temple relief itself, only a plate of it in a book about Indian art written by Heinrich Zimmer, whose work had not been brought to my attention as a schoolgirl in Calcutta because the missionary school I attended taught no Indian history, culture, art, or religion.

The plate of the temple relief showed the god Vishnu asleep on a multiheaded serpent. Above the reclining chief god were other, lesser divine manifestations, seated on lotuses or winged bulls. At Vishnu's feet sat his spouse, goddess Lakshmi, dutifully massaging the god's tired calf muscles. Below, separated from all the gods by a wall of serpentine coils, were mythological human figures.

I was entranced not by craftsmanship but by the inspired and crazy vision, by the enormity of details. Nothing had been excluded. As viewer, I was free to concentrate on a tiny corner of the relief, and read into the shape of a stone eyelid or stone finger human intrigues and emotions. Or I could view the work as a whole, and see it as the story of Divine Creation. For me, it was a reminder that I had almost lost the Hindu instinct for miraculous transformation of the literal. Not only was Vishnu the chief god, but the serpent supporting Vishnu was also the god Vishnu, given a magical, illusory transformation. My years abroad had made me conscious of ineradicable barriers, of beginnings and endings, of lines and definitions. And now, the preparation for the visit to India was setting off an explosion of unrelated images. Reptile, lotus, flying bull, gods, and heroes: All functioned simultaneously as emblem and as real.

As a very small child, before I learned to read, I used to listen to my grandmother (my father's mother) reciting ancient stories from the puranas. But after I started missionary school in earnest, the old gods and goddesses and heroes yielded to new ones, Macbeth and Othello, Lord Peter Whimsey and Hercule Poirot. I learned, though never with any ease, to come and go talking of Michelangelo, to applaud wildly after each scene in school productions of *Quality Street*, and to sing discreetly as a member of the chorus in *The Gondoliers*. School exposed me to too much lucidity. Within its missionary compound, multiheaded serpents who were also cosmic oceans and anthropomorphic gods did not stand a chance of survival. My imagination, therefore, created two distinct systems of cartography. There were seas like the Dead Sea which New Testament characters used as a prop to their adventures and which the nuns expected us to locate on blank maps of Asia Minor. And then there were the other seas and oceans, carved in stone on walls of temples, bodies of water that did not look like water at all and which could never be located on maps supplied by the school.

The mind is no more than an instrument of change. My absorptive mind has become treacherous, even sly. It has learned to dissemble and to please. Exquisitely self-conscious by its long training in the West, it has isolated itself from real snakes and real gods. But the snakes and gods remain, waiting to be disturbed during incautious sabbaticals.


## Identity

I had been away from Calcutta for fourteen years. My parents no longer lived there and I had never written letters, nor even sent birthday cards, to friends and relatives during this period. Yet after all these years, their first question invariably was: "Has Calcutta changed very much?" And my response was what I knew they wanted to hear: "No, it's just the way I remember it." Then it was their turn to smile benevolently at me and whisper: "You know, you might have a Canadian husband and kids, but you haven't changed much either." I was not lying, merely simplifying, when I agreed with friends I had not seen since our missionary school days that nothing had changed. Because in Calcutta, "change" implies decline and catastrophe; friendship is rooted in the retention of simplicity. The fact that after fourteen years away I was still judged "simple" was the greatest compliment my friends and relatives could bestow.

I was born in Ballygunge, a very middle-class neighborhood of Calcutta, and lived the first eight years of my life in a ground-floor flat on a wide street sliced in half by shiny tram tracks. The flat is still rented by my *jethoo;* the tram tracks still shine through the mangy blades of grass in the center of the street; and the trams are still owned by British shareholders most of whom have never seen Calcutta. Ballygunge remains, in these small, personal terms, a stable society. Wars with China and Pakistan, refugee influxes from Assam, Tibet, Bangla Desh, and Bihar, Naxalite political agitations: Nothing has wrenched out of recognizable shape the contours of the block where I grew up.

In those first eight years, though I rarely left Ballygunge, I could not escape the intimations of a complex world just beyond our neighborhood. I saw the sleek white trams (perhaps never sleek nor white) and I associated them with glamour and incredible mobility. My own traveling was limited to trips to the *mamabari* a few blocks away, and to school which was in the no man's land between Ballygunge and the European quarters. These trips we accomplished by rickshaw. My mother had a tacit agreement with one of the pullers at the nearby rickshaw stand, and whenever he saw her approaching with her three little daughters, he would drag his vehicle over at a trot. Rickshaws were familiar—the same puller and the same route over back streets with light traffic. Only trams promised journeys without destination. And sometimes trams promised drama. While swinging on the rusty iron gate that marked the insides and outsides of properties but was not intended to keep trespassers out, I had seen a man (a pickpocket, I was later told by an older cousin) flung bodily out of a moving tram by an excited crowd. And once I had seen the heaving body of a run-over cow on the tracks just in front of our house. The cow had drawn a larger crowd than the pickpocket. The head had not been completely severed from the body; I think now that a fully severed head might have been less horrible. I saw it as an accident, cruel, thrilling, unnecessary, in a city where accidents were common.

I saw processions of beggars at our front door, even Muslim ones, and it was often the job of us small children to scoop out a measure of rice from a huge drum in my widowed grandmother's vegetarian kitchen and pour it into the beggars' pots. I was too little to lean over the edge of the drum and fill the scoop, and for that I was grateful. The beggars terrified me. I would wait for them to cluster at our front door, but when they were actually there, I would hide behind my older cousin Tulu (now a geneticist in Hamburg), who would issue efficient commands to the beggars to stop fighting among themselves and to hold out their sacks and pots. It is merely a smell that I now recall, not the hungry faces but the smell of starvation and of dying. Later, my mother, a powerful storyteller, told me how millions had died in the 1943 Bengal famine—she did not care about precise statistics, only about passion—and how my father had personally organized a rice-gruel kitchen in our flat. I had no

concept of famine; I only knew that beggars were ugly and that my
father was a hero.

As a child in Ballygunge, I did not completely escape World War
II. My mother told me later, especially after we had been to war
movies at the Metro Cinema, that there had been periodic air-raid sirens in the fields just beyond the landlord's palm trees, and that my
father had set aside a small room as air-raid shelter for the forty-odd
people who were living at the flat at the time. She remembered the
tins of imported crackers, the earthenware pitchers of water, the bedrolls, and the complaints of the younger uncles who felt that tea
made on a hot plate in the shelter did not taste as good as tea made
on the regular open stove. She said she had not been frightened at
all during the raids, not even after the bombing of the Kidderpore
docks, and that sometimes instead of rushing to the shelter at the
first wail of the siren, she had settled us in, then raced to the street
to admire beautiful formations of the Japanese planes. The Japanese,
she insisted, meant us Indians no harm. She talked of prewar Japanese hawkers who had come to the front gate with their toys and
silks. I did not see the Japanese planes. I do not remember the sirens.
But in the last year of the war, as I was sitting in the first-floor balcony of the *mamabari* on Southern Avenue, I saw a helmeted soldier
on a motorcycle swerve around a car, then crash into a stalled truck.
His body was flung high (all the way up to the level of the second-
floor windows, my aunts said), before it splattered against the sidewalk. That is my only memory of the war: street children scurrying
after the dead soldier's helmet. My aunts said that the soldier must
have been drunk, that all soldiers were drunk and crude. I was
shocked that a soldier who was drunk could also be Indian. I had
never seen a drunk person.

And immediately after the war, when many British-owned Wolse-
leys, Rovers, and Austins bore gigantic white V's on their hoods, I
became aware of signs of violence of another sort. Funeral processions for teen-age freedom fighters passed our house. At the head of
these processions were bullet-ridden bodies laid out on string beds
and covered over with flowers. In those days, we thought of them as
freedom fighters and martyrs but called them "anarchists" and "terrorists," for we had accepted the terminology of the British without
ever understanding or sharing their emotions. Later still, during the

communal riots between Hindus and Muslims at the time of Partition, I saw from the roof (where we always rushed at the first signal of a possible invasion of our block) giggling young men loot a store and carry off radios and table fans. This was comic, but I knew that in other parts of the city, looters were vandalizing households and murdering everyone in sight. A week later, my father and the workers in his pharmaceutical plant were besieged by a Muslim group and had to be rescued by troops. The event might have been tragic for our family—and in fact, three workers were killed by the rioters before the troops arrived—but my father delivered the account with so much elegance and wit that I have never been able to picture it as a riot.

It is that Ballygunge which has not changed. It is still possible for my parents' separate families to continue renting the flats they have lived in since I was born, to conduct discreet and fairly stable middle-class lives, although each year the periphery of violence draws a little closer to the center.

I cannot claim that same stability in Montreal. In the last ten years I have moved at least five times, perhaps more. The few women I claim to know have undergone several image changes. They seem to have tired of drugs, of radical politics, of women's movements. Two have taken lesbian lovers. Two others have discarded their lesbian lovers. One rents a high school boy. To me they seem marvelously flamboyant. I envy them their nervous breakdowns, their violent self-absorption, their confident attempts to remake themselves. Having been born in pre-Independence India, and having watched my homeland change shape and color on schoolroom maps, then having discarded that homeland for another, I know excess of passion leads only to trouble. I am, I insist, well mannered, discreet, secretive, and above all, pliable.

As I told and retold, to friends and family, the story of our fire and car crash in the first months of our visit, I realized that it was not plot that fascinated me, but coincidence. I think there is such a thing as a Hindu imagination; everything is a causeless, endless middle. What oddity of fate or personality had brought one particular twenty-six-year-old Québecoise baby-sitter far from her home to my

kitchen in English Westmount on Thursday, February 22, 1973, so
that she could start heating Crisco oil for Bernie's french fries, lose
herself in daydreams, and inadvertently set the house on fire? I could
not remember how many fire trucks had been on the scene, nor how
long it had taken to put out the fire. I could remember the squelch
and crackle of freezing water on our queen-sized mattress, frozen
cedar shavings in a smoke-blackened gerbil cage, the sticky black
mess where the kitchen telephone had hung, and sticky white messes
where the stove and refrigerator had stood.

What mysterious design had trapped me, safety belt unfastened,
in the passenger seat of our Volvo on Thursday, April 4, so that a
housewife in a station wagon, missing a stop sign, could cause me to
crack the windshield with my head? Those few details spread out in
my imagination, obliterating everything else. But there was no
regret. A strange acceptance and then relief at the swift disposal of
sentimental baggage acquired over almost ten years; I was pained
only by what neighbors must have thought of us; we were careless
young people playing at professions. We couldn't afford competent
help, and we paid the price.

But my mother, from whom I learned very early the persuasiveness
of oral literature, has a more communal Hindu imagination. On the
first night Clark and I spent in Chembur in 1973, after the children
had finally fatigued themselves to sleep in strange hot beds, and after
we had told all we could about the fire and collision, my mother
gave us her version of the story of our fire.

She told us that she had had premonitions. Did I remember that
she was given to premonitions? So, my mother continued, she had
had premonitions of danger and had worried herself sick over our
well-being. And a week prior to receiving news of our fire, there had
been a fire in Chembur, a colossal fire at the nearby Esso refinery.
Plans had been made to evacuate everyone from the general neighborhood, including my parents and other residents of Calico Colony.
And my mother had stood at the open windows of her bedroom
overlooking the crazy distant flames, and she had panicked. Not because she had been afraid for herself, for at fifty-odd years she had
long been preparing to die, but because she felt *we* were in danger,
that we in Montreal were vastly unhappy. And in a week our letter
had explained the mystery. She had sensed our danger through men-

tal telepathy. Though we had been oceans apart, she had shared our misery. That was the point of her story. Drama and detail did not concern her. Nor causality, nor sequence: What mattered was her oneness with our suffering. It was as though we were figures in the same carving and the oceans that separated us were but an inch or two of placid stone. This is, quite simply, the way I perceive as well. In Deoghar several time sequences coexist in what appears to be a single frieze. *In the eye of God,* runs another quote from Zimmer, *mountain ranges rise and fall like waves on the ocean.*

Clark wanted to know how many tanks had exploded and how many rupees' worth of damage had been assessed. My mother did not know. She could not respond to his logical method of reconstruction. He separated the peripheral elements from the central, then forced such a swift, dramatic pace on the haphazard event of our fire that hearing him recount it moved me in ways that the event itself had not.

And, unlike me, my mother did not isolate details for their metaphoric content. For her the incident was indivisible from the general functioning of the universe; mental telepathy was possible in a world that fused serpent and God without self-destructing.

I often thought back to that story of mental telepathy when I later heard other Hindus—barristers, bank managers, sports writers, businessmen—confide to Clark and me that though they considered themselves rational, modern men, they believed in healers, palmistry, astrology, and miracles. Our talks with these men inevitably concluded with a reference to Sai Baba, the young South Indian saint, who, we heard, produced holy ash, vermilion powder, lockets, and even diamond rings out of thin air. For the West, the educated Hindu's belief in telepathy and psychokinetic energy may seem intellectually dishonest. But I am convinced that such beliefs have more to do with radically different ways of telling a story than with underdeveloped logic. Hindus entrust much less of the universe to logical explanation—and dismissal—than do Europeans. Belief in magic, miracles, and myth still causes very little conflict, even among successful scientists and businessmen.

On that first night in Chembur, I did not dispute my mother's claim of mental telepathy. I heard it as a call from a portion of my brain that I thought had long ago been stilled. But because talk of miracles, magic, and telepathy made me uncomfortable, I tried to deflect the mood; I chattered instead about the charred percale sheets and towels, the waterlogged suitcases full of my silk saris and photographs from my decade-long married life.

"At least I didn't have to worry too much about packing," I joked as my father poured me my second gin and lime cordial.

# ·৯[ II

## INTIMATIONS

My life, I now realize, falls into three disproportionate parts. Till the age of eight I lived in the typical joint family, indistinguishable from my twenty cousins, indistinguishable, in fact, from an eternity of Bengali Brahmin girls. From eight till twenty-one we lived as a single family, enjoying for a time wealth and confidence. And since twenty-one I have lived in the West. Each phase required a repudiation of all previous avatars; an almost total rebirth.

Prior to this year-long stay in India, I had seen myself as others saw me in Montreal, a brown woman in a white society, different, perhaps even special, but definitely not a part of the majority. I receive, occasionally, crazy letters from women students at McGill accusing me of being "mysterious," "cold," "hard to get to know," and the letter writers find this mysteriousness offensive. I am bothered by these letters, especially by the aggressive desire of students to "know" me. I explain it as a form of racism. The unfamiliar is frightening; therefore I have been converted into a "mystery." I can be invested with powers and intentions I do not possess.

In a life of many cultural moves, I had clung to my uniqueness as the source of confidence and stability. But in India I am not unique, not even extraordinary. During the year, I began to see how typical my life had actually been, and given the limited options of a woman from my class and from my city, how predictably I had acted in each crisis. And I see how, even in the West, I have acted predictably. My writing is a satellite of my marriage and profession; I have chosen, or fallen into, the role of bourgeois writer, limited to a month of writing in a year, or one year of writing for every seven of teaching. The American alternative, *Mama Doesn't Live Here Anymore*, remains unthinkable.

Only the first eight years were spent in Ballygunge, in a flat crowded with relatives, and friends of relatives who needed a place for sleeping and eating while they went to college in the city, and hangers-on, whose connection with my family I did not have the curiosity to determine. I was not happy in that joint family. Perhaps some of my mother's frustration seeped down to me. People say that I look very much like her. Certainly I am, like her, a collector of resentments and insults, and am stubbornly unforgiving. I suspect that in those early years, it was more important to me to retain my position as my father's favorite daughter (he had written a poem about me, titled "Treasure of the Heart") than it was to imitate, in proper fashion, the personality of my mother. But I am sure that from her I learned only to feel relief when we could close the door of our bedroom and shut out the forty-odd relatives.

It was a small room after the corners and sides had been filled with the bulky furniture of my mother's dowry. Two beds—one was the bridal four-poster, the other was a simple *chowki*—were pushed together for the five of us, two adults and three daughters. I recall that because of shortage of space, my father used to store an untidy pile of scientific books and journals on the bridal bed itself and that we children had to be careful not to kick the books in our sleep. In a household where no one kept his opinions to himself, this room was our shrine of privacy.

Sometimes there were invasions by cousins or younger uncles. Once my mother, sisters, and I returned from our customary afternoon visit to Southern Avenue to find that my eldest sister's British-made painting book and paintbox, which she had won as a school prize, had been vandalized. Another time, the lock of the wooden cabinet in which my mother kept her jewelry and small cash savings had been forced open, and some money was missing. I was taught to think of these episodes as an assault on our desire to maintain slight separateness within the context of the joint family, rather than expressions of mischief by relatives.

Within the small perimeters of that room, it became clear to me that if I wished to remain sane I should not permit myself to squander my affections on too many people or possessions. With overpopulation of that sort, possessions and relationships could at best be fragile. I learned also to be always on my guard, and because I was small, shy, and the second youngest in the family, to stay in the background, out of danger's reach. During communal meals, when all the children sat on the floor of the corridor surrounding an inner courtyard, I did not demand the prized items—eyes and brain of carp—because I knew that if I set myself no goals, there could be no defeat. I had, I felt, an intimate knowledge and horror of madness. There was a mad aunt in the family, and during a long stay that she, her husband and four children inflicted on us (because there was some natural disaster, probably a flood, in the part of East Bengal where they lived), I had seen her chase her husband with an ugly piece of firewood. I cannot recall if I had actually seen her hit her husband on the head with the firewood before I was hustled off by my mother into the privacy of our bedroom, or if the aunt had only been standing, weapon poised, about to hit him. I did not think of the uncle, whom I disliked, as the victim. But I thought of madness as grotesque, and as shameful, for I had been told by my parents that if too many people came to know about the craziness in the family, it would be hard to marry us daughters off. I resolved immediately to fight in myself the slightest signs of insanity.

I was released from all that terrifying communal bonding by a single decisive act of my father's, shortly after my eighth birthday. Because of certain circumstances in the pharmaceutical company that he and his partner, a Jewish immigrant from the Middle East, had set up, circumstances that he did not explain to his daughters though he probably did to his wife, he brought home colorful brochures one day of an all-first-class boat on the Anchor Line, and within weeks we left the joint family, and Calcutta, in order to make a new start in London.

We were happy in Britain and Switzerland where my father worked on his research projects, and where we went to school and were remarkable for our good manners as well as our intelligence, and where my mother took night courses in flan baking and basket weaving. But my parents did not make for themselves a new life. The partner followed my father to London, for a while installed us in a company flat at the corner of Curzon and Half Moon streets, vacationed with us in Montreux, and was, I suspect, persuasive about his plan for the pharmaceutical company in Calcutta. And so, after almost three years abroad, we returned to Calcutta, not quite where we had left off, and certainly not to Ballygunge and the joint family.

That period abroad is the only time I have felt perfectly bilingual. It was a time of forgetting Bengali and acquiring English until I reached an absolute equilibrium. But that gradual erosion of the vernacular also contained an erosion of ideas I had taken for granted. It was the first time I was forced to see myself not reflected in people around me, to see myself as the curiosity that I must have seemed to the majority—a skinny brown child, in stiff school uniform and scarred knees, who could not do cartwheels. The sense that I had had of myself in Ballygunge, of being somehow superior to my cousins, was less destructive than this new sense of being a minority on account of my color. I felt I was a shadow person because I was not white. We were an extraordinarily close-knit family, but since I had been brought up to please, I felt I could not burden my parents with these anxieties. It would have made them unhappy, and I could not bear to do that. I could count only on myself for devising strategies of survival in London, our adopted city. I became less passive than I had been among relatives and friends in Ballygunge: I began to regard facility in English as my chief weapon for bending my own personality and for making friends among the British.

In sacrificing a language, we sacrifice our roots. On returning to Calcutta, we found that our image of ourselves had changed radically. It was not at all a question of money. *Jethoo*, my father's oldest brother, owned rice mills and lumber mills in Assam, but he would not be comfortable outside Ballygunge. But to us, the thought

of re-entry into that closed, conspiratorial joint-family world was unbearable. So we sublet a flat in fashionable Chowringhee, the break
from the joint family being facilitated by a quarrel between my
mother and another relative. We changed schools too, from the
Anglicized Bengali school on the edge of Ballygunge to the most re-
nowned girls' school on Middleton Row, a school where, it was
rumored, Indian children had for a long time been denied admission.
And in our new school, the foreign nuns treasured us for our faintly
British accents which had survived the long homeward journey.

From our return to Calcutta after the false start in Europe until
the middle of 1959, we lived in the compound of the pharmaceutical
factory which my father and his partner had set up in Cossipore, on
the outskirts of the city. My parents now refer to that phase of our
lives as "the good days." I thought of the compound walls as the
boundaries of a small constitutional monarchy in which my sisters
and I were princesses. We presided at factory functions, such as
sports events, religious celebrations, variety shows for workers, and
looked on that as our necessary duty.

The pharmaceutical company had bought out the garden house
and estate of a refined Bengali gentleman after whom a street had
been named in happier times, but whose fortunes had now declined
completely. His botanical gardens—full of imported rarities—were
cut down and cleared, the snakes scared away, the pools filled, the
immense Victorian house converted into a production plant for cap-
sules, syrups, and pills. I saw the conversion as a triumph of the new
order over the old, and felt no remorse. Nothing would return me to
the drabness and tedium of Ballygunge.

For me, being part of the new order meant walking under arches
of bougainvillaea with my sisters and a golden spaniel we had acquired immediately after moving in, while neighbors gawked at us
from their rooftops. We were inviolable and inaccessible within our
walled compound. To our neighbors, we were objects of envy, and
probably freaks. There were screening devices to protect us: gates,
guards, internal telephones. We were at home to only those we
wished to see; others could be sent away from the front gate. Having been deprived of privacy in early childhood, I carried my privacy

to an extreme; I did not even learn the names of the streets around
the factory.

Every day we shuttled between this fortressed factory compound
and the school compound in an old gray Rover, once owned by a
British executive who had decided independent India was no longer
the best place for him. Our privacy was guaranteed on these trips by
a bodyguard who looked like Oliver Hardy. The ride from Cossipore
to Middleton Row and back is very long, and the cityscape unusually
unpleasant. I learned very quickly, therefore, to look out of the window and see nothing. During those rides, my sisters and I talked endlessly about the kinds of men we wanted to marry, and memorized
passages from Shakespeare or from the Gospels for the morning's
quizzes. My older sister, who is four years older than I and currently
is a childless, working wife in Detroit, was the most romantic among
us. She said that she did not care about money, but that the groom
would have to have excellent table manners and be perfect at
ballroom dancing. My younger sister and I knew what she meant by
that: She wanted a "Westernized" groom who had studied abroad,
and who could command for her a "Westernized" life-style in a
pretty flat on Park Street or Chowringhee. Like us, she did not want
to lapse into the self-contained vernacular world of Ballygunge.

During this period we were once visited by some female relatives of
Mr. D. Gupta, former owner of the garden house that we had converted into a factory. My father arranged for the visiting women to
be taken on a guided tour of the plant and then to have tea with us.
It was intended by my father to be, and therefore was, an amiable
occasion. We sat on the Georgian and Jacobean imported furniture
that my parents had extravagantly selected from auction houses on
Park and Free School streets, and we listened to the niece of the former owner describe how pretty the chute of colored syrups and cap-
sules had been. It was amiable because the old and new orders had
treated each other courteously. Confrontations would come later,
and my sisters and I would one day not long after that tea, on our return from school, have to walk through a crowd of striking employees who had blocked our car and who carried placards we were
too well-brought-up to read. This tea among the women of the former and current owners was an acknowledgment of another sort: the
vulnerability of individual heroes or families in the face of larger

designs. Having a street named after oneself was no permanent guarantee of dignity or survival.

That is why, on this 1973 trip back to India, when a newer order
has replaced us within the walls of that same compound, I chose not
to visit the factory, nor to walk once more under the flowering arches
where my sisters and I dreamed about our "Westernized" grooms
and "Westernized" life-styles. On this latest trip, I was told that the
neighborhood around the factory had become dangerous, and that
during the recent Naxalite agitations, workers had been beaten up
and that a chemist I recalled well had been knifed in the head a
block and a half from the factory gates.

For me the walled factory compound, the guards at the gate office,
the bodyguard inside our Rover, the neighbors staring at us from the
rooftops, are now emblems. We were typical of a class in the city.
There was surely nothing ignoble in our desire to better our condition. In a city that threatens to overwhelm the individual who is passive, there was nothing immoral in self-protection. But we had refused to merge with the city; we had cleared the snakes and
shrubberies; we had preoccupied ourselves with single layers of existence—getting ahead, marrying well—and we had ignored the visionary whole. And now, years later, those of us who left and settled in
far-off cities like Detroit and Montreal, as well as those of my school
friends who stayed and who now live in flats on Park Street or own
houses on Rawdon Street, are paying for having scared the snakes
and gutted the shrubberies.

My parents moved out of Calcutta long ago. But the impulse to
erect compound walls, to isolate and exclude, appears all around me
in Calcutta in 1973. My friends live in mansions that the British had
built in less volatile times to separate themselves from the bazaars
and settlements of the natives. These mansions, even now, are
fronted by spacious lawns, gravel driveways, enormous gates with
wooden watch posts, and one or more uniformed guards. The guards
are not always alert on the job. One rainy July morning as we swung
into the driveway of the home of a managing director of a former
British firm, we caught the guard urinating against the compound
wall.

The cry these days is more for protection than for privacy, and this cry is more shrill than I have ever heard. The women who live in these mansions and whom I meet very regularly for lunch and charity work, study groups and cocktails on the lawn, tell me about the "troubled times" when everything was "topsy-turvy" because the Naxalite gangs took over. With manicured nails jabbing the air, they describe to me how the Naxals scared the guards, sometimes invaded the compounds, threw gravel against the bathroom windows, tore up the lawns by playing soccer. One elegant young woman wearing a delicate pink nylon sari and Japanese pearls (it is hard for me to adjust to this new image, for I had last seen her as a pig-tailed schoolgirl with socks that kept sliding into her shoes) wants me to know that "the troubled times" are not over yet, that what I am seeing is simply a lull before the coming class confrontation. I do not disbelieve her; it is a common conviction all over Calcutta. A woman I had met a week before is now hiding out with her family in the house of another friend in order to avoid what she calls "mischievous acts"—acid bombs? sieges? kidnapings?—by striking employees in her husband's firm.

Here in Calcutta, my friends go out into the city in groups, beautiful women in well-waxed cars, and they pack pills for lepers for Mother Teresa. They supervise sewing workshops for destitute women, even clean streets in front of photographers and journalists in order to save and beautify Calcutta. "CALCUTTA IS FOREVER" announces a billboard on Ballygunge Circular Road, paid for by the Beautification Committee. "KEEP YOUR CITY CLEAN AND DESCENT" mocks a less-professional effort near Free School Street. They have made their commitment to this decayed and turbulent city. In exchange, they want protection for themselves and their children.

To protect oneself is to be sensible, I am told. It is a city-wide obsession. Even the Scholar's Guest House where Clark and I stay and which is run by the Ramakrishna Mission, a religious Hindu order, is set apart from the street by high walls. Outside the walls are the accouterments of Ballygunge life: hawkers, beggars, loiterers, squatters, sleepers, cows and pariahs, cars, taxis, buses, mini-buses, cycles, rickshaws, bullock carts, and heedless pedestrians. Inside there is greenery, flowers, a studied calm. The *durwan* at the gate sits on a stool and separates the two worlds. He has a register and pencil to keep track of all visitors. But still the brutal world invades the mission, and brass gas rings disappear from the secondary kitchen, and dissatisfied employees demonstrate on the edge of the judiciously kept lawn.

We do not seem to have heeded the message of the anonymous sculptor from Deoghar. We have confined ourselves to single obsessions. We have protected our territory, and posted uniformed servants to keep out the confusions of the city. We have forgotten that the guard himself is in an ambiguous position and that his loyalties may be fragile. In a city like this, an elderly relative tells me as he chews an endless mouthful of betel nuts, *You just can't be too careful. If you relax for a second, someone will snatch your gold necklace or your purse.* He advises me against certain doctors—there have been stories about nearly any doctor that I mention. *That man is too black, That man is unmarried, Never go to a doctor alone.* But to be so wise, I would like to answer, is also to distort.

Out there beyond our walled vision is a reality that disgusts and confounds the intellect, and a populace that is too illiterate, too hungry, too brutish, to be gently manipulated. Or, just as confounding, a populace too gentle to be brutishly commanded. The odds against survival for an individual are enormous, and rewards, at best, are uncertain.

*Merge,* commands the Deoghar sculptor, *there are no insides and outsides, no serpents, no gods.*

But at this time, we who consider ourselves more intelligent, more politically conscious, more sophisticated, more charming than the ancient stoneworker, know that to merge, to throw in our lot with Calcutta, is also to invite self-destruction. If we take down the compound walls and remove the ceremonial guard who relieves himself in the street and picks his nose while opening the gates to visitors, what will happen to our children?

It is at this point that I separate myself from the chorus of my old school friends in Calcutta. My sons will return to Montreal at the end of the year, study very little, ski a little more, watch Saturday cartoons on TV, and inherit the promises of the New World.

For the children of my friends who have chosen to remain in Calcutta, the range of future possibilities is infinitely more frightening.

Though we never discuss it, we all know that this city will yield its rewards only to the strongest, the smartest, or the most powerful.
*Bombay: May–June 1973*

For me, 1973 was a year of luxurious nostalgia. This nostalgia could be triggered by the smallest objects, such as a Venetian liqueur glass bought at Staynor's auction house during the "good days" and transported with love during the reluctant move from Calcutta to Baroda and Bombay. Nostalgia could overtake me anywhere and transform the immediate surroundings until my parents' carelessly furnished Chembur living room become once more the room stocked with Jacobean sofas that I had lolled on as a teen-ager.

But for many Indians, 1973 was a year in which nostalgia gave way to bewilderment and anger. The papers and periodicals were full of stories of misunderstandings. I read that an eighteen-year-old pregnant woman who had been cooking supper on the platform of a clean, new railway station was kicked to death by an outraged railway official. And that a starving mother threw her four daughters and herself into a well but succeeded in killing only two.

Then there were the standard stories of rage and frustration, of men killing each other in movie house queues, of knifings among street sleepers because a child had cried too loud and too long or one man had made a pass at another man's wife. The time for good humor seemed about to disappear. There were endless complaints about endless shortages, and short fierce strikes all over India, but no one had yet taken radical, irrevocable measures.

In Chembur, where we spent the first month and a half seeing my family and preparing for the trip farther east to Calcutta, I learned that fear is not an affliction; it merely is a way of ordering a confused world. The wives I met in Bombay relied on fear to give meaning to lives that might otherwise have seemed, even to them, banal. Like my mother, these woman lived in compounds of factories in which their husbands worked, in executives' quarters which were considered luxurious. The compounds had the usual paraphernalia of security: walls, sometimes topped with barbed wire and always with wicked shards of glass, check posts, emergency "hot lines" to the general manager, uniformed and ununiformed guards. These executives' wives thrilled to the lazy salute of the watchmen as they drove in and out of the main gate on their way to the bazaar: The salute was reassurance of status. These women were valuable while the millions outside the gates were not. The compound literally isolated them from the world of unassorted passions. The factory walls gave them their corporate identity, loyalty, and self-respect, created a calming communal village in a chaotic industrial zone. The women were grateful for the rigid security and for the group privacy, relieved to be cut off from the other Chembur in which degenerate or starving people burgled, murdered, cheated, used dirty words. They had intimations of danger each time they went to the bazaar in groups of two and three in private cars, or (because of gasoline prices) mostly in the factory's bus. More often than not the buses that bumped them along the narrow highways and city roads had windows covered with wire mesh to deflect any projectiles hurled by unhappy laborers.

Inside the compound, they lived in neatly kept houses, set in hierarchical rows, and separated from the noisy, smelly work site by trees or hill slopes or at least a bamboo grove. Their children watched television in the company's recreation room, and sometimes if there was a really good movie being run, the women joined the children for an hour or two, fighting mosquitoes that preyed on all the viewers. There was also a Ping-Pong table, and though none of the women played themselves, they took secretive, unacknowledged pride in the Ping-Pong skills of their husbands and sons. They did not worry that there were no telephones, except in the houses of perhaps the general manager and the managing director. Their husbands handled all their serious relationships with the outside world; all they needed was the factory intercom so that they could call each other to set up visits and call their husbands home for lunch.

The women I met in that preparatory period before Calcutta were friendly, anxious to let me know that they did not hold my eccentric marriage against me, though, when pressed, they admitted they did not want their daughters or younger sisters to marry outside their state and caste. Their friendliness took the form of solicitous advice to Clark and myself. They found us naïve, helpless, untutored in strategies of self-defense. So they became our eager tutors.

"Don't let Bart and Bernie go off to the park with the servant.

You never know what gets into servants' heads. They should post a guard there."

"Did you read about that murder? After six and a half years, a servant goes crazy and murders the lady when her husband is at work. I tell you, you simply can't trust anyone."

"Chembur is one of the worst areas, one of the very worst," agrees another.

"Chembur is nothing compared to Calcutta. I don't know why you want to go to Calcutta. It's so nice here."

"Never ride a taxi in Calcutta. Tell your old friends to send cars if they want to see you."

"Make sure Clark gets in first. . . ."

"Have you told them about that European who lost his passport? Don't ever leave your hotel room for a visitor downstairs—make him come up."

"During the troubles people would just walk up to you on the street in broad daylight and snatch your gold necklace. They would cut off your fingers to get your rings."

"Things are better now, I must say. Hats off to Siddhartha Shankar Ray. He's been good and tough."

"Maybe a little bit better for the local people, but Bharati and Clark won't be able to manage. They are too trusting. I see Clark and I say to myself he is so open, always laughing, what will he do in Calcutta? He'll take his big Nikon camera to New Market and the *goondas* will beat him up. You tell him to be careful."

They told more stories. A niece whose earrings had been torn from her ears, shredding the flesh. An old widow whose gold chain was clipped from her neck in plain view of fifty people on a tram. For her complaints, she'd been lectured to by fellow passengers for having provoked the attack by wearing gold.

"Bharati, you better not wear *two* gold chains like that in Calcutta. It looks very nice—you have a very nice throat and collarbone area for necklaces—but in Calcutta that's an open invitation to burglars."

"There are so many gold smugglers around and they'll do anything."

"I'll tell you a story that happened to relatives of a friend of mine."

"Is this the one about prostitute rings?"

"No, this one is much worse."

She began the story; Clark was nearby, reading. It was all in Bengali, with a cluster of executives' wives hanging on every word.

"These people were quite young and the husband had a good job. One day they went to New Market to shop. They had an infant daughter who also went to the market with them. She was fast asleep, so the parents—and this is fate—left the baby locked in the car while they went in for a second to buy something, I've forgotten what—"

"They have *very* nice petticoats in New Market," my mother said. "It was probably petticoats."

"Anyway, they went to the store, and when they came back, there was no sign of the baby."

"It is fate," suggested another neighbor.

"Car was locked you said?"

"Completely locked. So there is absolute pandemonium. They informed the police, interrogated those Muslim chaps who hang around New Market acting as porters and touts, but no trace."

"They are absolute *goondas*—Mex, you hear that?"

"So, anyway these people had some important connections, and a real serious search was made, but still nothing turned up."

"That is good. These days in our country unless you have connections nobody will care."

"Nobody cares, that is right. It is terrible."

"Never let Bart and Bernie out of your sight for a minute."

"Every day, they had to drive here and there and everywhere to look at babies, but it was always the wrong baby. It gives you an idea how many stolen babies there are. Meanwhile the poor mother was so upset that she was almost mad, unable to eat or sleep. Then they got a call from the police to come out to the airport where a suspicious-looking mother and child had been detained. The husband and wife rushed out there, and sure enough, the mother recognized her daughter, and threw herself on the kidnaper—"

"Oh, thank God!" the women exclaimed.

"No, no—here comes the worst part. It was their baby all right, but she was dead."

"No! *Baapré-ba!*" They touched their foreheads.

"*Yes.* The smugglers—they were Muslims trying to get back to Abu Dhabi to get more gold—had taken out the baby's intestines and stuffed the cavity with gold bars, then sewn the stomach flaps back. Go ahead, translate it for Clark." He raised his head at the mention of his name. "*That's right,* Clark, *Calcutta no good. Calcutta full of goondas and very bad behavior.*"

My mother likes to lock doors. Also windows, safes, cupboards, closets, trunks, valises. Her closest friend in Chembur has installed a padlock and chain around the door of her refrigerator. Foodstuffs such as sugar, gram flour, cloves, cardamom, and cigarettes that cannot be fitted with locks are poured into plastic canisters and placed in neat rows inside lockable cupboards. Keys to locked cupboards are stored in other locked cupboards. My mother carries only one key on her person; it is frail and black and hangs limply from a knot in her sari, just below her left shoulder. Heavier rings of keys, the ones that issue insolent challenges to potential burglars—for example, the ring of keys to get to the purse that contains the key to another cupboard and to another purse which holds the key to a steel cabinet with a safe fitted with a double lock where my mother has stowed my scratched German leather purse full of passports, health certificates, and the children's photographs—these remain out of sight.

Clark considers this paranoia. He tells me that since the gate office of the factory compound screens all those who try to enter, this elaborate security system is designed to discourage only the live-in servant and part-time maids who come to wash the dishes, do the laundry, and to clean floors and toilets. I know, of course, that Clark is wrong. He does not understand the apocalyptic vision of my mother. He is annoyed that he cannot get to his tape recorder without having the women unlock several cupboards, or that when he is ready and waiting in the car for the long drive downtown it takes my mother and me several extra minutes of co-ordinated effort to give him his traveler's checks and identification cards. I explain to him that if the servant wanted to burgle or murder, he could easily do so during the siesta hour. My mother, though heavy, is not at all strong. She is totally at the mercy of any sinister intruder. Locking is her way of integrating belief in karma with belief in individual resourcefulness. She is alert to the conditions of modern India; she assumes that disaster, which in her childhood had seemed to lie in some unrealizable future, is now about to occur in her lifetime. Perhaps she remembers those wooden cupboards back in the joint family, when the forcing of a door was an attack upon all her defenses. She will not set herself impossible goals about reversing her fate or the country's; she will simply use her common sense to minimize the personal effects of disaster.

We suffer an unacknowledged crisis over Bernie's electric train, which we bought in Geneva en route to India and which we cannot permit him to play with guiltlessly in Chembur because of the factory's policy of "voluntary" power restraint. Bernie, who is obsessed by trains and planes, lies on the cool floor of his room and pushes his locomotive with his finger. My mother would like us to store the train set in a locked wall cabinet whenever Bernie is not playing with it. Clark refuses to do that.

"But that *chokra*-boy will wreck it in no time," my mother objects (to me, never to Clark). "He's a very curious and careless boy."

"It's a toy, for God's sake," Clark explodes with undue passion.

He is correct; he wins the round. We leave the electric train set out, and in a matter of weeks, the monsoon deposits rust flowers on the tracks, stealthily adventurous fingers leave dents on the underpinnings of carriages (it is Rajan who encourages Bernie to pry the tops off the passenger cars; it would not surprise me if Rajan had expected miniature people inside, reading their German newspapers), and the locomotive seems clogged with fluff and hair balls. And so my mother and Bernie conspire to save the train from further damage. They wrap the broken set in an old cotton sari and place it on the top shelf of a cupboard; it is transformed from a toy that functions to a souvenir of a nearly perfect visit by the family of a favorite daughter. I try once more to explain the episode of the train to Clark. I paint him a middle-aged woman with an overwhelming sense of doom. A middle-aged woman who no longer reads, sews, goes to parties, sees films or television, visits friends, and whose children now lead independent lives in far-off cities or continents. Locking out hazard, locking in happiness. To deprive her of that would be brutal.

My mother has raised precaution to a high art. She has not only experimented with locks of various sizes and brands—on trips abroad to visit me or my sister, she has spent meticulous half-days at the key and padlock counters—but she has also extended the range of items to be locked out. In Chembur she locks out sunlight, insects, bats, toads, pariah dogs, servants' chums, and cobras. She is full of cautionary tales about the cobra that had slithered into the neighbor's bathroom because a window had been left unlatched. All her windows are still covered over with the heavy black paper that had been given out to all residents of the compound to block out house lights during the Indo-Pakistan war. During the war, she had supervised the cutting and pasting, making sure the servant did not let a single sliver of light slip through. You could develop film in some of those rooms, even in tropical daytime. Now when she shuts her windows during the day—and she does that by nine o'clock to keep out industrial soot and smells, heat, undesirable creatures—the house is peaceful, dark, and cavernous. With doors and windows battened down, and with her hands on the panel of fan and light switches, she can control her universe. Manipulation of breezes and light, she construes as a triumph of will over chaos. Each time she bars a window, causing the papered-over panes to cut off the sun, she sees it as a stalling of a future disaster.

The wartime paper, as it turns out, is destined to go. Clark does not like the paper; he cannot work behind closed windows. He likes to work, and he is more self-reliant than anyone else in the compound. Also, he has allies in the servant and the chauffeur, whose full names he, rather than my parents, has been the first to find out. After three weeks of writing longhand in bed under a ceiling fan that scattered his writing materials without cooling him, he has the chauffeur drive him out to the bazaar, where, without engaging in acrimonious and exhaustive comparison shopping, he buys a metal desk and a metal chair, and installs them himself in front of windows in our bedroom. Then, with Rajan's help, he rips aside the company curtains, unlocks the windows, peels off the black paper, takes a long gulp of the outside air, and writes uninterruptedly for five hours.

My mother looks in now and then and says in the direction of the servant, "Don't interrupt. *Sahib* at work here."

But to me she says, "Are you sure he'll be all right? All that black stuff from the factory chimney will make his eyes sore. Ask him, does he need anything? Shall I bring him some mangoes or sweet lime? Or how about tea? He needs to eat more."

Over the next few days, the servant continues with the paper-removing work that Clark began. The curtains in all the bedrooms start to bleach in window-sized rectangles. Those of us who suffer from nervous sick headaches in the sun suffer them more than usual. Clark, whose desk looks out over the rise and the chimney, develops itchy eyes and has to return to his original writing position on the bed under the fan. The children suffer continuous hay fever. Dust from the open window covers his desk, typewriter, arms, hands, and papers; he can't erase without smearing the page. The servant mops a great deal more than he has before. A window has been opened and a foreign element permitted indoors. Clark does not yet understand an Indian's relationship to "nature"; he still suffers from the American myth of nature's benevolence.

When it is time for Clark and me to fly from Santa Cruz Airport to Calcutta, I am not afraid to leave Bart and Bernie with my mother. She will, of course, be even more overprotective when she is their sole guardian. My father will be at his office until the boys' supper hour; so she will see herself as their principal custodian, and love will make her more fearful than usual.

I hear her shout as I pack my bags, "Bertie, don't play in the puddle. Hookworms will get you." And five minutes later, "Barnie, come back here darling, big, big cobras outdoors." These, I know, are her ways, and perhaps her only ways, of expressing affection to her stranger-grandsons. To love is also to minimize the beloved's exposure to danger. And, having been brought up in monsoon country, I know that hookworms and snakes slither in and out of maladied, middle-aged imaginations. Bernie has already shown me, five yards from our front door, six dead baby vipers (he called them "fat worms, Mommy"), washed down the hillsides by the heavy seasonal rains. So I do not shout out counterinstructions to the boys to go out into the rain and find their own adventure, to be resourceful and independent and not bother the grown-ups. I do not whisper to my mother to disguise or restrain the force of her love. This will probably be the last time that the boys, my hardy North American boys, will experience familial affection and not consider it burdensome.

But for many Indians, the excellent balance between fear and love is part of nostalgia. Extravagant, unrestrained love can no longer be expressed and extravagant fear has come to replace it. Only partially hidden under the stiff Indian-English of newspaper journalism, I see the spurts and flares of private terror in this year of threatened famine and deteriorating nerves.

Mr. Suprio Das, in *The Statesman* of August 1, 1973, writes that while out on the V.I.P. Road for his customary evening constitutional stroll, he had stumbled upon a decomposing corpse bearing obvious knife wounds, and that though he had done his civic duty by calling the police, he had not been able to arrange for immediate corpse removal. Three days later the corpse had disappeared, thanks to the efforts (he believed) of neighborhood pariah dogs and vultures. And now, the writer wants to know of the editor of that respected newspaper, what should he do if during another evening stroll, he happens on another corpse full of knife wounds?

In Habibur area, in the district of Malda, a sixty-five-year-old landlord (*jotedar*) wins posthumous notice by becoming North Bengal's first fatal casualty during the crop-cutting and harvesting season. He is rumored to have been shot full of arrows by a tribal group who did not want him harvesting in that area..

Hungry or simply immoral youths, in large gangs, attempt to hijack loaded trucks in the Siliguri area, by blockading the highway with boulders, then by throwing stones at the windshield of the stopped truck in order to injure the driver and his guard. This results in an organized protest by truck drivers who tie up traffic on Highway 31 and demand better protection. The protesters are finally persuaded to cease their demonstration in time for the motorcade of West Bengal's Chief Minister, Siddhartha Shankar Ray, who is making an official visit to Kalimpong.

In India, then, for some people at least, it is a year of eroding faith in inevitable destinies. The daily newspapers, still uncensored, publish scorching indictments of official pronouncements and heap abuse on ministerial fiats. The workers at Calico go out on strike. It is to last only a week, but it drags on and on, sharpening into a show of force. Six months later, after a death and several beatings, the workers will return, accepting the company offer. Force alone still carries the greatest respect.

# ᦰ III
## CALCUTTA

I had no clear idea of what I wanted from Calcutta the night I arrived after an absence of fourteen years. Perhaps I merely wanted a place where I could completely relax. The plane had been full of slim but potbellied businessmen carrying briefcases, one or two off-duty stewardesses in tight slacks and imported T-shirts, and an extraordinarily handsome young West Bengal cabinet minister. I wondered if it was obvious to them that I had been out of Calcutta for a long time. In India one's questions are almost always miraculously, though not satisfactorily, answered. And my unarticulated question too had been quite lucidly answered by the man who had given up his window seat to me and who had told me before immersing himself in his files that he was a senior executive in a tobacco firm. In response to my calling the air hostess who had just served us snacks and to my telling her that there was a hair in the sweetmeat she had served me, he had turned in his seat and laughed, "Madame, I can tell you must be a resident alien in Canada. Here we've learned not to let little things like that upset us." How he could gauge my foreignness so precisely I was hesitant to ask.

Bengalis, especially those from Calcutta, are arrogant about their subnational identity. They do not seek connection with a larger world, except on equal terms. It pained me, therefore, to discover even before I had landed in the city that my connections with North America were so obvious.

But Calcutta is a tolerant, open, friendly city. The American consulate is on Ho Chi Minh Sarani. Respectable businessmen share the sidewalks with pariah dogs that look half-jackal, and everyone shares everything with crows and cattle. In Calcutta people dream of the present or past, but never of the future. Here the girls are pretty but lack the brash artifice of girls in Bombay, and the boys of Calcutta think of themselves as hopelessly intellectual. For those who have come from elsewhere, Calcutta is only a transit stop; for those who were born here, Caclutta is the generator of fierce and contradictory passions.

In Calcutta it is impossible to deny the geometry of one's birth. And I found myself in a difficult position since for me the city was both the original home and a rest stop. So I exploited the friendliness of the city, called up old Loreto House school friends who swiftly called others, and soon I was absorbed into the daily texture of other people's lives. Every day I met with one or more of these old and new friends, drove in their chauffeured cars (gleaming little Ambassadors fitted with fans or air conditioning, and vintage Austins and Rovers), accompanied them to their clubs, sat on their lawns or terraces illuminated with pale blue bulbs, shared hors d'oeuvres with their guests, with steel tycoons, tea brokers, tea planters, accountants, barristers, hoteliers, generals, journalists, film stars, race-horse owners, former maharajas, tennis players, and visiting knighted Britons. Clark was astonished by the elasticity of this society, compared to the narrowness of ours in Montreal. As for me, I felt sheepish that I was now so eager to explore the social life I had once regarded with irony. The years of tortured adaptation to other people's attitudes and rhetoric receded; dark and massive like storm clouds, they threatened my simple pleasures.

I reminded myself that it was too easy to satirize my friends. *While Rome burned*, etc. They didn't fiddle, but their daughters sang Christmas carols as we hurtled through beggars-and-traffic-clogged Calcutta streets. And they spoke with cloying affection of the preparations for Princess Anne's wedding. From the perspective of Montreal where my own life was smooth and modest, the extreme contrasts of Calcutta could only be handled with irony. The poor had to be seen as starving, spectral brutes, and the rich as arrogant and unthinking. In Calcutta the people I met acted simply as human beings, and they were sometimes insane and sometimes noble, but just as often they were banal or irritating. There was no neat curve to their daily lives that they exposed to me. Nor were there dizzying zigzags. It was I who was at fault for having set myself up as a professional interpreter of the slightest signs. Calcuttans had learned to respond only to the crudest stimuli, to hoard rice, lentils, cooking oil, milk powder for babies in the face of ever-increasing shortages, to exude from poorer villages to a poor metropolis, to clutch their billfolds tightly while walking on crowded sidewalks.

Within the first few weeks I began to feel guilty that I had allowed irony—acquired from excessive familiarity with British novels, and from a too-long association with departments of English—to invade and conquer me quite so completely. Once back in Montreal, thinking about my friends on their gently lit lawns and the sidewalk dwellers who were always just out of reach, I realized that no matter what I might write about them, my reader and I will exchange a conspiratorial wink. But my point is that in India I forgot to wink. Rich and poor alike concentrate on survival and on minimizing humiliating personal defeats. Irony is the privilege of observers and of affluent societies.

"Bharati, I can't believe that you of all people do your own dishes, cook, clean!" giggled Anjali, my closest friend from Loreto House, that first morning of reunion. "I remember how spoiled you three sisters were. You couldn't even tell when water had come to a boil."

The way she collapsed against the cushions on the deep, wide sofa, her shoulders still shaking from laughs that sounded almost like sobs, suggested to me her regret at the circumstances that had taken me so far from the comforting, circumscribed life for which we had been trained in our home town. I tried to reassure her with talk of electrical appliances and convenience foods purchasable in supermarkets where there was no time-devouring ritual of bargaining.

"I don't care if you have a washing machine," she protested. "You still have to put all the laundry in and take it out yourself. You have to go to the store yourself and carry home your sack of TV dinners." Anjali herself had three imported refrigerators, two in the kitchen and one in an alcove off the larger of two living rooms. Another woman I met through her kept her imported electric range in the dining room, an aggressive intruder among Indian antiques, useless in this city of frequent power cuts. It was not that these women were unfamiliar with appliances, but they conceived of them differently. To them, a freezer or range or washing machine was a widely accepted shorthand for status, and had no connection with labor-saving. Since the housework was done by servants who quite often were not to be trusted with sophisticated and difficult-to-replace gadgets, the idea of saving labor held little meaning. The household staff *was* the labor-saving device, freeing the women to pursue with dutiful meticulousness their full-time threefold careers as wives, mothers, and civic leaders.

I asked each of my friends if she would prefer to live in another country or at least in another Indian city. Their answers never varied. They were the luckiest people in the world; Calcutta was fatigued and neglected, but its neglect by other Indians made them love it all the more fiercely. I assumed that for them love was synonymous with choosing to stay rather than to flee. And the fainthearted had left, they told me bitterly. Did I remember Meenakshi, the girl with the greasiest braids in school? Well, her husband had padlocked his factory gates during the troubled times and snuck off to Bihar in the middle of the night. Was that fair to the workers or to the city? But they had stayed. And they had all suffered during the Naxal-dominated regime. They had been sick with fear whenever their daughters had not arrived back from school at the precise, prearranged hour. One of them had stepped out of the bathroom one morning and found a Naxal youth in her bedroom, waiting to solicit for a neighborhood religious festival. For *his* neighborhood, not hers, could I imagine the cheek? The watchman at the gate had not dared stop him from entering, and it had been up to her to send the young man away with ten rupees.

They had stayed because Calcutta is the ultimate test of one's self-worth. And they carried on as usual. They wanted me to know that during the chaotic days of the United Front Government, they had not given up swimming or golf. A woman whom I had just met at a fund-raising session asked me if I had heard that bodies used to have to be picked up from the pond in the Royal Golf Club. The city was tranquil now thanks to the firmness of the current Chief Minister, Mr. Siddhartha Ray, and the police inspector, Mr. Ranjit Gupta. Decisive, authoritative, these men had purged the city. I had met them both, hadn't I? Weren't they sophisticated and witty in addition to being firm? I realized that for my friends the Chief Minister and the chief police official were not abstract symbols and wielders of power, but men they thought of as so-and-so's first cousin or so-and-so's husband who had restored normality to the city they loved. And I had indeed met Mr. and Mrs. Ranjit Gupta and they had both been intelligent and charming on each of those social occasions. I had not met the Chief Minister on this trip, but long ago in his capacity as barrister he had pleaded a case involving my father, and in the dining room of Palm Beach Hotel in Gopalpur, Orissa, his wife had evoked happy blushes in us all by calling us three sisters exceptionally well behaved.

I did not argue with my friends about the appropriateness of firm handling of political dissension or terrorist activities. At first my reticence probably had something to do with my having been well-brought-up. It would have been discourteous to argue with my friends who had welcomed me so warmly and who had stayed through the confusing period and kept faith while I had preoccupied myself with the banalities of literary research, publication, and academic promotion. At no time had I been forced to fear for my family's physical safety. Later, during arguments with Clark, I heard myself defending my friends' faith in authoritarianism as the only prescription for the troubled city. I wanted to show him how thinly spread had been my acquisition of liberal sentiments, and how fast the process of unlearning could become. To defend my friends was to assert my right to differ from him. It was for me a self-gratifying, vicious game, not an argument about politics. Much later, after the inchoate cynicism had touched us also, after we had seen for ourselves how shortages of food or of gasoline could mean violence flaring at quiet intersections, after we had realized how hard it was to work because of the unpredictability and frequency of power cuts, after we had learned to be cautious and to anticipate disasters, to keep a stock of candles handy, to avoid going out during city-wide *bandhs*, to hide our Nikon on certain streets, I began to think of "toughness" differently than I had in Montreal. If toughness meant not only safe streets, but efficiency, I was willing to welcome it. I was learning to look at concepts like "democracy" and "democratization" in non-North American ways. I felt that finally I was shaking off intellectual imperialism by indulging in purely Indian clichés that "conceptual democracy" had to be interpreted differently in chaotic, developing nations. My friends were not self-conscious about their support of "law and order." They left arguments about politics and principles to men. They knew that the city owed them stability and they were not hesitant about demanding that minimal security.

I heard them say over and over, until repetition accumulated in my mind the force of prophecy, that hard times were ahead for the next generation. I suspect that they meant that not only would refrigerators and freezers disappear from their daughters' lives but that the daughters' attitudes might suffer radical surgery. In the meantime, while Russia grew more and more appealing to middle-class youth by making available cheap Russian books, language lessons, and scholarships abroad (even a cousin of mine was being tutored in the Ramakrishna Mission by a Russian lady, in hopes of getting away to Moscow), my friends continued to send their daughters to Loreto House and to bring back T-shirts with comic imprints from annual trips to Western Europe and the United States. They did not intend to fight their children's battles; they simply wanted to prepare them for the crises that now seemed unavoidable.

Over the months as I tagged along with them and followed the daily structure of their lives, I felt an accumulating embarrassment about the self-absorption of my own life in Montreal. I worked with no charities, had no connection with neighbors, or with ethnic and professional groups. Depression and joy were limited to promotion and tenure, acceptance or rejection of manuscripts. Friendships were limited to other writers and other English professors. In contrast, my friends in Calcutta were hard-working, and modest about their achievements. If they had social status in town, they seemed to be saying, it was because their parents had chosen their husbands prudently. A decent and successful husband was the reward for an adolescence of obedience and self-discipline. They had learned to work out their identities initially in terms of their fathers and afterward in terms of their husbands and their communities, and so most of them did not bear the scars of personal ambition. In Calcutta, being the wife of a socially and professionally prominent man was a full-time career. Being a woman physician or lawyer was not, for them, a preferred alternative. Their careers as housewives (chatelaines is almost appropriate) demanded certain skills: managerial shrewdness, physical stamina, diplomacy. Dressing immaculately when they would rather lounge at home, making small talk with visiting dignitaries, taking the wife of a foreign consul to lunch at the Bengal Club, all this was part of their professional duty.

There were the automatic memberships on governing boards of service clubs and charity organizations, the obligatory official entertainment every evening to advance or maintain the husband's business status, and servants to supervise, children to help with homework, older relatives to placate with visits. I watched my friends organize sewing workshops for destitute women, package medicines for lepers, work in adoption agencies for unwanted orphans, visit slums, sweep the filthy Calcutta streets as part of the city's beautification program, and arrange premières of Hindi popular movies (which meant entertaining the Bombay film stars who had agreed to come), in order to raise funds for favorite charities. Almost without exception, they seemed unalienated·from their daily routine. And those who expressed boredom appeared to do so because they thought that was what I and my bearded, professorial husband wanted to hear. Their habit of pleasing was so deeply ingrained that it included us as targets to please. Boredom, I remembered from my own adolescence, was not a sign of disaffection; it was an expression of a refined, Edwardian sensibility.

Underneath their stubborn simplicity and professionalism, I sensed deep and bizarre passions that kept them confined to a city which had begun to act toward them with the maliciousness of a bitter dying relative. In retrospect I realize that our conversations were meandering and often pointless; or more correctly, our conversations were more "innocent" and more "simple" than the chatter I am used to hearing from my women colleagues and friends in Montreal. In Calcutta there was less dissembling, and little or no irony. But it is important for me to get across the sense of wonder, even envy, I felt for women who could preserve their innocence in the midst of city-wide misery, without any morbid inward-turning. I am aware how reprehensible such sentiments can sound in the West, but here I am expressing my own unlapsed Hinduism; it is the Hindu concept of saintliness, after all, that reveres a man for plucking diamonds from the air, for standing on one leg for twenty years, for holding an arm in the air until it atrophies, and for retiring naked to a cave for fifty years. Whatever a Hindu is, he *is*, above all, without guilt. His saintliness implies no social commitment. If one is rich and well fed, the last thing in the world he would feel is guilt. Once I returned to Montreal, however, the daily lives of my former school friends began to resemble serialized episodes from an imaginary Indian soap opera. The people who had seemed to me so simple, innocent, and normal in Calcutta were now quite unreal. Such innocence was neither believable nor desirable (and perhaps not even possible) in the New World.

Also, I realize now that my friends were homogenous only in the way that housewives in need of deodorants, paper towels, rug shampoos, furniture polish, liquid soap for dishes, in TV commercials tend to blur and merge. My Calcutta friends shared attitudes toward poverty, upbringing of children, Calcutta and its exploiters, strong government, and Naxal agitators. But there were hairline cracks within the group. They ranged in age from early thirties to mid-forties; some were Bengali Hindus, other Bengali Brahmos; others were not Bengalis at all but had relocated with their husbands from Punjab or Rajasthan (Marwaris) or Madras. When they did not think of themselves as embattled Calcuttans, their differences magnified enough to elicit from them nasty remarks about each other, but not enough to get in their way or ruin friendships. They were all realizers of the collective upper middle class Calcutta dream of material comfort without becoming assembly-line bourgeois.

One of my new friends is Veena, who lives in a huge, renovated mansion on a short, fashionable lane off Park Street in what once used to be thought of as the city's "European quarters." Though Veena has not told me herself, I know that she comes from a North Indian princely family. (I am amazed at how much I have come to know and how quickly; I have filled in the blanks of fourteen years in a matter of weeks. I do not feel as exposed, as helplessly foreign, as I do in Montreal.) Her husband owns a cement company and is a prominent man in town. I have met him at humorless cocktail parties on other people's lawns. I know nothing about cement and he pretends to know nothing about fiction. So we have talked of the artist Krishna Reddy and of the musician Vilayat Khan. Veena and he have three children, the oldest of whom is away at school in the United States. A girl is in middle school at Loreto. The youngest—a dour-faced boy whom I have seen riding a red tricycle in the family compound—is in nursery school.

Veena is a pale, serene woman, and her high-ceilinged house reflects her serenity. There are marble staircases; there are enormous wooden doors with brass knockers that cut me off from private spaces; there are at least four living areas and cream-colored walls that are hung with paintings and prints (I recognized two Krishna Reddys), faded Persian rugs, and giant stone gods and goddesses. Her calm exaggerates my own anxiety. Sitting on her chintz-covered porch furniture or lolling against raw silk bolsters in her air-conditioned living room, I often feel a strong desire to declare my envy. Veena has made a fine art of homemaking. To me she is an unusually lucky artist whose medium and talent are not in conflict with her life.

One afternoon, at a lunch in honor of the wife of a Finnish colonel stationed in Cyprus, as the other guests were descending Veena's marble staircase to return to their cars for the drive home through the careless heart of the city, and for a rest at home before the evening's entertainment, Veena smiled at me and asked me to stay back.

I stood with her at the head of the stairs until the last elegant woman—translucent in chiffon sari—had floated out of sight. Then she led me back into the living room, past the beautiful textures of upholstery, tapestries, canvases, coffee tables and end tables, and antique musical instruments, and thrust open with more violence than I expected her to possess a heavy wooden door fitted with a brass knocker and brass latch. Behind the door was a small air-conditioned private sitting room with a glassed-in view of the back garden, the high compound walls, a park full of beggars and small children with their maids, and half-finished condominiums. The walls were lined with banquettes covered in beige silk. There were no books, no plants, no paintings. I guessed that this room was Veena's final retreat. Even beauty was not permitted to distract or please her in this room.

"This is where I do my meditation," Veena said. "You probably don't approve of meditation and things like that, but you know, I'm still an old-fashioned person."

I assured her I had nothing against meditation, and that my father in Chembur spent about three hours a day on meditating and chanting and rocking back and forth in front of rows of gods and goddesses. We sat across from each other on the banquettes.

"Do you think Calcutta has changed very much in the years that you've been away?"

"Not really," I said. It was the automatic response; only the timing of her question surprised me.

"Well, it *has* changed," Veena said evenly. "We pretend it hasn't to make things easier for ourselves."

Then she told me the story of her three days in 1969 when her house had been blockaded by strikers (the technique is known as *gherao*). Her husband had not been in town, and it had been up to her to keep the children and the servants from panicking. (As she spoke I made a slipshod count of the number of servants on the premises, and came up with sixteen including the two chauffeurs and the domestics for her widowed mother-in-law who lived on the floor below and had her own kitchen.) Veena said that her prescription for sanity had been simple: She had confined the family to the small air-conditioned room in which we were sitting—the noisy air conditioner shut out the slogans from the street—and she had played Scrabble and Monopoly with the younger children. For three days they had done without bread or milk. For three days they had slept on mattresses on the floor or on the narrow banquettes.

"I'm not a smart woman," Veena said, leaning forward. "I'm not a Ph.D. or writer. I'm just a timid housewife looking out for my husband and children."

She went on about the three days in 1969. It had been a time of class warfare, she felt. Otherwise what could explain her husband's workers blockading an innocent mother? The only way to deal with the fury of the strikers had been to deny their very existence. She was convinced her strategy was correct. If she had gone downstairs to talk to the strikers, there might have been a dreadful episode. Had Anjali and Rina and Nalini told me about the troubled times of the United Front Government? Had I heard that the manager of the "Tolley" (the Tollegunge Club) had been killed by his own "dog-boy"? Had Rina's husband regaled me with the story of how he had barely escaped being mutilated by a pipe gun on a golf course?

Outside, beyond Veena's head and the compound walls, I could see the overcrowded park. All the benches were broken. An itinerant monk, his trident beside him, was asleep on the balding lawn. Two little boys ran to the sleeper, threw handfuls of grass on his exposed belly, then ran out of my sight. Under a mangled park tree, two men were about to fight but could not seem to make physical contact. I was relieved that the air conditioning cut off the noise from the street and the park.

I thought I was beginning to understand the secret of Veena's serenity. Playing Monopoly while angry laborers laid siege was just the kind of unspoken advice I too had received as a child from my parents and from the Loreto House missionaries. This same impulse had compelled my sisters and me in the early fifties, when our car had been blocked outside the factory by workers wearing red kerchiefs, to thrust open the car door and walk, unhurried, toward the safety of our gates.

Ignoring the adversary had worked for us, and it had worked for Veena. In Loreto House, I knew, it was still being passed on as a powerful tactic. A few days earlier, I had visited my old school and talked with the principal—in my years at Loreto she had been a lay person and my French teacher—and she told me how *she* had dealt with the "troubled times" and with the enemy. In her case, the enemy had been a gang of politicized college boys who had invaded Loreto House and demanded it close immediately in support of a general strike. She had refused, and had promptly marched the boys into the prayer room. In her precise, soft voice she had told the leader either to stay and join her in a prayer for peace ("doing something constructive") or to leave at once so that the Loreto House girls could proceed with their study. Had the boys chosen to stay and pray? I don't know. The specific conclusion had not interested the teller or the listener. Perhaps it can be explained away by tribal differences in our narrative structures. Only the "middle" of the episode remains—adversaries about to come to blows but missing—the cause of the particular strike that had angered the boys was never mentioned.

That afternoon, between the lunch for the colonel's wife and a teatime appointment with Bengal's leading woman mountain climber, Veena and I sat in her monochromatic sanctuary and she told me anecdote after anecdote about militant Naxals. She rang a brass bell and ordered a servant to serve us lemonade on the porch.

That was the only time that Veena took me into her undecorated, small sitting room, and as far as I can remember that was the only time she talked to me about class warfare. On the porch, we slid easily into safe topics and safe debates about the woman's place being in the home. Veena said that she knew that in America mothers are often not back home from gallivanting when their children come home from school. Between sips of lemonade, picking fresh lime pulp off her reddened lips, she asked me if I knew any such irresponsible mothers. I confessed that I did, but said nothing of our baby-sitter and the fire. I tried to distract her with an account of Clark's and my visit to Loreto House. If one looked very hard, I laughed, even at Loreto, where independent social thinking was simply not encouraged—or even suspected of existing—there were hints of rebellion. Had her daughter told her that some progressive girls were conducting a discreet battle with the nuns about a certain "unsuitable" poem in *Palm Leaves*? I had a special attachment to *Palm Leaves*, the school magazine where my early tales of Napoleon in exile and Roman soldiers had earned me the principal's commendation, of having "a gift of the pen." The girls had selected an appropriately autobiographical poem by the Bombay Jewish poet Nissim Ezekiel, about his own private school days, "a slavering Jew among the Muslims" (if I recall accurately) in a rigidly English (Catholic) school in Bombay. Ezekiel is ironic about his Jewishness, his Catholic schooling, his (mainly) Muslim classmates, and the lines of the poem about all three had been deemed "unsuitable." I tried to interest Veena in this story. What *exactly* had been unsuitable: possibly the "communal" ring of Ezekiel's irony? The irony toward the Christian schools in India? His Jewishness? Or its ragged, manifestly *Indian* subject matter? English schools in India had never courted too much Indianness. Veena didn't see the conflict. That is, she didn't see why the girls wanted to publish such an ugly poem. I was never to know what the nun had found offensive; "unsuitable" is another locked-door sort of word in polite Calcutta society.

We finished the lemonade, dried our moist lips on crisp pink linen napkins with wide crocheted edges, and traced idle designs with our oval, shiny fingernails on the frosted outsides of our lemonade glasses. At the time, this signaled nothing more ominous than the end of one social engagement so that I could rush back to the Ramakrishna Mission and remind Clark about the lady mountain climber. But now, since memory forces patterns and revelations in the blankness of daily events, I am tempted to read into that simple scene permanent "unfinishedness" to which women like us have been condemned.

"It's ridiculous, our way of life," laughs Anjali. "You realize, of course, that it's dying." I know she does not mean that as censure, only as acknowledgment of change.

Except for the years that I have been away and in which I have not written to her but heard occasionally of her marriage and social prominence from traveling friends and relatives, I feel very close to Anjali. Our families have been friends for a long time, and our fathers went to college together. We went to the same school, learned the same code of conduct from the same nuns though we have applied the code very differently in adult life. The summer I turned seventeen I had been prepared, during a lazy picnic in someone's garden house, to fall in love with Anjali's older brother who had returned to India for his summer vacation from engineering school in Britain, and who, that day, had looked very handsome in a Paisley ascot and white slacks. Falling in love was something heroines did in garden houses in English Victorian novels to which I was partial that summer. But I have always been parsimonious with my love, and I did not fall in love that day. I bring it up now only to stress that my fondness for Anjali is not detached from history, as are my friendships with many other women in this city. Our families had been reflections of each other, progressive enough to send us to

Loreto House, but not liberal enough to let us go to parties where there might be boys and dancing.

Anjali is a tall, well-built woman in her early thirties, who married before she had finished her first year at college, and now has two very pretty daughters. Her husband is the managing director of a company that had formerly been British, and which retains an extremely British spirit though all the employees are now Indian. The business associates she entertains, especially from November through March when the weather is pleasantly cool, include many British former directors and their wives. She can, therefore, listen as knowledgeably to small talk about antique pistols and water polo (a recurring topic with retired British India-hands) as to chatter about the price of prawns and hilsa. She says that it is her wifely duty to make her husband's business associates feel relaxed.

But there are times, she confides, when she feels that even in Old Ballygunge (formerly a favorite residential area for the British) she is being invaded by a foreign culture. And that is why she is so militant about preserving certain Bengali rituals. She still insists on chopping the day's vegetables on the traditional Bengali *bonthi* (which is a large floor-mounted knife with a curved blade sharp enough to slice off any distracted or unpracticed finger); she still personally selects from the freezer the day's supply of meat and fish. For her this household work is symbolic; she has eight servants, including two gardeners and a chauffeur, so it is her way of explaining to people and perhaps to herself that she still has a hold on the traditional roots and values of the Hindu wife.

It is only between ten and noon every morning that she need please no one. So, in this free time, she pleases everyone. She visits relatives who live in the more crowded, the more "Bengali" streets of Ballygunge, relatives who cannot be invited to the lunches and dinners she hosts for visiting Britons but who would feel justly neglected if she cut them off completely; she shops for her household; she does volunteer work. At noon she tries to be home for her younger daughter's return from school, for like most women here, she is convinced a mother's physical presence must be strong, loving, constant. In the afternoon, there are board meetings to attend for she is on the board of all prestigious service organizations, and there are friends to visit. In the evenings, there are dinners or large cock-

tail parties to oversee at home, or two or three parties that her husband and she must attend, to be served similar drinks and hors
d'oeuvres by interchangeable waiters, and to be talked to by the
same guest list of prominent people in town. It is a world based on
the small-capital diplomatic model, where etiquette and protocol
and rank have become oppressively demanding, due perhaps to the
slow hemorrhaging of Calcutta's prestige and importance in the past
half century.

"Do you know that I have to go to two hundred and seventy-six
parties a year?" she laughs. "No one can tell how bored I am sometimes. Our kind of party is such a curious phenomenon. I can't invite just any old person I want to, it has to be people from Nikhil's
rank. You know, only the Number Ones in business firms and the
top professionals."

I am disconcerted by this information. The society that I had assumed was marvelously elastic and open and friendly is also simultaneously rigid, hierarchical, and exclusive. In a city where there are no
natural outsides and insides, the phenomenon of the party, like the
walls of the compound, is a strategy of self-definition.

Anjali drinks her lemonade in long gulps. "I have too many
friends, that's my trouble. One gets flooded with friends. One
doesn't know how to cope."

We discuss her charity activities, her membership on the governing boards of a school and of several service organizations, her membership in all the fashionable clubs, and it becomes obvious to me
that in all these activities she has championed the status and dignity
of Indians in an upper-class society that was, and still is, oppressively
colonial. She tells me that in one of the service organizations, of
which she is now president, she is only one of two Indian women invited to participate so far. It is important, she sighs, for her to stay
on and nominate more Indians.

This is a woman who is too much in demand. Her children, her
husband, her extended family, her servants, the workers in her husband's company (she knows their first names and distributes gifts to
their children after the annual office party), the city's poor and destitute, all need her help, and she gives unselfishly, because she is the
ideal Indian wife.

As we reminisce over our lemonades in the smaller and cozier of her two living rooms, the veranda tailor (paid by the day to sit in one's veranda and living room and sew), who has been working all morning on a pair of slacks for the lean and sexy older daughter, interrupts us with a question about style. The telephone rings, and it is a friend making discreet inquiries about job possibilities for her son. Then the servant (whom I remember from nearly twenty years before, and he remembers me) announces lunch and wants to know how many people to expect for dinner.

"You know, it's paradise when we sit at home and don't have to dress up," she giggles as we go into the dining room for an elaborate lunch which includes my favorite East Bengal item, prawns cooked inside green coconuts. "By the way, remind Clark that for tonight lounge suit is essential. In the tropics, my dear, we still like to be very British and very formal."

It took me a month or two to recognize that in this small group of women, who were not typical of women in other classes and parts of the city, I was witnessing a non-American definition of women's liberation. These few women were successful and ambitious, but like Sita of the Hindu legends, their virtue was demonstrated in the service of their husbands. The economy of the developing nation established them as rich enough not to feel personally responsible for the shininess of their floors or the rings around their husbands' collars. If there was any dirt on the floors, or on the shirts, the failure could be construed as historical and not personal. The Naxals had spoiled the servants with their talk of class warfare, and though the Naxals had lost power, there remained unpleasant residues such as domestic workers' unions in some high rises. Besides, they complained, everything these days is adulterated, detergents are not as effective as they used to be. Or perhaps the detergents are effective but the servants are corrupt, cleaning their own clothes by stealing from the amount rationed out by the housewives. When they made conventional small talk about the dishonesty of servants, the general deterioration of moral fiber, and the woman's place being in the home, they intended no irony. Their audience was a small, unembattled one, made up of women much like themselves. No persuasion, no explanations, necessary. At least on the surface, faith in karma (since their husbands had been chosen for them by their parents) seemed to absorb any resentment of economic dependence on the husband. Long hours of communal work among the unpacified and unbeautified poor dissipated the self-indulgent loneliness that is the frequent reward of liberated women in North America.

I never found out what these women thought of sex. We talked quite often about happiness and love. But, in spite of the Kama Sutra and the Khajuraho temple, it is not a culture (particularly in that Edwardian little circle) that encourages conversations about sexuality. At school, the nuns had exposed us to expurgated editions of Shakespeare. I now realized these women had never stopped self-expurgating. It would have been impossible to expect from even my closest friend in Calcutta confidences about frequency and quality of orgasms that I received in Montreal from women I barely knew. It is not that these Calcutta women denied knowledge of sex; barrenness is sinful in Hindu women, and being dutiful, they had all borne at least one or two children. But it was not yet a fit ("suitable") topic of conversation among polite ladies. From what Clark would tell me, Indian men were far less reluctant to discuss sex. Once, well after midnight, Anjali's husband, Nikhil, drove us through the red-light district of fashionable downtown Calcutta, stopping the car to talk to the girls. Anjali kept up a steady, amusing conversation throughout the entire episode. I do not know if on annual trips abroad the women made a point of seeing movies like *Last Tango in Paris* (the men alone certainly would), or if they brought back *The Joy of Sex* hidden skillfully among their new Jean Patou shirts.

Judging from the sterile nightwear that is popular in the trousseaux of young women from this class, and which is quite often designed by my friends as part of their charity work in sewing workshops for destitute women, Marabel Morgan's "Total Woman" prescription for thrilling husbands has not yet penetrated Calcutta. I once showed my friends an old copy of *Ms.* magazine that contained an article by Letty Potgrebin on consciousness-raising among a group of intelligent, middle-class New York women. My friends were shocked by the article, especially by the advice that a C.R. session might include taking off all clothes and admiring each other's bodies. I did not dare tell them that in some groups, participants are urged to bring hand mirrors and admire parts of the bodies the existence of which I think my Calcutta friends would deny outside the privacy of their bedrooms.

These, then, are very "innocent" women. And their innocence is guaranteed by the absence of wide-reaching media. If there had been private commercial TV networks in the city, it is very likely that these women would have been made models for "the good life" (men like their husbands serve as models for cigarette ads accompanying popular movies), or they might have been cruelly satirized. If TV, wherever it existed in India, had not been government-controlled, it is possible that they might have become victims of guerrillas and crazies obsessed by media-attention. But spared of powerful media, they were spared of conversion into rigid symbols. They kept their fantasies and follies private, inviolable.

They were self-professed happy women. But their happiness was mocked by the faces of the women on the fringes of that group. Faces that showed the strain of having tried hard to get on committees and boards of governors, and failed. They too were impeccably dressed in floral print nylon saris, but there was an edge to their greetings and gossip. Though they admitted no bitterness in front of me, I suspected that they blamed their karma for denying them the final dignity of being the wife of the Number One man in a reputable business firm.

Now and then, in restaurants on Park Street or in children's sections of bookstores or at informal teas in former school friends' homes, I thought I recognized some of those faces from my long years at Loreto House. There was one recurring face that intrigued me, heart-shaped, thin-lipped, and suggesting an unusual degree of hardness. When I asked my friends about her, they told me her name and capsule biography. She was the younger sister of a Loreto girl I had known. She had, apparently, married against her parents' and her husbands' parents' wishes. Her husband was a clever engineer, but in spite of his cleverness he had not yet become the top man in the construction company where he worked. During the very earliest weeks of labor unrest, he and his assistant had been ringed by strikers and brutally beaten. Not long after, at his own request, the company had transferred him to a small town in Madhya Pradesh. The company quarters were gracious, and the air there was probably fresher than in Calcutta, but the wife had refused to live in a small town. Besides (and this was the reason my friends forgave her conduct) she had her eight-year-old son's education to worry about. So this woman had returned to Calcutta with her son, leaving her husband to travel across the country whenever familial affections overwhelmed him.

I met this woman once, at a Chinese lunch that someone I hardly knew had had catered to welcome back someone else just returned from a five-week trip to London. I remembered this woman as a nervous girl who had carried off too many prizes at school and talked of studying law. I cornered her as she was retreating to the terrace with her plate of egg rolls and chili sauce. She did not offer any excuses or apologies for not having become a barrister. She told me about her son and the entrance examination he had taken to get into St. Xavier's school. The examination had not been easy, but thank goodness the boy was clever like his father. Did I know that the situation had so reversed itself now that mothers like her preferred to have daughters because it was easier to get them admitted to Loreto House?

If her son had not made it into St. Xavier's, his career would have been ruined before it got started. Was it not awful that one's life was so predetermined? I agreed it was sinister that small boys should have to compete so fiercely and for such serious stakes. It might have been cruel to describe the permissive atmosphere of my sons' school in Montreal—cruel or absurd. We also talked about the chocolate birthday cake she had baked at home for her son, and recipes for tea sandwiches. She thought it was funny that both of us who had been considered smart but clumsy had become such finicky cooks. She filled me in on mutual friends I had forgotten about; her remarks were abrasive, entertaining. She made no overt reference to loneliness or depression. But as we returned to the buffet table to serve ourselves fried rice, chili chicken, and sweet and sour pork, she whispered to me, "It doesn't pay to be too intelligent in our group. The girls who fill the medical colleges are all a little bit poorer and a little more Bengalified than us. All the smart girls went away and some married Euopeans to stay away. I don't think that's any solution, do you?"

I love these women; I was one of them.

But by some fate having to do with my father and with the way I was raised—the intense Bengaliness of my childhood that left me with a horror of its coarseness, and the suspended dream world of my adolescence that shattered so completely I would distrust all attempts to restore it—and the "gift for the pen" that did not tame itself like other teen-age passions, I became a different person. Something is fraudulent in the way I live; too little money to give up working; too much ambition to really want to. And who am I—a Ballygunge girl raised just like Anjali and all the others—to be nodding wisely as intense young ladies at McGill babble on about their lesbian lovers, group sex, and multiple orgasms?

And something is terribly, terribly wrong with the world I came from in Calcutta. What is unforgivable is the lives that have been sacrificed to notions of propriety and obedience. I met only the upper crust, only the ones who wanted to be met, who had something good to show me. Many more were in a kind of hiding. My class is refining itself into extinction, almost like the Edwardian British who were most responsible for creating it. The upper classes of Calcutta in 1973 were still cherishing souvenirs of Mark Phillips and Princess Anne's wedding. Like the Edwardians, exquisite social refinement and stunning social obtuseness will be our downfall; we have evolved to such pinnacles of presentability that we are in danger of losing the most precious legacy in the Hindu tradition, our gifts for improvisation and adaptation.

We were in a taxi on Park Street when a wizened little boy darted into the middle of the street and flung a palmist's brochure through our window.

### YOU ARE WHAT YOUR HAND REVEALS

The palmist was listed as Professor J. K. Sahni, "celebrated seer" and "master of the language of the hand." His office address was given as 11 Dr. M. Ishaque Road (formerly Kyd Street). Twenty-six years after Independence the brochure still listed the old and new names of the street, conceded the coexistence of the colonial and the national in our affections.

Though I am pitifully vulnerable, like all Indians, to the enticements of fortunetellers, and though Kyd Street was in the immediate neighborhood, we did not go to Professor Sahni and discover our futures that morning. I liked to think that I was *not* what my hand had revealed to the first palmist whom I had visited at the age

of thirteen. That palmist—a thin man with rotund, hairy nostrils—
had said that I was destined for a middle-class Bengali woman's life,
to please my husband and elders, to be intelligent without being ob-
noxiously opinionated, to have two or three children and to run a
clean, decent home, to be shrewd about household budgets, and to
pray to the household gods. By agreeing to go abroad, and then by
marrying Clark on the first day of the school year in Iowa City in
1963, I claimed to have "cheated" fate. I did not want to risk being
told by a famous seer named Sahni that that impulsive act too had
long been prerecorded in the faint mapwork of my palm.

So Clark and I did not test our faith in the triumph of free will.
Instead we let ourselves out of the taxi on Park Street close to the
corner of Middleton Row where years ago I had gone to school, and
as we did every noon hour in Calcutta we walked under jutting balconies, stepped delicately over muddy puddles, drying phlegm, and
crimson *pan*-spittle, vendors' trays, pariahs with pups, and beggars,
crossed the street near Kwality's restaurant and were nearly run over
by a heedless Fiat; then lingered in the paperback section of the Oxford Book Shop where a very strange and satisfying assortment of
books eddies into the backwater of Calcutta, to remain and yellow
for uncounted months until a keen-eyed academic spots a John
Hawkes title, or James Leo Herlihy, along with full collections of the
various Indian paperbacks. And then outside Oxford's we stopped to
joke with the vendor of periodicals—never have *Time* and *Newsweek* and the bundles of two-week-old *Herald Tribunes* been more
welcome than they were that Watergate summer. The vendor spread
his merchandise on the front steps of other people's stores; he'd held
that spot for thirty years, and his father before him (he was proud to
tell us) for thirty years before that. After sixty years at the same loca-
tion his entire overhead consisted of five jute mats and some collapsible steel racks—a very late concession to the movie-magazine trade.
On normal days, by the magic that makes commerce so personal in
Calcutta, he would spot us from a taxi as we cruised by, and he would
take those few seconds to hold up the new arrivals—*Stardust*, the
American papers and weeklies, a new Travis McGee novel—and we
would know to stop the taxi and dash across. Other days he would
only shrug as we looked his way. We would stroll on up Park
Street, to buy Clark's skin ointments, to buy my Anacin, to buy our

diarrhea precautions, and to weigh ourselves (Clark in pride; I in mortification), then to stop at Trinca's or at a Chinese restaurant for lunch. We were a permanent noon-hour fixture on Park Street; after two weeks it was as though we'd been there all our lives; after four months we knew the vendors and their families, and the children on the street who lived by scampering for taxis knew us and had fought whatever battles among themselves were necessary to gain exclusive rights to our free-spending whims. By Indian standards, Clark and I were scandalous overtippers.

But the truth is that in Calcutta we are rarely allowed to escape what our hands reveal us to be. Looks can sometimes alter one's destiny a little, and in this city, in 1973, I was bizarre-looking. Loiterers, the endless rows of unemployed youths who lean against fences or cluster around outdoor teastalls, made a point of commenting on my huge tinted gold-rimmed spectacles. "Look at that, look at that, she must be from *p'horen!*" as if I had no history prior to going abroad. And dark-suited businessmen with wives whom I met for the first time at the Calcutta Club or the Bengal Club or on some friend's canopied and carpeted cocktail-hour lawn, would say within five minutes of our meeting, "You say your maiden name was Mukherjee? You must be from Sir Biren's family then." It was as if my short hair, my protruding collarbone, the brevity and fit of my *choli* blouses, my impatient walk, the slightly arrogant arch of my eyebrows, the frosted eyeshadow and transparent lip gloss made me seem too progressive, too Westernized, and therefore too rootless, to be a predictably middle-class Bengali woman born on an unexceptionably middle-class Ballygunge street. And when I hastened to inform them of my scores of uncles, aunts, and cousins who still lived on Rash Behari and Southern avenues, these businessmen smiled as if to indicate that they were on to the hoax.

Calcutta seemed to me to be made up of separate walled villages between which there was only defective communication. Through friends like Veena and Anjali, I met the Number Ones of the city. But through my relatives I met women who wanted me to stand on my grandmother's back porch so that they could take a look at me from their own gardens or balconies and shout out to my aunt, "My, she married a foreigner? She doesn't look like a foreigner!" The same women grumbled constantly about the price of carp or hilsa and the gritty coarseness of rice available in most ration shops. But there was also the Calcutta of the Ramakrishna Mission dining hall where I sat silently worshipful of visiting Bengalis like Amartya K. Sen whose brilliance and sophistication had been legendary in Loreto House when I was growing up, or where I listened to hairy-eared scholars describe local library facilities as I passed the salad or pickles. And where, quite by accident, I heard the question that shaped my second novel: *What do Bengali girls do, between the ages of eighteen and twenty-one?* asked casually by a visiting Columbia professor of history. To the waiters at the mission I was an Important Personality because they saw chauffeured cars drive up to the gate for me every morning; and there was the Calcutta of the USIS where I was a quasi-American novelist to be taped and interviewed.

Traveling in and out of these walled villages were marauding foreigners, white men and women (Australians, the new Europeans, suddenly discovering Asia), tourists who lost their tempers in banks because they felt they had been waiting too long to cash their traveler's checks, groups of college students led by fatigued professors who passed out pills for every occasion. They were essentially harmless, even friendly, people, but in that time of sliding convictions they asumed in my mind sinister stature. I suspected them of being contemptuous of Indian know-how, of being clannish when they sat together and giggled at long tables in the dining hall, of being patronizing when they wore saris or *kurta-pajama* which they always wore like costumes at a fancy-dress party. No white foreigner, not even Clark, was exempt from my growing disgust. Only the Japanese —and there were three of them in the Scholars' Residence across the lush green lawn—seemed to have escaped the cruelties of colonial games. I had no need to convert them into uneasy symbols. They were unobtrusive in corridors and dining hall; they spoke both English and Bengali poorly; among themselves they practiced baseball. Only now could I begin to guess why my mother, in those unusual days of World War II, had felt no rancor toward the Japanese pilots in spite of their bombing of the Kidderpore docks, and why she had rushed out into the unprotected street to admire their silvery formations. The Japanese had been foreign enough to be mysterious, exciting; they had proved to women like my mother who grew up during stern British rule that Asians were capable of efficient technology and that self-hate was a colonial construct. Sometimes, to preserve my sanity, when bushy-haired Englishmen trying to recover from nervous disorders made jokes about the puniness of Indian laborers, I would turn on them shrilly and point to their accusatory plates piled high with rice, vegetables, and mutton stew.

And sometimes, in the flickering darkness and heat of our guest room during power cuts, propelled by the same misplaced bitterness, I quarreled with Clark, accusing him of having forced expatriation on me. Could he live out his life in Calcutta where he would have to learn a new language, a new way of making friends, where he could not expect his readers to understand too well the intents of his fiction? Could he give up his little quarterlies, and Hockey Night in Canada and baseball at Jarry Park? He did not understand that I was fighting for my sanity. He thought of it as a fight for domination, and used the only weapon he had: common sense. He asked me how I thought he could find a job in Calcutta as an instructor in creative writing, and support a family of four Canadians. He couldn't of course—like me, he practiced a useless profession.

It was, of course, impossible to explain to a North American, no matter how decent he might be, that for me it was a time to subvert memory, to hunt down sly conciliatory impulses. His role could only be a slight one, that of being witness. I trained my mind to speed down two parallel highways in which no U-turns were permitted. When we visited relatives and flats I recalled from long ago, I would fill Clark in on structural changes (which were rare), and on histories of our relationships—who had suffered bursitis, who had been operated on for an inflamed appendix, whose daughter had been expected to do brilliantly in the university exams but had instead done rather poorly. But when I entered those flats, took my Italian platform sandals off near the entrance, answered ritual wisecracks about my skinniness (I was skinny only by Bengali standards and was rapidly growing plump on constant Bengali diet), my adult composure was bruised by the memory of myself as a neurasthenic child given to reading in dark corners and to nursing sick headaches. It was not a memory to be shared with a co-operative husband or with thick-limbed relatives who wanted to know if we had really gone with Satyajit Ray to Indrapuri Studios for a private screening and how much I had paid for my sandals and Saurashtrian tote bag.

It was for me a simple matter of privacy. This visit to India was forcing old wounds to the surface, and since I was now a Western Woman, I wasn't content to nurse them, even coddle them in the traditional Indian manner. I induced my anger to flare: against the West, against Bengal, against my family. I have never been given to undue confidences, and when I have appeared to confide, it has almost always been a trick for hiding a deeper secret.

As a child I had thought privacy was possible only if one could scout out and stake claims on secretive spots behind heavy furniture or dusty curtains. In the flat on Rash Behari Avenue, my favorite hide-out had been between the parental four-poster and a chalky green wall with barred windows. One of the bars had been twisted slightly apart by (we suspected) a timid burglar, and cast crooked striped shadows on my bare legs. So when Clark and I, at my uncle's request, visited the room where I had spent the first eight years of my life, I saw superimposed on that uncluttered and recently painted bedroom wall the image of a wavy-haired, narrow-shouldered child crouching under the barred window, her skin powdery with green paint. But even as a child in that sun-striped room I had moved from the literal to the metaphoric in my pursuit of privacy. Survival from too much love: That was what privacy meant to me. But in middle-class India, to escape love is practically impossible; however disastrous, however murderous, it is still love. And I had survived by becoming a compulsive reader and by inducing sick headaches. I read indiscriminately, but I loved the Russians best—Tolstoy and Gorki in Bengali translation—who enveloped me in a world that I did not understand but which I took to be less trivial, more extravagant than mine. The Russians were great squanderers of passion; whereas I, even as a small child in a large joint family, had learned that frugality of feeling was my best defense against assault.

I loved my headaches. Later, with a Bengali's typical love of adumbration, I added to that a love of vomiting, of slipping a long delicate finger over the rough-grained tongue and down the silky, fleshy walls of throat and gullet until I was rewarded by an·arc of fluid which I watched splatter against the rusty grid of the old-fashioned bathroom drain. Headaches meant that I would be made to lie down with a cold rag (dipped in my father's 4711 cologne) over my forehead and eyes, while my mother would try to snatch as many minutes as she could from her cooking for the enormous family tribe and knead the pain out of my forehead. Of course I wanted the pain—which was often severe enough to make me want to die— to go away; but for the duration of the pain I could lie guiltlessly passive in a crowded room, temporarily freed from habitual watchfulness. On this trip to Calcutta I have asked my former school friends if they are afflicted with aches and pains, and without exception they have denied intimate knowledge of any physical pain.

Were the headaches the earliest sign that I would escape abroad and marry a foreigner? But fate sent confusing signals to some of us who were born in the decade in which Britain relinquished her hold on India. We were born both too late and not late enough to be real Indians. In the colonial ambiguities of the mid-forties we acquired our monstrous habit of loving paradoxes. We loved both the freedom fighters and the red-faced officers who carried bullets and pistols. And on Independence Day, on August 15, 1947, when I stood on the balcony of my grandmother's flat which had been exuberantly decorated by my youngest aunt with paper chains and flags, we thought ourselves totally unmarred in spite of the brittle oxymoron buried in our hearts.

On this trip, when I visited the same grandmother who is now an almost sightless invalid, and I stepped out onto the same balcony, there were no festive chains and flags, only the day's wash hung out to dry and bird droppings on the wrought-iron railing and ants scurrying along cracks on the cement floor. And below, on the sidewalk and on the grassy boulevard embedded with tram tracks were embattled settlements of refugees and beggars, the sad new inheritors of freedom. In the poverty that is general in Calcutta, their poverty did not seem to me overwhelming. I saw women cook, feed, and scold their children, get beaten by their husbands, pester motorists for handouts. One day I saw two well-dressed women pull up in a sleek black Toyota (never longer and more luxurious-looking than in India) and their chauffeur distribute several boxes of sweets, which caused a near-riot, until older boys appointed themselves as monitors. And at the close of every day, when the men would return with enormous jute sacks crammed with paper they had scavenged from the street, I would watch the ritual of the women and children pouring water into the sacks—probably not a drop more than the informal law tolerated—since the paper would then be sold by the kilo to the pulpers. They had set up a village inside a metropolis: That was their remarkable triumph.

But when I thought back to that August dawn in 1947 when I had stood on that balcony in my stiffly starched frock waiting for my mother to braid my hair so that I could join the victory procession of cousins and neighbors, organized by my Aunt Minto, when I recalled how the sidewalk and street had been full of flag-waving people, I wanted to weep. National dreams turning sour was, I knew, common enough to seem inevitable, but that knowledge did not make the pain any less personal or bearable.

Though my mother braided my hair with tricolored nationalistic ribbons that August morning in 1947 and though my older sister who was my aunt's confidante checked my dress front for breakfast stains and my thickly polished Keds for scuff marks, I could not join that procession. After having practiced the slogans until the Jai Hinds came out in just the right ringingly sincere tones, and after having practiced marching down the corridor (*left, right* is one of the hardest things for Bengali girls to master), at the last minute I developed a headache and had to stay home. I now realize how extraordinary that mood of celebration must have been if it could have persuaded girls like me to shed our timidities and think of marching down Southern Avenue. In the fifties, after we had moved out of Ballygunge and eased ourselves into a very "Westernized" orbit within the city, we would rarely walk on a public sidewalk, and on those rare occasions when we might have to go to a stationery store or a lending library, the car would be parked as close as possible and we would be accompanied by the formidable-looking khaki-clad bodyguard who kept secret from strangers the gentleness of his disposition.

All that was a long time ago. It is enough for me now that I *had* wanted to go with my sister and Aunt Minto. It is enough that I had held a small silk flag in my fist and that with my forehead pressed against the rusty railing, I had witnessed other marchers walk, run, and shuffle. It had been a city—I like to think—so crazed with love that for the moment it had flung off its old gentilities and not yet dreamed up its new taboos.

On this trip to Calcutta, I saw myself through the eyes of others, and realized that the paradox remains but tears none apart. To my relatives—who accorded me the status of an honorary male by urging me to eat with Clark and the uncles at the first shift at the dining table, instead of on the floor on the second and third shifts with my aunts and girl cousins—I was the embodiment of "local girl makes good." And I was also an intimidating alien, a raspy-voiced woman who was not content to be simply a schoolteacher or charity organizer (which were appropriate enough women's work), but who argued with male relatives about tax breaks and inflation and who was not prepared to accord automatic homage to Sai Baba.

It was my knowledge of conversational English that they envied; fluency in English (especially with an American accent) rendered me a special creature, made success abroad possible, gave me access to a bottomless strongbox of Canadian dollars. I was a career person, which meant that I had the right to independent thought without incurring censure, while the middle-class Bengali woman was locked into a woman's world of gossip and speculation. The young working-women I talked to in Ballygunge—women between the ages of nineteen and twenty-five from genteel families that were finding it hard to remain genteel because of inflation—seemed to think of working for a living as slightly shameful. In an ideal world, their shy gestures suggested, they should have been plucked out of the griminess of actuality by bright young men with promising futures.

Working outside the home as secretaries or bank tellers exposed them not so much to excitement as to danger—possibilities of being mugged on the bus trip to and from the office, of being propositioned by an unscrupulous boss, and of being scolded for inefficiency by a testy superior. An unemployed father of four daughters, who was living on the rent he collected from one tenant and on handouts from relatives, told me about his oldest daughter. "She has been offered a job as the personal secretary to a male school principal. But I shall not permit her to demean herself that way. As long as I have any pride left, I shall not allow her to take such an extreme self-sacrificing measure." And I saw enough evidence of job dissatisfaction or indifference—women in crumpled cotton saris fast asleep with cheeks on desk tops cluttered with brochures, women with perspiring make-up curtly dealt with by the boss in front of a long line of customers—to understand that in these middle-class families, quite often, a sister or daughter going to work only threatened masculinity and brought pleasure to none. It was not that there were no glamorous jobs for women in the city, but those jobs seemed by custom reserved for women of the upper middle class, women with flawless English and with style, women who had gone from girls' colleges to secretarial schools in their confident, giggling clusters and who became secretaries, receptionists, and administrative assistants in multinational corporate offices and consulates in the fashionable downtown district, women who in between their work schedules fitted in appointments with hairdressers and sari-buying expeditions and lunch dates with junior executives who very quickly succumbed to their charms and installed them as nonworking wives in spacious company flats.

Once when I was slipping into my sightless grandmother's hand a hundred-rupee note, my token ritual gesture of appreciation (made years too late) for the courageous encouragement she had given my mother, my sisters, and myself when most women of her generation and background were hostile to women's education, my quiet action was spotted by a female visitor. The visitor looked at me with rancor. "You are a rich Canadian, you can afford to show off. I'm just an ordinary Bengali giving private math lessons to local dullards. People like us can't give more than fifteen or twenty rupees to elders we love. My sister in the States just sent forty rupees to my grandmother. She said it was from her assistantship pay check. She and her husband are studying genetics in Utah."

And the point of it was that her bitterness was directed at my economic independence; my career had freed me from having to please my husband or any other future male provider. I was accountable to no one except myself for whimsical gift-giving, and this made me unique in her experience. I was not afraid of what my husband would say if I spent money without consulting him because I would never become skill-less, destitute, and lonely, even if he decided I was unbearably disagreeable. Ours was not a clash of old and new feminine sensibilities. Nor was it a difference of opinion about men.

It was, I suspected, a collision of separate ways of acquiring and expressing power. The bitter visitor felt imprisoned by her habitat: A glamorous job, such as being an air hostess with a foreign airline or a stenographer for a multinational (*any*thing foreign lends its cachet), seemed completely unavailable to her. As a private tutor of math to local children she had no way of feeling important, and no way to buy herself an exceptional future. Her sister had escaped by being attractive enough to be married off and by being intelligent enough to have been given a teaching assistantship in the States. But what of the millions of other young women, the women like her who were sensitive enough to feel cheated but neither pretty nor smart enough to arrange for their own salvation? It was a brutally naturalistic world in which only the fittest survived. She resented me because I was a survivor and because I had expressed my survival by giving a bill of one hundred rupees (approximately fifteen dollars); for her, that was the equivalent of at least one hundred dollars. If I had given a sari worth the same amount, that would have been an inoffensive gesture. But by giving money to a woman who never went out and who had a loving son to provide her with material comfort, I intended to say, "Spend it any way you wish or don't spend it at all. I trust you to make financial decisions."

And so the gesture was really to reinforce my own embattled conviction. It was because I felt I was suffering from the chilly flimsiness of incomplete memories. As a child, sitting in corners reading Gorki, I had heard endless stories about an aunt who had been humiliated by in-laws for bringing what was considered an inadequate dowry. I had heard of women committing suicide by setting themselves on fire or tying themselves to train tracks or jumping into wells. Then some aunt of mine would discover me crouched in a corner, book in hand, listening to them talk, and whisper, "Not in front of children, please." And I had heard, while visiting a friend in a narrow street near Dhakuria Lake, a woman scream; I had rushed to the window and been told by the friend's mother, "Oh, that's just the people next door. They're always beating up the new bride. I'm afraid one of these days she is going to kill herself or go back to her father." *That*, to the culture into which I was born, was the potential tragedy. To be a woman, I had learned early enough, was to be a power-less victim whose only escape was through self-inflicted wounds.

It was my mother who had hinted at another solution. I had heard her shout between sobs (I cannot remember the precise cause of the fight nor the identity of the chief adversary), "Just wait until the girls are a little older, I'm going to tell them everything, I'm going to make sure they're well educated so no one can make them suffer." And that was the first time I had felt that someone was about to remove a part of my brain in order to make me a different creature than I was, and I had collapsed in tears. But over the next few years this threat to tell us all and equip us with a formidable education be-came the commonplace of family squabbles, a signal to keep out of the way of grown-ups; and later still, during what we called "the good days" when we were in schools that pleased parents as well as daughters, it became a subterranean memory waiting to be given firmness and shape so that it could emerge as a clear prescription for my own liberation.

Visits to relatives throughout those eleven months in Calcutta in 1973 released in all of us, hosts and guests, unpredictable emotions. One afternoon, as Clark and I sat in an elderly uncle's living room (this uncle had considered living rooms a newfangled Westernized idea when I had last been in the city), being served a lavish high tea by his college-educated daughter-in-law, my uncle had expounded on the correlation between modern Indian architecture and the breakdown of family love. "They build small apartments nowadays so that parents can't come and stay with the young people for too long. It's a conspiracy," he had said. "Nobody cares for the old, nobody wants to live together as a joint family anymore. This society is going downhill because everyone is too selfish, too modern."

Because I had heard him advance that theory on earlier occasions, I deflected his attention from any evasive answer that I might be forced into by asking the daughter-in-law, "Why aren't you sitting down for tea with us? You've worked so hard!" And I had been lov-ingly rebuked by the uncle who had gone to enormous trouble to make sure his wife and daughter-in-law cooked items that were im-pressively numerous but did not require ingredients that were likely to upset Clark's stomach, "Don't be silly, women don't eat with us. There's plenty of everything, she'll eat later." And that, I realize now, is the essence of the Ballygunge I was raised in; the only possible mortification for either the male or the female would be in not having provided enough to eat. To demand anything more is simply alien.

It occurred to me how extraordinary—how liberal—this scene also was. This was an uncle who was by his own admission an orthodox Hindu, who had been pleased when I had confided to him my new aversion for mutton and chicken, and who was rumored to have had a tantrum of heroic proportions when one of his sons had married a woman from a different caste. But, in spite of that, he had welcomed me, the wife of a white man who was outside all caste computations, to sit and eat like an equal—like a man—under his family's ministrations. It was, I thought, one more proof of the elasticity of Hindu convictions.

And, better still, it was an indirect tribute to my mother's courage. She had filled out secretly, with the help of a non-Brahmin young man who would later become Aunt Minto's husband (because in a tightly structured society, every rebellious act has unforeseen implications), application forms to an Anglicized Bengali school which, after our return from Europe, we would learn to treat with condescension. In those days, when my mother was still in her twenties, she had been ambitious for us. She had tied white taffeta ribbons in our hair and taught us to recite, "How do you do?" in answer to someone else's "How do you do?" and "I'm very well, thank you," to the question "How are you?" She had supervised our English reading and spelling and unwittingly engendered in me fantasies about my British counterparts, who according to my schoolbooks went with their parents for picnics in the country and to the zoo to see elephants and tigers and whose mothers baked them chocolate cakes and whose fathers drove motorcars. (We had been to the Alipore Zoo, of course, but we had felt sorry for the bony, dispirited animals.) My mother had loved us enough to risk the wrath of elderly relatives, and through the perversities of love, I had squeezed more selfish pleasure out of life than she could ever have dreamed, but I had also lost belief in the self-sufficiency of Calcutta and made a foreign continent my battleground for proving self-worth.

"Good for you," a playwright said to me on the telephone during one of the respites from power cuts. "You struck a good one for women's liberation in that interview in *Desh*. I think that chap did a very decent job on you and Clark."

After the first seven or eight weeks in the country, I had come to realize that familiar phrases like "women's liberation" could be applied to unfamiliar contexts. For instance, it might be used to describe a time-saving recipe in a women's periodical, or a protest march by enraged women consumers. The playwright who telephoned me, I soon realized, was talking about a little incident involving Clark, me, and a teapot.

The incident itself was trivial. What struck me was that several friends mentioned it to me in discussions afterward. During the course of the interview, while the journalist had been asking me questions about *The Tiger's Daughter*, and while the photographer had been crouching in dusty corners of our room at the mission to "trap" my very elusive charms with his imported camera, and while I had been permitting myself the smug smiles of a superstar, the mission bearer had brought in the customary tray of afternoon tea. I had paused in my answers only long enough to order two extra cups, and when they arrived, Clark had poured the tea. Few actions in India seem to be regarded as matters of simple convenience. Clark's pouring the tea was regarded by the playwright and several other readers as emblematic of the power relations between the Blaises. In a Bengali home, I was reminded by friends, a husband would consider it demeaning to get himself a glass of water (especially in front of guests) or to pour his own tea. A woman university lecturer, who I knew had studied abroad, told me bitterly that although her husband had stopped nagging her about her need for an academic career, he still expected her to spread butter and jam on his toast at every breakfast. An older woman confided that her husband had been furious because she had bought an expensive item like a pop-up toaster without first asking his permission. And a Bengali husband in his seventies, in describing passionately to me what he considered the degeneration of Bengali culture, illustrated his point by telling me that nowadays his wife, daughters, and daughters-in-law did their sari-buying in the daytime (when they could be imprudently swayed by the fraudulent pitch of salesclerks) instead of waiting for him to accompany them in the evening.

All this might have seemed to me amusing if I had not also been made aware of the underbelly of such experiences. There were the endless stories of wife beatings and suicides. And they weren't always about strangers. A young woman I had met years before and who was now an architect in Germany had fled India (it was said) because her husband and mother-in-law used to beat her. A woman who herself was rumored to have been given a hard time by her in-laws told me scathingly that her daughter's sister-in-law had gotten a separation simply because the husband had been a moron but nobody had told the bride or the bride's parents ("Where was her patience? Where was her wifely virtue? After three years she just headed back to her parents saying she had had enough!").

Again and again, among middle-class Bengali women I would hear, "She is a lovely, docile girl, she's never given us any trouble," or "She is not at all independent, she'll do whatever her husband tells her," and these remarks would be offered as compliments. One afternoon, while sitting in someone's balcony overlooking a narrow alley in Ballygunge and trying unsuccessfully to get a twenty-five-year-old unmarried woman to tell me why she had stayed in college despite her obvious dislike of studying, I was interrupted by her father, "You're making a big mistake, madame. Bengali women do not engage in serious thought. Their conversations are about gossip or budgets, and they sometimes seem to flirt with their brothers-in-law. But if you're looking for answers, you won't get them from decent Bengali girls. To please you they might fabricate an answer or two, but don't believe them. You say you are a novelist; well, then, you must have insight, insight into truth. Why don't you invent their answers."

The trouble, it seemed to me, was that even in the India of 1973–74 with its woman Prime Minister and its impressive lists of women in politics, medicine, law, journalism, and labor unions, the average woman modeled her life not on these modern examples, but on Sita and Savitri of ancient Hindu literature. The stories of Sita and Savitri were kept alive by oral tradition, while the modern models were accessible to only the urban few who could read newspapers.

Sita was the daughter of King Janaka of Videha. Her hand was won in marriage—the prize in a great archery contest—

by Prince Rama, the eldest son of the powerful, aged King Dasaratha of Kosala. Sita and Rama lived happily for a while in Ayodhya, the capital city. But the machinations of one of his stepmothers drove Rama into exile for fourteen years. He was accompanied into exile by his devoted wife and a loyal brother. Shortly after, his father died. During the period of exile, while living as hermits in a forest, Sita was abducted by the demon King, Ravana of Lanka, and imprisoned in his palace on his island kingdom. After a long search and a fierce battle, Rama with the aid of an army of monkeys defeated the demons, slew Ravana, and rescued Sita. Though Sita had not allowed her thoughts or her person to be in any way corrupted by her captor, Rama, in accordance with the religious and social customs of the times, was obliged to banish her from his side for having lived under another man's roof. Sita, refusing to live with her honor thus stained, ordered a funeral pyre to be built for herself, and in full sight of the courtiers threw herself on the burning pyre. But the fire god intervened and saved her. For the assembled subjects of Rama, the ordeal by fire was proof of Sita's purity and innocence. Rama, whose royal mandate was to please and serve his subjects, was thus able to take his wife back and establish her as his Queen in Ayodhya.

In the last book of the *Ramayana*, which contains this story of Rama and Sita—this book is regarded as a later addition by many scholars—there is a cruel sequel. It appears that even the ordeal by fire did not fully convince all subjects of Rama, and that Rama eventually yielded to pressure from the populace and reluctantly banished from the court the pregnant Sita. She found refuge in the hermitage of Valmiki, where she gave birth to twin sons. Years later she had a brief and accidental reunion with King Rama in the forest, and had the satisfaction of seeing him acknowledge the twins as his sons. Finally, as the ultimate proof of her innocence, she asked Mother Earth to swallow her, which Mother Earth did.

To the Hindu girl-child, Sita is an exemplary figure. The lesson is clear, uncomplicated: The wife's role is one of self-abnegation.

Sita's loyalty is tested by the blandishments of the evil King Ravana, by the ignorance and cynicism of the subjects of Ayodhya, and by the unimaginative nature of Rama's devotion to his people. But she never hesitates or questions. In this context, to ask why Sita should be made to suffer for Rama's failure to protect her from abductors is to ask an irrelevant question.

> Another legend tells of Savitri, the beautiful daughter of a King who had fasted and prayed for over eighteen years in order that the gods might cure him and his Queen of barrenness. When she reached marriageable age, because she remained unwooed, her father sent her off in a chariot to roam the countryside and bring back a suitable bridegroom. Savitri selected Prince Satyavan, whose father had lost his kingdom to an ancient enemy and who had, as a result, been brought up in the forest as a woodcutter. Both she and her father were warned by a seer that Satyavan was destined to die at the end of a year, but the threat of death did not deter Savitri from marrying him. At the specified time, while Satyavan, accompanied by Savitri, was cutting wood in the forest, the Spirit of Death, Yama, appeared to carry him off. However, the fearless and loyal Savitri reminded Yama that a wife's duty was to follow her husband no matter what the destination. Yama was so overwhelmed by her wifely devotion that he revived Satyavan and restored him to Savitri.

To me, growing up in Ballygunge, Savitri and Sita were not colorless figures out of books in which worms had eaten away too many words. They were the creatures of my dreams. They were the stuff of exciting theater. In fact, during theatrical evenings at my maternal grandmother's, my cousins and I loved to mime the story of Savitri and Satyavan. We took these evenings very seriously; even Aunt Minto, who must at that time have been an undergraduate at Lady Brabourne College, helped us make tinsel swords and crowns, rig up curtains from torn silk saris, and erect a wobbly stage in the widest part of the corridor. I remember now that I always played the part of Satyavan and spent my moment on the stage lying as still as possible while a younger cousin held my head on her "wifely" lap and an older neighbor glowered ferociously under her "Spirit of Death" make-up.

"We mustn't be in too much of a hurry to condemn, you understand," the wife of an advertising executive said to me as Clark and I sat in their small living room and admired their art collection. The carpeted floor was littered with framed and unframed paintings, posters, and prints. "That's what a lot of women's liberation types don't seem to grasp." She pulled out a poster from under nineteenth-century prints of Calcutta scenes and pointed to the grouping of the two figures on the poster. "Look at this carefully," she instructed in her slightly professorial English. "This is obviously an upper-class married couple of another era in this city. The husband is sitting on the chair. The wife is sitting on the floor at his feet. In front of her is a plate strewn with flower offerings, et cetera, you see."

The figures on the poster were exceedingly handsome, their cheeks, jaws, and eyebrows had extravagant curves. The husband sat in a European-style chair in the middle of a hall full of arches and pillars. His back was very straight. His sacred thread fell over the magnificent convex of his naked belly. The foot of one leg was cocked confidently on the dhoti-covered knee of the other. The wife sat with her head bowed over the plate, and covered with the wide, glittering border of her sari. She wore gold bangles, gold rings, and a gold hip chain.

"Now, then, Mrs. Blaise, please do not be rash and call us sexist. You see, the impulse to worship one's husband should be seen as a short cut to the worship of God. How good is your Bengali? Can you read the inscription below?"

The inscription, loosely translated, advised this: if husband is pleased, pleased is god/husband is life/husband is pride/husband is the only jewel.

"It sounds funny now, but at the time it was meant as good advice. Perhaps some women in the United States and Canada could still use it."

I could not determine the tone of her voice, and so I could not make a rejoinder. There was a pause, a little too long to be dismissed as natural but not long enough to hurt or embarrass. After the pause, she showed us prints of nineteenth-century Calcutta by D'Oyly Bart.

We sat on the floor so we could better see the detail: a dhoti or bed sheet hung out to dry on the roof of a building, a child retrieving a ball, English gentlewomen under parasols sitting in horse-drawn carriages which were trapped forever in motion on streets with exotic names such as Dhuramtollah or Chitpore.

Ideas, scenes: Nothing seems lost in this strange city. Now, instead of the English ladies under pale silk parasols, there are women like me in bright silks and expensive cottons speeding in crowded Ambassador cars down congested Chitpore Road. I am with friends; they are, more correctly, friends of my parents, and they are taking Clark and me to the ugly theater district to explain to us the marvels of a Bengali musical. The fat housewife beside me in the back seat of the car jiggles her weight from hip to hip and tells me without rancor, "I want you to write this down in your book, okay? Write down that Indian women are born to suffer. Why should girls be taught to cover their heads in the presence of older men and speak softly and never look boldly into their eyes? It's women who go through all the pain of labor and then the child carries the name of the father. Write down, Bharati, that in modern India there are many pockets of anger." She giggles into a loose end of her cotton *tangail* sari to minimize the seriousness of her remarks.

"You see how modern my wife is," the host shouts to us above the random noise of Chitpore Road traffic. "But don't let her give you a distorted picture of our women." Then he turns in his seat to scream at the driver of a '57 Buick, "Eh *sala!* Are you blind? Who do you think you are? The viceroy during the British Raj?" After which he turns a half circle to smile indulgently at Clark and me jammed on either side of the fat housewife, and says, "You see what kind of driving we have to put up with," and speeds us toward the Bengali rendition of *Ali Baba.*

During that year I was, of course, aware of a few outspoken women but I am not sure that they shared anything with women like that fat housewife in the tightly packed Ambassador. I had read of progressive women such as Kamala Bhasin. Bhasin, who edited *The Position of Women in India*: Proceedings of a seminar held in Srinagar in September, 1972, wrote in her introduction: "The position of women can be reasonably compared with the plight of the millions that make up the so-called scheduled [i.e., former untouchable] castes and the depressed communities of India." And in a paper entitled "The Predicament of Middle Class Indian Women—An Inside View," she wrote with greater feeling: "The road that Indian womanhood is expected to travel is dark, dangerous and forbidding. . . . The oppression, suppression and consequent depression that women have come to suffer from has eaten deep into their vitals to an extent that makes them accept their present condition as being the destined duty of their sex. The ideal of service becomes their monopoly and even finds expression in literature and art."

Placing anger in Bhasin's context was still light-years away from the Ballygunge and the women I knew.

I had intimations of small clusters of radical women existing in the city. In the middle of innocuous Loreto House gossip I would often be told that so-and-so (to me they would always remain shadowy creatures in crumpled white school uniforms and untidy braids) had become a Naxal and gone underground or that so-and-so had become "weird" and spent most of her time explaining the right of women to own property, work, study, vote, divorce, and remarry.

"Do you remember Malati?" a friend might say to me in her living room as we sipped iced coffee which the white-liveried bearer had just brought in. "I think she was your partner in the Lancers dance sequence in *Quality Street*. Well, can you believe that her younger sister is a rabid women's lib type? Each time I see her she's fulminating about . . . get this!—Manu! That's right, Manu the Lawgiver! I think that's doubly funny since we hardly learned any ancient Indian history from the missionaries!"

I did succeed in catching Malati's sister in the corner of a fussily decorated balcony at a cocktail party toward the end of my trip to Calcutta. She told me that her anger against Manu (ca. 500 B.C.) bore resemblance to the intensity of the anger of some American feminists against Freud. Then she said that Manu deserved our wrath and recited in a singsong, sententious voice:

> Though he be uncouth and prone to pleasure
> though he have no good points at all,
> the virtuous wife should ever
> worship her lord as a god.

When I asked her what had become of Malati, she told me in the same sententious tones that Malati had married a diamond merchant in Bombay and become incredibly fat.

And so it was not surprising that in 1973 an inconspicuous village widow named Bitto made it into the front page of *The Statesman* with her tragic contribution to women's liberation. The story of Bitto is a story of love and death in a millet field near Agra where tourists come in carloads to see the Taj Mahal, which is itself a magnificent monument to death and to love's triumph. At the time of the episode Bitto was twenty-four years old, widowed since the age of sixteen. To be a widow in Hindu India, especially in rural areas, is to lose all social status. It is to disclaim all lust, to make oneself as physically unattractive as possible, and to devote the rest of one's life to prayers. Widow-remarriage, to orthodox village Hindus, is an ultimate obscenity. For the first eight years of her widowhood, Bitto was said to have followed the Hindu model. She had lived in her father's house, probably grateful to have her chastity safeguarded by her father and brothers. But at age twenty-four something had gone wrong. She had permitted herself to fall in love with a visitor from another village and had tried to run off with him. Her flight had been blocked by her more orthodox relatives, and in the ensuing struggle between tradition-bound villagers and the impulsive lovers, a sister-in-law received a gunshot wound, and an uncle and a policeman had been killed. The villagers pursued the lovers into the millet fields, and there, aided by police, they killed them.

For a long time I had nightmares about Bitto. Not because romance had failed but because a whole village had resisted a young woman's dream of personal happiness. A Hindu widow had dared to fall in love instead of worshiping the memory of the dead (and in this case, adolescent) husband: That was the real transgression. And being in love, she had actively sought out a new life with a new partner in a new village. She had chosen to be selfishly modern. Even in death, she had not been forgiven; the police had had to arrange the lovers' cremation, since the family would not. There could be no clear-cut heroes and villains in this story of colliding world views and expectations. No one had gained, everyone had lost, a lot.

Even in cities like Bombay there were occasional disastrous confusions. For instance, during that year a women's periodical, *Femina,* carried the story of nurses in a well-known hospital organizing wild-cat strikes and immobilizing the institution because a sweeper had allegedly assaulted a young staff nurse in the hospital's dimly lit base-ment. The victim had been apparently discovered with lacerations on her body and with her ring missing and with red welts around her neck, suggesting to some that her gold necklace may have been forci-bly torn off. The journalist's reconstruction of the sequence of events revealed that at lunch that day the staff nurse had reprimanded a sweeper for attempting to join her at her table in the hospital cafete-ria; three hours later she had been brutally assaulted by an unknown assailant in the dark and dusty basement where she normally changed out of her nurse's uniform before going back to her flat. The reporter referred to "the insolence and bad behaviour of the me-nial staff." The menial staff had been insolent; the lower class had not known its place. Perhaps that was what *really* hurt. But the inci-dent had mobilized the nurses to act as a group and agitate for bet-ter protection and facilities.

For me it was a time to share that anger and that confusion; it was not a time to judge.

# ·ᢌ IV

## FOUR DAYS

I was leading two lives that year; set against each other, they suggested a painless but mocking harmony. In Ballygunge I was the dutiful relative who paid Sunday morning visits to the family, ate rice and curried delicacies with her fingers, and sat on the edge of a bed gossiping with aunts or listening to the *Bournevita Quiz* on All-India Radio. But in downtown Calcutta, especially on Park Street or Chowringhee, I was the Indian *memsahib* with a white escort to be lewdly stared at, or to be whispered "good day" to by elevator-boy-pimps. These lives—my lives—were separate, contiguous; they impinged but did not collide. In Calcutta, I could not help thinking, hundreds of thousands saw themselves leading craftily welded lives. I was one of many. I saw my Calcutta days as transparencies—the banality of quotidian encounters reduced or enhanced by the photographer's trickery. Sometimes when I held a transparency up to the light, the microscopic suggestiveness of what I saw—a woman pouring tea or offering a platter of cucumber sandwiches, a woman in diamond-drop earrings speaking into a microphone on a stage with film stars and politicians, or a woman in poorly fitting pants playing golf and smiling in the direction of the camera—was comically obvious. But sometimes, because the light was too dim or because the photographer too subtle and too malicious, the little squares of my full but aimless days brought me no comfort, no revelation.

## The Talk of the Town

Kamala, a banker's wife I had come to like very much, called me after breakfast, minutes before a power cut, and asked me to go along with her to her weekly packaging-medicine-for-Mother-Teresa's-lepers session later that morning. Because by now I had grown suspicious of my own need for privacy, and because I was eager to intersect increasing numbers of Calcutta lives, I quickly agreed.

Kamala's chauffeur called for me punctually. He swaggered into the mission's reception room where I had been chatting with the telephone *babu* about Canadian immigration, looked contemptuously at the mission staff and at a white scholar in *kurta-pajama* discussing his bill, and told me that his *memsahib* was waiting for me in the car. It was clear from the way he held his liveried body aloof from the mission staff that he could not square my life as an academic with my (to him more familiar) life as a cocktail-sipper on his *memsahib*'s lawn. I followed him out to the Fiat where Kamala was sitting on the white slip cover of the back seat and looking unusually hot and nervous.

"It's been a perfectly horrid morning," she said apologetically as I climbed in. "I've been interviewing English-style cooks and they all want to make me something called baked carp à la anchovy sauce! I don't know that I can even find canned anchovy in Calcutta, let alone afford it."

She said that the "English" cook was her husband's idea. He had spent a year in London for training and he had returned with an inconvenient love of English cooking. They already had two *deshi* cooks—two men from her maternal uncle's home town—who were reliable if a little unimaginative. She would probably have to let one of these men go. She would probably be scared stiff of whichever

"English" cook she hired. She was sorry that she was burdening me with her domestic squabbles. How had my talk with the woman mountaineer gone? She just couldn't imagine a Bengali girl deciding one fine morning on a career of mountain climbing—could I?

I reminded her that she herself was a career woman. In an unused part of the servants' quarters in her compound, Kamala had set up a small workshop for hand painting and hand printing saris. It had started as something she did for her friends and then developed into a profitable business. Now she had four employees, and recently she had painted a sari for a film actress.

"Oh, come on," Kamala giggled. "That's not at all the same thing. All I've done is turned a feminine accomplishment to profit. But for a girl to want to climb mountains, well that's really weird. You've really got to want that career to be any good at it. I mean you can't stumble into it accidentally as you did with teaching or me with painting saris."

The medicine-packaging session was held at an Englishwoman's flat on a gracious and hard-to-find street. The hostess was an old India-hand. Her furniture, her deportment, the controlled enthusiasm of her speech, suggested the endless adjustments she must have made so that Britain and India could coexist in her life. She greeted Kamala and me at the door, asked me if I had been told that my hands would get messy, then led us quickly through the living room, past a room divider studded with rosettes and ribbons her children had won at annual horse meets and swimming meets, and into the dining room where we were to sit.

"You won't find this difficult at all," the hostess said to me as she took the chair beside me. "We use powdered medicine nowadays and packaging powder is a breeze. Kamala, do you remember the days when we used to work with pills instead?"

"Of course, wasn't it awful?" Kamala agreed. "I always had a hard time cracking pills in half before packaging."

"We had a visitor once," the hostess went on. "I think she might have been Canadian in fact. Anyway she cracked the pill in half and the two halves popped into her cup of coffee!"

"I remember that," Kamala laughed. "Bharati, you should have

seen her face. She took one look at the coffee and I thought she was
going to get sick."

On the dining table directly in front of me was a pretty glass bowl
(the kind that holds candies on coffee tables). It was three-quarters
filled with a dull, whitish powder. The hostess' eleven-year-old son,
in T-shirt and short pants, explained that the bowl contained the
leprosy medicine and that it was his job to refill the bowls, and did I
think that I would be the first to request a refill? Next to my bowl of
medicine was a stack of newspaper rectangles. I was to measure a
tiny scoop of powder (the exact amount specified by the hostess),
place it in the center of the paper rectangle, and fold it carefully.
The boy stood behind my chair for several minutes, then demonstrated his mother's instructions for correct folding.

For the others—there were nine of us altogether, three whites and
five Indians, and the boy with short pants and ice-blue eyes—the
medicine-packaging session that morning may have seemed commonplace. For me it was especially disquieting. I was accustomed to a
more North American, give-at-the-office concept of charity. On a personal scale, charity meant to me a bike-a-thon or a fast-a-lunch, and
mailing money to make haggard waifs in magazine ads (who were
often Bengali) a little less unhappy. On the national scale, it meant
watching on television the airlifting of food and clothing to disaster
victims. But in this crazy city the connections between the coiffed
women and the lepers were intimate, continuous.

I asked the women what they thought of the critics of Mother
Teresa. There were enough critics—students, radical journalists, tea-
stall habitués—who had hinted to me that all the energy and publicity directed in the name of Mother Teresa should be deflected from
the leprous and dying to the poor and homeless.

"Mother Teresa is a saint," an Indian woman said.

"Bharati, how can you ask such a question?" Kamala pleaded.
"She's an Indian saint. How can you not understand about Indian
saints?"

And of course as soon as Kamala said it, I made the connection
between Mother Teresa—an Albanian Catholic—and the Indian
saints revered by my family. She was a saint, a condition that transcended mere nobility, simply *because* she had concentrated her
efforts, her love, on hopeless cases. To help the dying in a despairing

city was an *acte gratuite*; it was pure love, without definition or degree.

"People have such misconceptions about lepers," the hostess said as she rang the bell for refreshments. "About lepers and crazies, about the whole lot of these poor dears. Mother has made them rethink the situation. What will you have? Coca-Cola or coffee?"

The women around me gossiped as they folded package after package for the clinic. Between them they covered Calcutta's housing shortages, the inadequacy of hospital facilities, the insolence of domestics, and women's movements.

"I think Germaine Greer is so tiresome," said an Englishwoman.

"I understand that all this women's lib business is no longer so popular in Britain," said a plump South Indian whose cousin had just returned from Liverpool after a five-year stay.

"Do you need more powder?" the boy in short pants asked me. "Any call for this magic powder? Other weeks I fill two rounds before the Coke and coffee break."

To please him, I asked for more powder. My fingertips were grimy from the newsprint. I cupped my hands and poised the dirty fingertips above his creamy white shirt in a flippantly threatening gesture. He backed away in mock fright. He was not much older than Bart. I assumed that he had won at least some of the ribbons and trophies I had spotted on my way in. In twenty more years, I wondered, would he think back on his job as a refiller of leprosy medicine as silly and exotic, a concession to his parents' willful exile? And what of Bart and Bernard? Would they, with typical liberal guilt, blame me for running away when most of my friends had stayed?

"Bharati, what do you think? Shall I cut my hair?" Kamala asked, "I hate having to put it up all the time." She ran her dirty fingertips through the wavy hair on her crown. "But my husband will kill me if I cut it."

I did not think it odd that Kamala could define Indian sainthood and discuss hair styles with the same anxiety. After all, she had not invested the medicine-packaging session with symbolic significance. It was clear that for all the banality of our chatter, I was witnessing, that morning, a group of dedicated people. They loved Calcutta. In helping the lepers they pledged loyalty to a city to which most Westerners applied words like "hell" and "desolation." Their rhetoric

was neither pompous nor metaphoric. They had personalized the
city's problem. The problem of the lepers was *their* problem in the
same way that finding the right domestic or the most pleasing hair
style was.

I knew that I was not yet prepared to love Calcutta in their ways.

I went back to the mission, prepared for a formless afternoon of
reading. In the evening, I was supposed to help some aunts, uncles,
and cousins select saris for Jaya's wedding.

It was becoming harder for me to read the books that we had
brought from Montreal and then carted across India. They seemed
to have become the paraphernalia of a sealed and remote life. I
could not believe that I was expected to return to it.

Clark sat on his day bed, reading and swatting mosquitoes. Behind
his head lizards scurried up the walls. When the lizards retreated too
close to the ceiling to be comfortably spied upon, I went to the window that overlooked a straggly street, a garbage dump, and a decayed
mansion with squatters, dogs, and crumbling garden statuary. A
young man stood at a ground-floor window of the mansion and
waved to me. Earlier on this trip to India I would have been shamed
by this acknowledgment from a squatter. I would have wanted to
pretend to myself that we inhabited contiguous but opaque win-
dowless worlds. Now I could approximate my friend's strategy for
survival, stand my ground at the window, even smile faintly at our
coexistence. But I could not wave back to the man. Only American
tourists could do that, the perfect innocents who came to India in
the summer months, noisily in the mission dining rooms, and took
pictures of rickshaw pullers and refugees.

A boy in undershirt and short pants walked stiff-backed under my
window. He carried a heavy metal container on his head. Just before
disappearing from the arc of my vision, he stopped, pissed against
the garden wall of the mansion, then continued his journey. He had
not taken the load off his head to piss. The young man at the window was still waving to me.

Anjali called me. "You'll probably think I'm bonkers but could we
persuade you and Clark to come to the *Bobby* première tonight? We
have tickets for you people. But I don't know, it's not likely to be in-

tellectual enough for him." And when I had assured her that we would be thrilled to go to the première, she added, "We'll pick you up early. It's bound to be a madhouse. You know how these *pan-wallahs* and *biri-wallahs* get when a Bombay film star arrives. Raj Kapoor and Chintu Kapoor will be there. But I wish there was some way of telling the throngs that Dimple Kapadia isn't coming."

"You're kidding!" gasped my cousins when I called to let them know that I would not be accompanying them on the sari-shopping expedition.

"What luck! you're actually going to see Chintu in person? It's not fair, I'm the Chintu fan and you two get the invitations. I wish you could smuggle me in."

There were, of course, no ways to smuggle oneself in. That was a lesson I had learned. You had to be a civic leader and fund-raiser like Anjali whose name added glamour to printed programs for pre-mières. Or you had to be lucky, like us. Or you had to demand the right to enter, you had to prepare yourself to storm police lines, break down all doors of the movie house, burn a few parked cars as an exemplary gesture, threaten to paralyze the city.

Our success is mocked, a little, by the failure of others. I had not thought it possible to see such a crowd on Chowringhee. It was like a dramatization of the city's overpopulation, volatility, and despera-tion. I could not believe that for so many people, watching other people arrive at the Metro Cinema could be so thrilling. The rich and the poor, the lucky and the unlucky, were separated from each other by a thin line of policemen. Contiguity and conflagration: I prayed we would not lose our lives that evening. Outside was the dark, shapeless crowd, surging forward and being pushed back as cars emptied. Inside was a glitter of diamond earrings, brocade sari bor-ders, sequins, sleeked hair.

Later, a beautiful woman would say, "I thought those people were going to rip off my diamond earrings. I covered my head with my sari so that no *goonda* got bright ideas about the earrings. But they must have thought I was a film star. They reached out to touch me."

There were speeches by politicians, organizers, Bombay movie stars, snatches of a popular song from *Bobby*. The most beautiful of the charity organizers, another Loreto girl of my vintage, stood be-fore the glittering thousands of Calcutta high society to welcome

Raj Kapoor, and forgot all her lines. After that embarrassment, Raj Kapoor himself took over and began auctioning signed albums of *Bobby* sound tracks: The first album went for an astonishing five hundred rupees. The second for an incredible two thousand. The third album was won, like the other two, by a young Marwari boy willing to pay five thousand rupees, nearly seven hundred dollars.

Farther down the aisle, a dark man in a shiny green suit said very loudly, "Just look at these young Marwari chaps! They come with five-thousand-rupee notes tucked into the pocket of their tight pants."

"Shh," whispered his companion, a woman with a rose in her elaborate chignon. "You know whose son that is. I bet his father gave him the money just before he went on the stage to pick up the album."

"These fellows have bought up Calcutta."

"Well, it's our fault if they have. In any case the money goes to charity, remember?"

It sounded to me more a ritual than an acrimonious exchange. They had come to have fun in an auditorium packed with well-dressed people determined to have fun. A good part of the fun was to swing the neck in sweeping arcs and feel oneself a glittering part of a special pageantry.

When the hall was finally darkened it came as a letdown. The crowd had not come to see the film that had sparked such national hysteria; it had come to revalidate its sense of being the city's elite. *Bobby* with its marvelous sentimentality about interclass and intercommunal triumphant love, its heady tunes, gorgeous sets and costumes, and exaggerated acting was aimed not at this crowd but at the crowd on the street outside the theater. *Bobby* presented a pageantry of another sort; to love *Bobby* required leaving the pageantry of the auditorium behind and entering the pageantry of Raj Kapoor's magically vulgar imagination. But many of us could not yield ourselves so completely to that magic. We were listening to faint scuffle sounds in the back. We were thinking of our prearrangements to leave at the intermission; there were other happenings or parties to go on to. Would we find our friends in that crowded lobby? Would we make it safely out of the building?

We did find our friends in the lobby, at the appointed time and at the designated spot near the imposing staircase. We did make it safely out of the Metro Cinema, past the still-surging crowds, and into Anjali and Nikhil's car. But not before Clark and I had witnessed firsthand the not-so-gentle ejection of an intruder. The intruder had walked in confidently in his tight-fitting pants and pointed shoes. It was his swagger that had fooled us. He seemed interchangeable with the cool young men who had earlier paid their thousands of rupees for *Bobby* records. But his confidence had not fooled the police officials. He had been challenged, grasped firmly by the shoulder, and escorted out, to be reabsorbed into the applauding dark anonymity from which he had emerged. For a few minutes he too had been a star. I thought that it was perhaps a tribute to the magical atmosphere of *Bobby* that this intrusion and ejection had not led to a riot.

An amateur socialite, I was happy to go with Anjali and Nikhil to Raj Kapoor's party in the Park Hotel. In Montreal it would be hard to explain to colleagues the guiltless pleasure I felt at being invited to Raj Kapoor's party. To them Raj Kapoor would be no more than an unknown film actor turned director and producer, parochial compared with a Satyajit Ray. But Raj Kapoor is the king of Indian films, and in India, films are the national passion.

I no longer cared to discriminate between the silly and the serious after so many months in Calcutta. It no longer seemed necessary to feel outrage at the condition of beggars, nor to probe and explain away tiresome disaffection. It was enough to be in the presence of a national hero in a hotel ballroom. We were photographed with the hero, and his handsome son, Chintu. The hero said, "Music is my passion," and, training his beautiful blue eyes on us, he sang a song from his old movie *Joker*.

Anjali said, "My brother used to love your films. He was always singing songs from *Joker*." Then turning to me, she added, "You remember how *dada* used to sing songs from *Joker*?"

Of course I remembered. Now *dada*, the boy in ascot I had been prepared to fall in love with, was an engineer in England with an English wife and English kids and he probably no longer sang Raj Kapoor songs.

Nikhil said, "Raj, I want to tell you something special. I touched your hand thirteen years ago . . . no, it must have been fifteen. I wasn't married then."

Anjali said, "Fifteen years ago you were probably like that boy they threw out of the Metro Cinema this evening."

Chintu Kapoor, the heartthrob of teen-agers like my cousins, said in response to someone's question that he had always been interested in acting, there had been no question of any other profession. I saw a very pretty woman waiting to move in toward him, but he left the party early, forcing the woman to practice her charms on someone older.

The party lasted long enough for me to see a discreet Bengali woman stumble from bar to buffet, red-eyed and deliriously drunk. The beautiful Loreto House girl was still mortified for having flubbed her lines. The second-prettiest woman in the room, I learned from another old Loreto girl, had once worked as a secretary in a foreign consulate, then married well, and was now rumored to be promiscuous. A consular secretary who was stunning enough to have starred in a Raj Kapoor film left the room, I was told, to throw up.

A very large man in British tweeds said to me, "Who *are* you? I saw you last in the lobby of the Sheraton-Oberoi in Bombay. That time you had two little boys with you as well as the gentleman." In these circles, India is an underpopulated country.

Raj Kapoor said that he had always had faith in Satyajit Ray, and that while their talents were so different he had never doubted Ray's genius.

Nikhil said, "You and Ray should make a film together. That would be such an historic venture."

Raj Kapoor laughed. He said that that would be like Bernard Shaw making love to the proverbial dumb, beautiful blonde.

Nikhil and his business friends were clustered around Kapoor; I'd never seen grown men act so thrilled. And suddenly I realized why: Raj Kapoor was a fellow Number One, but a Number One from the industry that transcended all others in India. Next to Raj Kapoor, Satyajit Ray was just another bright local boy with neither money nor power—and those were the only standards the Calcutta business world acknowledged. The men had been transformed.

One of Nikhil and Anjali's married-couple friends said they were leaving for some food—did we want to go? Sure, sure, we said; we always said yes. Anil, the new Number One who had taken over the further entertainment of the Blaises, drove at fashionably high speed and dropped off the secretary, then the general's wife who was Raj Kapoor's cousin and who lived in Fort William. I was sorry the party was over. But actually the party was not yet over.

"Who's ready for kabobs?" Anil asked. "I'm starved, didn't eat a thing at Raj's."

"You're crazy," I told him; he was a reckless sort, a little shorter and older than Nikhil, but with a Loreto House wife a few years younger than Anjali and myself. "Who can eat at three A.M.? They had a fantastic buffet at the hotel—why didn't you stuff yourself there?"

"I wasn't hungry then. I'm hungry now. Let's go to Nizam's."

"Bharati, you remember Nizam's, don't you?" asked the wife.

"Of course. We used to sit in the car and order *anda paratha* and a fat man used to bring it to the car."

"A fat man still brings it to the car," she laughed.

Nizam's is an unpretentious restaurant behind the New Market in a predominantly Muslim area of Calcutta. It has long been popular with Loreto House girls, and at least one Loreto College picnic that I attended was catered by Nizam's. For a Hindu woman to eat in such unflinchingly Muslim surroundings, I considered not simply chic, but a sign of liberal temperament.

At Nizam's we waited in the car. A fat man lumbered down the steps of the restaurant and salaamed Anil as an old and prized customer. Anil ordered *pasinda* kabobs for all of us. We professed not to be hungry but allowed ourselves to be persuaded.

The kabobs, when they arrived, were indeed excellent. But while they were being readied in the restaurant kitchen, Anil decided to entertain us. He got out of the car, leaving the door slightly ajar, and walked down the wide quiet street, a majestic little man, slightly drunk. The shapeless gray bundles on the sidewalk stirred, revealing just-awakened sleepers. It was close to 3 A.M.

Anil spoke to a dirty, bushy-haired woman. Then she began to run up and down the middle of the street, touching a broken hydrant to mark off each lap.

"What's going on?" I asked.

"Oh, she's a madwoman, a *pugli*. He must have asked her to run. He's always doing things like that."

"Please tell him to come back. And close that door before something awful happens."

"Don't be boring, Bharati," she said good-naturedly. "Really, America's made you as bad a fuss-pot as all the Englishmen we keep entertaining."

The *pugli* stopped, and looked expectantly at Anil who was standing near the hood of the car. The restaurant lights washed his soft features with a bluish radiance. "More," I heard him say. "Keep going." The *pugli* began to run again.

Then he turned his attention to a rickshaw puller who had just turned the corner and put the handlebars down on the sidewalk so he could rest. Anil's voice, clear and uncharacteristically harsh, carried easily to the car. He was demanding the puller's name, address, and age. He was acting the role of a police officer checking the man's permit. Why didn't the picture on the permit look like him? Was he telling the truth?

"Come closer to the light. I want to see your face."

"My God, he's going to get us killed. Please tell him to stop it."

"He's always full of life like this. He must relax, he works so hard."

"*Saab*," pleaded the rickshaw puller, "I swear it is really me. The picture is a little dark. But I am the picture."

The *pugli* came to a rest. Anil commanded her to run some more.

We hate others because of our own cowardice, and I hated the man in the restaurant kitchen for taking so long to make the kabobs, thus keeping us prisoners to other men's fantasies. I hated him because I knew I ought to get out of the car and tell the rickshaw puller to ask Anil for *his* credentials. Because the rickshaw puller near Nizam's was suddenly not just a Muslim resident of a Calcutta slum, but he was also me, a timid, brown naturalized citizen in a white man's country that was growing increasingly hostile to "colored" immigrants.

The food arrived. It was explained to the rickshaw puller that his license had not expired and that we believed he was the man he claimed to be, and that we had played a joke at his expense. The *pugli* was instructed to stop running. Both were given *baksheesh*, some coins from the kabob change, nothing like the rupee notes that Clark and I sometimes distributed. They retreated to different corners of the sidewalk, counting the rewards for participation in a rich man's diversion.

I cannot pretend to understand what it was that I witnessed. For Anil and his wife it was nothing more than entertainment, being director, audience, and actor, simultaneously. Deprived of television, cinema, plays, or movies, the upper-class Calcuttan finds *people* his only sure entertainment. Perhaps his choice of scene and his cast of characters were nothing more sinister than fashionable eccentricity. Or perhaps Anil and I, in our separate ways, were as insane as the *pugli*, but without the comfort of communal recognition.

On the drive back I was relieved I had not given into any hysteria and interrupted the game. The players had all known their roles; improvisation might have led to violence. I was not innocent enough to enjoy it and I was not wise enough to discriminate intelligently between malice and play.

"You're driving too fast," the wife said to Anil on Gariahat Road as we raced back to the mission at an unscholarly hour. Daredevil speeding by well-placed executives, long after their cautious chauffeurs had been dismissed for the night, seemed an unvarying component of Calcutta *macho*. "He's always showing off his driving."

"Do I give you advice about your work" he asked. "I don't need advice about my work."

"Just make sure Clark and Bharati get back safely. Bharati has to give a speech to a ladies' group tomorrow." Clark looked none too well, after the movie, the reception, the street performance, and now the drive. "He's really the best driver in town, Clark, so you've nothing to worry about."

The night *durwan* of the mission let us in around 4 A.M.

Nirmala, a rich Marwari woman, sent her car and chauffeur to fetch me for my speech to the ladies' group. The first time I met her she'd insisted on telling me that her husband, whom she called K.B., had not deserted Calcutta during the Naxal troubles. Nor, even more valiantly, had he interrupted his daily round of golf.

Nirmala's servant was out on the front steps to greet me as the chauffeur pulled into the carport. He told me that his *memsahib* wasn't yet ready and that he was to show me into the living room. There were, I noticed as I walked into the cool still interior, two living rooms, one furnished "European-style," with sofas, armchairs, and coffee tables, the other "Marwari-style," with a *gadda* mattress. The servant led me into the air-conditioned European one and brought me a glass of freshly squeezed lime and soda on a silver tray. Obviously, to the servant, I projected a foreign image.

I was admiring the view of Nirmala's walled, uniformly green lawn from behind the slightly parted living room curtains when she came down the wide stairs and stood in the doorway. "Good," she said, "the servant has already brought you fresh lime and soda. And don't worry, you can trust the ice cubes in our house." I followed her into the Marwari living room, where she unlocked a built-in cupboard and took out measured amounts of spices for the servant.

"Could I have a couple of cloves and cardamoms?" I asked. In Bengal, cloves and cardamoms and betel-nut slivers are conventional breath-fresheners, and (according to an aunt of mine) precautions against nervousness. Besides, I was glad to linger in the austere informality of the Marwari living room. "I love *gaddas*," I said. "In climates like this, they make much better sense."

"You like this room better?" Nirmala asked. "Oh, I'm so glad. It makes better sense in any climate. It's so much friendlier, you can just loll around and relax on the *gadda*. I use the other one for my 'proper' guests, you know what I mean, for foreigners, and K.B.'s business associates." She dropped a fistful of cloves and cardamoms in my palm. I knew from my mother and aunts how expensive these spices had become. Nirmala was a very generous woman.

"I *knew* I should have had the servant bring you straight into this room," she said.

In the car on our way to the meeting of the ladies' group, she asked me, "Are you nervous about the speech? Rina has told us so much about you. Weren't you her classmate in Loreto House? Isn't she grand? Isn't she a first-class organizer?"

I answered no to the question about nervousness and yes to everything else. Rina was grand. Rina was a first-class organizer. But more than that, which I could not explain to Nirmala, she was about thirty years ahead of her friends. She was not content simply to supervise her family and servants, go shopping with friends at New Market, drink iced coffee at Flury's, and pose worrisome questions about what to wear and what charities to help. While others, discontented, might have moped or made bitter, flippant jokes about the uselessness of leisure-class women, or fumed that their parents had not trained them to be lady doctors and lady lawyers, Rina had taken a level-headed measure of her strengths. She was amiable, knew a large number of important people in the city on a first-name basis, was good at managing household crises, had a flair for clothes and a B.A. (English Honors) from Loreto College, Calcutta University. Then she had found herself a part-time job—organizing cultural programs for the wives of Calcutta's most powerful businessmen— that still left her time to take her younger children to the Calcutta Club for swimming every day.

"Rina's a very unusual person," I said. "I like her even better now than I did when we were in college."

"Let me see, you might find one or two of your old college friends in this morning's group," Nirmala said slowly. "But on the whole, they'll be wives like me. We got married long before we were college age."

Nirmala's chauffeur negotiated wide streets and narrow lanes with equal impatience. Then, narrowly missing an accident with another ruthlessly waxed Ambassador car, he brought us to the entrance of a newish office tower in Calcutta's unprepossessing business district. In an air-conditioned board room of that building, I was to tell the assembly of prominent wives (billionaires' wives, my cousins had joked) how I wrote my novels.

Once in the board room, I thought it best not to tell all. My obsessions with opening paragraphs, tone, texture, pacing, my practiced lectures about fiction being metaphoric and synecdochic—how every little detail must carry an enormous weight—would seem to them, I feared, academic, and tiresomely cultured. I skimmed over the nuts and bolts of fiction, landed gingerly on the mechanics and sociology of publishing, then lost myself in the swamps of being a "Third World Woman Writer" in North America.

The question period drew a blank until a plump woman said, "You have such a lovely voice. Do you do much public speaking?"

"Well, I'm a professor, you know. I have to do a lot of talking."

"That's it, that's why you weren't nervous. I would have been nervous. Wouldn't you have been nervous?"

Rina reminded them that Loreto girls had all taken compulsory elocution classes. Many of them agreed that Loreto prepared the Indian woman to face the modern world.

"But I just can't stand up in front of everybody and lecture," objected the plump woman. "That's why I like doing charity work, you're in the background."

"Except when you are on the stage. What about that poor lady who fluffed her lines at the *tamasha* for *Bobby?*"

We left the board room for refreshments. Five of us went to a dimly lit, overcooled restaurant on Park Street.

Nirmala and I ordered sherry, and I realized only after the waiter had shuffled back to the bar that it was likely to be imported, and therefore hideously expensive. Two of us in the group had been at the *Bobby* première the night before and were asked to give details of the event. I guessed that there was a rivalry between different groups of fund-raisers for charities. Not everyone in this group had been to the *Bobby* première, and those who had, had not all been charmed. Wasn't the parking impossible? Wasn't the security system ineffectual? Weren't Bombay film stars a headache? Some of them were so *strange*. They had heard something about a riot and that the party had fizzled. But everyone agreed that Raj Kapoor was a dear.

By the time the sherry arrived I had already recounted all my anecdotes about Raj Kapoor, tipsy ladies, dumb blondes, and Raj Kapoor's unfailing gallantry. I gave no names, but everyone knew who the tipsy lady had to be.

Over lunch we talked about the aunt of one of the less-sedate women who had been at Raj Kapoor's party. The aunt, apparently, was the life of all parties she attended.

"That woman is such a life of the party that she has to check into a nursing home for a change of pace."

Someone recalled, giggling, that she had visited her in a nursing home and had found her sitting cross-legged on the bed, drinking raw gin and smoking. Another woman remembered her playing golf at a hill station.

"It was hilarious. There she was, waddling along on the green, followed by a woman caddy and two maids."

"Why the maids?"

"One was for carrying an umbrella, and the other for carrying a stool and massaging her legs between strokes."

After that, the greens chat became too technical for me. Everyone at the lunch played golf. It was all part of "women's lib"; they were proud that Indian women were finally getting off their behinds and getting some exercise. Golf was the sport of progressive, liberated women. My mother, aunts, and cousins would never expect to play golf; golf had a powerful symbolic significance, for men as well as women.

When the check arrived, I reached for my billfold, thinking we should split it. Nirmala told me to put my billfold away, after they had admired its pockets crammed with credit cards.

"When Nirmala says she's buying, we don't argue with her. She's quite easily the richest person here."

Nirmala was a very generous woman.


The next morning I called to make sure that Jaya, my Nagpur cousin, and her mother, Kola-mashi, had not changed their minds about going to the jeweler's. Clark and I waited forty-five minutes for a taxi to take us to the *mamabari* where he dropped me off. All the empty taxis were on their way to tea stalls where drivers congregated for longish breaks. Each time Clark spotted the yellow and black hump of a taxi coasting toward us from the direction of Jadavpur Bridge, he darted out into the middle of Gariahat Road and yelled, "Taxi! Taxi!" After several minutes, a group of the young loiterers who had been sitting on the bench of an open-air tea stall across the road began to mimic Clark's accent. "*Saab*, you want taxi? I get taxi? We go Chowringhee, you go Chowringhee?" chanted their leader. His friends continued to shout, "Taxi! Taxi!"

"Don't worry about us," Clark shouted back. "We'll manage." And the youth, laughing, went back to his friends on the bench. They stopped calling out for taxis; they had guessed we were unwilling to play.

And so, whenever the familiar old Sikh taxi driver was not parked in his accustomed stand near the mission, even a simple chore like getting a cab to go from Gol Park to Southern Avenue could be an exhausting ordeal. The "pace of life" one hears so much about is slower in Calcutta than in the West, but not necessarily any more restful.

In Montreal I can leave home, buy the week's food, return and put it away, then go out again by subway to the department stores and shop for five or six items, meet a friend for lunch, go to my office, answer letters, teach a class, meet students, return in time to cook a meal, change, and then go out again for the evening. In India, to do more than one errand in a day, to go shopping for more than one item, or to go visiting more than one person is virtually impossible. Arrangements are made—except in the most Westernized circles—three or four days in advance, and very little social activity can be spontaneous or improvised. And that, of course, changes the whole nature of social contact, even when it is intended to be simple and natural.

At the *mamabari* not everyone was ready to go to the jeweler's. So I accompanied Jaya and Anju who were on their way to shop for underclothes for the trousseau.

"You're sure you'll be able to walk, Babloo-didi?" Anju asked me. "You know that our streets aren't like your Montreal streets."

"Of course."

"Good. Now you can tell us all about Chintu Kapoor. Remember we want to hear everything, don't leave out any details. We want the whole atmosphere."

"What did you wear, Babloo-didi?" Jaya asked.

I told them as much as I could remember, censoring out the inebriated women and the games near Nizam's.

It turned out that Jaya was shopping for fancy panties. "I wish I had known," I sighed. "I could have brought you half a dozen from Montreal." I had started to say "Paris," but that sounded a bit too suggestive.

The first four shops we tried had only underpants with drawstrings.

"I want elasticized waistbands," Jaya said.

The fifth store, on being asked, brought out men's white cotton shorts with elasticized waistbands.

"No, this isn't quite right," Jaya said. "I want a different kind of elasticized band. Thinner band, you understand?" The rest of us delicately said nothing.

"Oh, I see," smiled the shop assistant. He put back the box of men's boxer shorts, then brought out a neatly folded stack of panties. "You see, *didi*, I keep only the best." And thus the Ballygunge girls were modest and their modesty was eventually rewarded.

"I hope you aren't too tired to go to the jeweler's now, Babloo," Kola-mashi said when we returned to *mamabari*. "You're not used to running around in this kind of weather."

Since there were so many of us, we took two taxis. My Nagpur uncle carried what looked to me like a bowling bag, for bringing home the jewelry. "We're not taking full delivery today," he said to me. "Only some items. If it'd been full delivery, the proprietor would drive us back. A taxi wouldn't be safe."

The jeweler's watchman let us in through the iron gates, then locked them behind us. I feared the faces looking at us from the street. Locked among displays of gold and precious stones, I felt myself the target of collective envy in cluttered Bhowanipur.

The young assistant welcomed us. "Ah, you've come to help carry, or you've come to buy another necklace for yourself?" he joked as he laid out bangles for Jaya to try on. Clark and I liked to talk to him. He had not always worked in a jewelry store, he had told us. He hoped one day to be an auto mechanic and run his own garage. From gold salesman to auto mechanic would be a strange career pattern in the West. He had not lost the gift for transformation. He was a sensitive young man for a would-be mechanic; he told me that watching Clark write left-handed sent a chill down his spine.

The assistant laid out three pairs of earrings, one of them enameled and studded with diamonds; four gold necklaces; two more gold necklaces with matching earrings and rings; one pair of gem-studded *bauti* (wide bracelets); and one pair of gem-studded thin bangles.

"Which of these earrings are you going to wear for the wedding?" I asked Jaya.

"Well, actually, all of them. There's a professional bride dresser here who can fix up to six pairs on a bride's ears."

There were three other customers trying on necklaces and bangles. One was a very fair woman in a cheap cotton sari. She had pale brown eyes and pale brown hair. In a culture that prizes fair skin but despises light eyes (except in Raj Kapoor) and fair hair, I couldn't tell if she was considered pretty. She coyly tried on heavy necklaces and simpered in the mirror.

"How can so many people be buying such expensive stuff?" I whispered to the assistant.

"Black money," he whispered back.

The watchman was signaled to let us out through the collapsible iron grate. We stood in the gutter hailing cabs, caricatures of casualness, holding Jaya's future in a zippered little bag. I was not unaware of our comic peril at that moment; even a cluster of child-beggars tugging at our elbows seemed more sinister than pathetic. We stood in the gutter for fifteen of the longest minutes of my life. When we finally got a cab, we kept it all the way out to the mission where we picked up Clark, then rode it back to the *mamabari* where we dropped off relatives, and then on to the Bengal Club where Clark and I had a luncheon date.

The Bengal Club is the most exclusive in Calcutta, and it was Anjali, again, who invited us there to meet a businessman she thought might interest us.

"His origins are a mystery to me," she had said on the phone. "He sounds very British, but he could easily be an Anglo-Indian. Or a Jew. Anyway, he's in tobacco."

The businessman was waiting for us in the comfortably crowded bar of the Bengal Club. In appearance, his ambiguity persisted. He looked passably English. How Indian, or Anglo-Indian, he might have appeared in London was impossible to say. He radiated an effortless authority; also mystery, in a society which had an incurable impulse to locate and fix. He seemed to know everyone. They sent deferential nods in his direction as they discussed, quite noisily, import licenses, patent laws, labor agitations, and the races.

"Would I know your father?" he asked me as Anjali ordered scotch for the men, gin and lime for me, and a soft drink for herself.

I told him that he probably would not. Calcutta seemed to me a dim episode in my father's life. But all the same, because the tribal memory of the city never ceases to amaze me, I mentioned my father's name and the name of the pharmaceutical company in Cossipore. Yes, he *had* met my father, but he had known the partner better. Hadn't there been a swimming pool, and a tennis court, a guest-house-cum-bar with Omarr Khayyám murals? We were both relieved; I had passed the necessary test.

We were now free to go on to small talk. "I fear we're not dining in distinguished company today," he said. "That chap over there is known to secure young women for visiting dignitaries and young boys for some of the residents. . . . And I knew *that* chap when he was rigging football matches." He asked us if we had been to the races yet, and when we confessed that we had not, he urged Anjali to call the secretary of the Turf Club and make the necessary arrangements for that Sunday. "A most splendid chap, I assure you."

The talk turned to Americans. As Canadians, we were spared his general disapproval. Calcutta, after all, is still a *British* outpost. We persuaded ourselves to be intrigued by Americans. I expect that our guest, who called my husband "Clark Blaise" throughout the lunch, thought of the name as hyphenated. In any case, to most Calcuttans in that class, Canadians were quite distinct from Americans, more familiar, less respectable, and far less intimidating.

"I don't understand the people at American Express," he sighed. "They are catering to the under thirty-fives and"—he cleared his throat and glanced about—"our friends from Rajasthan." He was referring to Marwaris. He lamented the new "Americanized" climate in business circles; Calcutta, the most British of Indian cities, should have been spared. The new climate was epitomized by a lavish party that American Express had given to which he had not been invited.

"You weren't invited?" Anjali looked shocked. She and Nikhil, we knew, had attended. "Gosh, I can't believe that."

"True, my dear lady, I assure you. Americans pride themselves on having invented public relations, but they don't know anything about getting along with people."

We moved into the dining room, which was impressively gracious, and began our meal by nibbling on toast with pâté ("Quite bearable, I assure you"). We made our way through cream of asparagus soup. After that I turned down the ham, spaghetti with chicken liver sauce, and cold meats and salad, and settled instead for the prawn curry, rice, and *dal*. Over the ice cream with butterscotch sauce, and the cheese and crackers, we talked of hunting and shooting boxes. He liked to go to a shooting box down in the Sundarbans, the jungle area south of Calcutta. I did not talk about the vanishing tigers; it might have seemed American.

We drank our coffee in the Reynolds Room, uncannily reminiscent, but for its giant Reynolds canvas, of the dated elegance of McGill's Faculty Club. The club and the businessman were sturdy, persistent cultured ghosts. We were the intruders. After coffee, we parted friends. We knew we would meet again, at the Sunday races, at Anjali's or Nirmala's parties on dimly illuminated lawns.

"Do you ever think of leaving Calcutta?" Clark asked as we shook hands. "Did you ever think of settling in Britain?"

"I love this city, Clark-Blaise," the man said, and then he was gone.

Anjali, Clark, and I lingered in the club library. While Anjali checked out a book of essays by Ved Mehta for Clark, I fanned outward into another era, to books on military operations in Afghanistan, and zamindary settlements of Bengal, and the tomb of Tutankhamen, and the "heart" of England. This, then, was that spot forever green—the Bengal Club in 1973. I thought I ought to make a point of reading *Indian Alps and How We Crossed Them* by "A Lady Pioneer," but I also knew I was so absorbed by the lady pioneers around me that I would not get around to reading the book.

On our way to the car, Anjali showed us the prints by Daniells and Bart of late eighteenth- and early nineteenth-century Calcutta, in the lobby of the club. "Can you imagine Calcutta was ever like that?" she laughed. And as we closed the car door behind us, she said, "By the way, did I tell you that the club took its name plate off during the Naxal days? Things were that bad. Do you want to stop for a cup of tea at the house before the driver drops you at the mission?"


As a result of our lunch at the Bengal Club, the following Sunday instead of going for dinner to the *mamabari* we went to the races.

Anjali had called the Turf Club, and the "splendid chap" had arranged for us to go as Nirmala's guests in the owners' enclosure.

"I'm really offended," Nirmala said with a mock pout. "Why didn't you ask me directly?"

"I should have known you owned race horses, Nirmala. But I didn't know I might even *want* to be invited to the races until a day ago."

It is from my mother that I have acquired a middle-class Bengali's distrust of gambling. Except for one visit to the race tracks in Darjeeling during a summer vacation, my parents had never been to the races. Not that they disapproved of lotteries; they bought a ticket every year for the Irish Sweepstakes. But buying a ticket in Calcutta for a horse race on another continent is not the same as going to the tracks and developing an intimate physical connection with gambling.

To some, I knew, the races meant glamour and social position. As a schoolgirl in Loreto House, I had heard gossip about whose parents had won how much the preceding Sunday. And I had seen news pictures of Englishmen in top hats and ascots sitting imperiously in uncomfortable-looking enclosures. No Englishman need feel lost, even now, in the owners' enclosure of the Calcutta Turf Club.

"Well, now that you are here," Nirmala said, "let's introduce you to the others. Anjali, have Clark and Bharati met the Maharajah of Burdwan?"

We followed Nirmala and were introduced to the Maharajah, who, as judge for the event, sat in a special seat, higher than all the others. Then we met Nirmala's other friends, business associates of her husband, in the two boxes that seemed reserved for her. There were Indian men and women whose sartorial splendor had become familiar to us after these months in Calcutta. In India, appearances count, and the ambition is to show off the best that you've got, as many times a day, or week, as possible. There were a few Englishmen in the paddocks (returned to Calcutta for the winter season) whose leathery masks of tropical service probably branded them in England as surely as they did in India, and one Briton in a blazer who made me think of the word "cad" out of nineteenth-century novels of manners.

"I think I'm going to take a loaf down there," said an Englishwoman wearing thick make-up and very dark glasses, pointing to the direction of the stairs. There was an enormous crowd below us and to our right. But this crowd seemed to me more nakedly greedy, less sinister, than the crowd outside the Metro Cinema.

"Most Sundays I'm here," Nirmala said to Anjali and me as the Englishwoman strolled away. "My husband always has some guest or other to entertain here. Next time you must call me directly."

A compactly glamorous young woman whom I recognized as a former school chum of my younger sister told me that she had spent two years in New York with her husband, and that in those two years she had not worn any of the fancy saris that her mother had helped her pack ("I think I spent the entire time in faded blue jeans," she giggled). She was in fancy silks that day; America had given her at least one sophisticated tale to tell.

A very attractive woman beside Nirmala leaned across her to tell me, "Only thing that's gone down in recent years is the price of tickets." She swept her delicate long fingers in a gesture that took in the ragtag crowd in other enclosures. "From ten rupees to five rupees." She wore her raven-black hair in a long pageboy made famous in India by Maharani Gayatri Devi of Jaipur, now one of the leaders of a conservative opposition party. Under the rich emerald sari with gold border, her frame seemed unusually lean and unflabby for an Indian.

Clark and I watched six races, betting token amounts to display a mood of gay incaution. We were rewarded with a small win in one Quinella.

"My horse always seems to come in second to the last," Anjali said. "I should have asked that Chinese man for tips. Have you met him yet? He owns the biggest Chinese restaurant and he's good about giving tips to helpless ladies like us. Nikhil never comes to the races. I don't know why but he's absolutely adamant."

The seventh race did not take place as scheduled, because of a riot having to do with the photo finish of the sixth race. In the next enclosure, people rushed toward the frail white fences.

"It's fixed! It's fixed!" shouted a corpulent man in a three-piece suit with a yellow rose in his buttonhole. His graying hair was slightly too long. "We don't believe the photo finish!"

"Fixed! Fixed!" chanted the crowd in the enclosure.

The corpulent man kicked the white fence that separated our enclosure from his. Some people tried to heave him on their shoulders, but toppled back on the grass before they could lift him. Others tried to scramble over the fence and were urged back by the police who had formed a single file along the fence at the first hint of trouble.

The riot had started so far away, and over such a tiny incident, and on such a beautiful day, that I had found myself unwilling to treat it seriously. But within minutes hundreds of frenzied rioters were pushing against a fence a few dozen feet away. Given leadership, they could have easily stormed our enclosure. Perhaps if I had not been among men like K.B., Nirmala's husband, who had not missed his customary golf during the worst days of Naxal terror, I might have been the first to panic. As it was, we retreated decorously to the upper grandstand, which afforded a better view.

"These people can't accept defeat," someone said bitterly to Clark's questions about what was going on. "They want to know why did the number two horse go so wide in the turn. They think that there's some hanky-panky going on."

"This is probably the most honest race track in the world," asserted the lean, attractive woman. "These people are quite mad."

The police, wearing helmets and carrying riot shields and *lathis*, successfully discouraged the angry crowd from scaling the low fence and storming our enclosure. Rioters surged in another direction, scaled the fence that separated the horses from the bettors and spectators, and lay down on the tracks to dramatize their anger.

"What can you do with people who bring such a crass attitude to the races?"

The officials had a workable Calcutta solution. They canceled the seventh, which was also the final, race. The cancellation meant we were free to stroll down to the restaurant on the premises. We left our vantage positions on the balcony; we left the riot to the rioters.

"They serve very nice tidbits with tea," Nirmala told me as we ambled toward the restaurant. Her husband and the man from the Bengal Club brought Clark and a leathery Englishman bulletins from the tracks. The corpulent gentleman had apparently been beaten up by the mob, losing his vest and jacket and tearing his shirt. The mob was now beginning to disperse.

"He should know that mobs can turn on their leaders," said the businessman from the Bengal Club.

The attractive woman turned to Clark and said, "You're a journalist, aren't you? You must write this incident up. It's so disgraceful. Some people haven't a clue about what we have to face at the race tracks. If you write it up, I can arrange for its publication."

Her hand was still poised in the air, unstudied contempt rippling from finger down through wrist and forearm. The crowd was dispersing, even the protesters on the track. Beyond the crowd were the bamboo structures of enclosures and white blooms climbing to their roofs; beyond that in the silvery distance of Calcutta's cool weather were trams; then conical shapes that someone told me were army tents. This was another Calcutta. The track was a dazzling green. Beyond the track were green pastures and rows of dark green trees. This was a green and silvery Calcutta of immense spaces, and humans confined by class and wealth into manageable enclosures.

At lunch the next day in a new restaurant for us, a stranger from the adjoining table leaned over and smiled. "I trust you had a profitable day at the races yesterday, Mr. And Mrs. Blaise," he said. "And that your book is going well." We did not learn his name. He was a Calcutta presence, simply announcing himself.

The next morning, a survivor of the race tracks, I accompanied Rina to the home of Meena, a very rich and very young Marwari wife with whom I had chatted briefly after my speech on creative writing.

Like Anjali, Rina often played a tireless Virgil to my grateful Dante. Rina and I had gone through Loreto House school together, then later Loreto College. In those days I had thought her an enviable free spirit. She'd had an unexceptionable Bengali name, which masked the fact that she was only half-Bengali; her mother was from some unidentified (my sense of geography has always been vague) South Indian city. Even back then she had worn very short hair, gone out with boys, and smoked. To these accomplishments she had now added driving her own car and marriage to a Punjabi. The elasticity of her heritage, I had felt in those days, had freed her from a predictable Calcutta future. When I heard later about her marriage, it seemed aesthetically appropriate. Her younger sister married a European, and her two closest friends married Englishmen, one of whom owned a London town house.

"I like my job," she said as we cruised down Gariahat Road in her husband's Fiat. "I'd have to sit at home all day and wonder what I was going to wear for dinner that evening. I don't care what Bengalis say about Marwaris, I think the Bengalis ought to take a good hard look at themselves." Her work as organizer of the ladies' group brought her in touch with Marwari women who combined, in proportions different from Anjali's or her own, the disparate native and modern codes. She knew at least two women whose sons had decided to sign up for hotel management programs instead of the conventional liberal arts courses.

Meena's servant was not at the front door of the three-storied house when we pulled into the driveway. But the door was open, and Rina and I cautiously entered the empty hallway. Underpopulated hallways seemed inauspicious in a Calcutta mansion. "Meena's fantastic. Very unusual. But the rest of the family might be kind of hostile," Rina warned.

I saw a tidy pile of sandals near a door. "Should we get rid of ours here too?" I asked.

"Might be a good idea," she said. "We have to go up to the top floor where Meena and her husband have their own apartment."

We walked past rooms that looked like kitchens, where women crouching and chopping vegetables looked up from the floor and quickly looked away. On the next level, through open doors, I saw the huge white *gaddas* of the typical Marwari residence. We kept climbing the staircase and were greeted in the hallway of the third floor by Meena. She was wearing a printed silk sari and her hair was loosely knotted at the nape of her neck.

"Why did you take your sandals off?" she said in a soft, persuasive voice. "You didn't have to, you know." I glanced surreptitiously at her feet. She was wearing ankle socks and no sandals.

She led us into the living room of her private apartment within the joint-family residence. It was not a large room, and there was no *gadda*; instead there was a sofa and armchairs, a glass-topped coffee table (under the glass were imported humorous cards: YOU CAN'T FOOL ME—I'M TOO STUPID and IN GOD WE TRUST, REST STRICTLY CASH); a wall system for displaying knickknacks and sparsely stocked with books, a large Rajasthani painting on one wall, and ivory figurines and miniature paintings on occasional tables. She ordered lemonade and refreshments to make us comfortable.

"I went to Loreto College," she said after the servant had disappeared. "I studied English literature. I liked what you said about writing the other day. You were so honest about what it is like to be an Indian writer in America, I immediately told Rina that I'd be happy to meet you."

She started, hesitantly, to describe her schooling. She had gone to Marwari schools before being sent to the Loreto nuns. Loreto had opened up a world of new ambitions.

"I even did debating there."

But when she was seventeen her parents, who were known to be powerful and progressive within the Marwari community, had married her off to a young man from a conservative Marwari family. "For these people an educated *bahu* [bride] is scandalous," she said. Her in-laws had not wanted her to continue at college; her husband had been neutral on this issue. She had interpreted his neutrality as permission to fight the in-laws. And she had won. She had not only passed her B.A. examinations but had completed course work at Loreto for a postgraduate teaching degree. In two months, if everything went smoothly, she would be equipped to teach school.

"But it's going to be a very hard battle," Meena said. She had striking eyes, and their bold stare brought out all the awkwardness and inadequacy of my responses.

I could hear the servant in some other room as he prepared our refreshments.

"How can I explain to you, Bharati, what an orthodox Marwari home is like? Even reading a book is considered criminal. They think I'll spoil my eyes and have to wear glasses."

I told her that Rina had taken me to visit another Marwari woman who had confided to me that at first her in-laws would not let her read the newspaper.

"They're afraid books will take me away from my husband. A *bahu*'s duty is to serve. They think education gets in the way of husband worship."

"How did you get away to the lecture?" I asked.

"Well, the group that Rina's organized has a lot of social status, so they are quite happy for me to be in on that. They even refused to make the car available on time when I had to take exams so that I'd fail."

Her voice was flat, as if she had passed beyond anger.

She talked of the fasts that she was expected to observe. To refuse to fast (which was generally dedicated to the increase of the husband's well-being) was to assert oneself as an atheist. The food observances were so strict in her house that if she ever wanted an onion or garlic she would have to smuggle it in.

"How many people are there in this house? Can you and your husband move out into your own place?"

There were twenty-five people whom she counted off on the joints of her delicate fingers. No, her husband would not consider moving out. They had lived briefly in Bangalore—he had been working on family business there—and that had been a happy time. She had done volunteer work with widows. But her husband had not wanted to stay so far from his friends and from his community in Calcutta. "I think he's overdependent," she said, then looked embarrassed by her own words. He was not a bad person, just very traditional. That was the impression she had meant to convey, but her unhappiness had come through. "Anyway, you're a writer, you have intuition, you can fill in what I leave out. He gets upset if he has to fetch water for himself, you know."

She told us more about her husband. Like most young men from his community, he had studied business administration in the United States. He was fond of certain signs of Westernization. He wanted her to have mod hairdos and wear mod saris.

The servant brought in two trays full of hot and cold midmorning snacks. "Try the vegetable pizza," Meena said, once more the gracious hostess. "Everything is homemade, so you have nothing to worry about."

Rina and I tried all the snacks. I told myself that it did not matter that I was putting on so much weight in India. Here food was a shorthand for love, and for the first time in my adult life I was feeling a capacity to give and reciprocate love. I would diet when I got back to Montreal. There, I knew, I could easily lose the twenty-five to thirty pounds.

"I would like to have been a writer," Meena said as we were get-

ting ready to leave. "But that is impossible. Now I'm determined to
be a teacher, to modify my community." The phrase slid out with
the uncertain ease of long and private practice. "That is imperative.
I must modify the Marwari community. If they don't let me teach, I
shall be at the end of my tether. I shall do something drastic. But I'll
do it. I really will."

I cried when I got back to the mission. I was writing a second
novel, *Wife*, at the time, about a young Bengali wife who was sensitive enough to feel the pain, but not intelligent enough to make
sense out of her situation and break out. The anger that young wives
around me were trying so hard to hide had become my anger. And
that anger washed over the manuscript. I wrote what I hoped would
be a wounding novel.

There was only one problem, my problem; how could I explain
this anger to critics in New York or Montreal who did not know that
a young Bengali woman could rebel by simply reading a book or refusing to fast?

## Gossip

In Hindu Calcutta, to be a wedding guest is to be a participant in a
psychodrama. In December I was a wedding guest. The bride had a
sweet disposition. I had praised her skill in arts and crafts, which was
on aggressive display in living room cabinets. The groom was a slim
and handsome pilot of whom everyone said, "He's very, very fair,
just like Clark, he can pass for a *sahib*." The bride and the groom,
however, were assigned minor roles. In the days before the wedding I
sometimes saw the bride packing new saris in a shiny trunk, or folding and refolding (at the request of her cousins) her new and almost
elegant underclothes, or simply standing in a corridor and staring at
crows. She seemed dazed, as if the wedding preparations had slipped
beyond her control and become too complicated. Only months before, I had seen her with her parents in another town, and she had
helped me shop for local curios, had bargained spiritedly for two
kilos of apples. Now she talked little, and when she did it was to
confirm details of the wedding preparations.

"Yes, we've checked out the rates of two bride dressers," I heard her say to one of her aunts. "One wants eighty rupees, and the other wants one hundred. But they'll both bring their own make-up kits, and I think that includes doing the bridal hairdo."

Sometimes she asked questions. "Shall I use hairspray? What do you think, Babloo-didi? Shall I use it just for the night of the wedding so that my hair isn't mussed up or anything?"

"It's not the groom who scares me, it's the groom's mother," the bride's mother said in tears.

"You should have stood firm about the dowry from the beginning," said one of the bride's many uncles.

"But she is our only child," sobbed the bride's mother. "If her mother-in-law isn't happy, then she won't be happy."

"What can she do since they won't be living in the same town?" the uncle protested. "It's only a matter of sticking out the first two to four weeks."

"But she's a tough lady!" wailed the bride's mother. "She might not let our daughter come and visit us too often."

The bride, who was an older bride than I had been, or any of her cousins had been, remained silent throughout these discussions. Tradition demanded passivity of Hindu brides, and though in her case tradition had been slightly bruised—hers was an intercaste marriage —she seemed not yet willing to rebel.

These discussions were inconclusive and interminable. At some point, the bride's mother would turn to me with a desperate look and interject in the middle of some relative's monologue, "If only *your* father could have been here! He wouldn't have let any of this happen! Everyone respects him and he always knows what to do!"

And even the relative whose speech had been interrupted would say to me without bitterness, "If your father were present here, I wouldn't fear anything. I'd just let the tough lady negotiate with him. He's so good at disarming tough people."

But my father could not attend the wedding. Nor could my mother, and Bart and Bernie. The strike situation in Chembur had worsened. It was impossible to request leave for even a week to attend a family wedding. My mother had explained it all in her neat, bulbous handwriting, and sent a cash gift. I repeated the latest bulletins I received on the strike situation, and echoed the bride's family's regret at the absence of my father. It was not his negotiating skill that they needed, it was his physical presence, the confidence that he radiated with his potbelly and his loud, guttural laughter. They needed a leader who could help them to open up and get in touch with their innermost feelings, who could anticipate trouble and force it to the surface and settle it without causing any permanent injury. A Hindu wedding is only incidentally an occasion for a bride and groom to be married off in the presence of others. Communal catharsis through communal drama: That seems to me its main purpose.

Sometimes we sat on the bed in the dining room (there were beds in every room to accommodate the assembled joint families) and drank hot tea and talked of the complicated etiquette of the wedding.

"We need two more married women to hold the brass plate for the wedding-morning rituals. How about you, Babloo? Will you join us or are you going to turn your nose up at such *tamasha?*"

I was glad to be asked to hold the brass plate. It meant that though I had lost my "full-Brahmin" status, they were willing to show their support of me in public. Being glad, I was able to turn down the invitation. "I think you ought to count me out. I don't really know any of the rites, I'd end up doing the wrong thing at the wrong time."

"No, no," said the bride's mother. "I know why you're refusing. I insist on your taking part. I don't care what people say, let them talk as much as they want to. They're already saying nasty things about this marriage being an intercaste one, and you see how I'm not paying any attention."

It was true that there were ugly rumors about the intercaste aspects of the marriage. It was rumored that an aunt had said to the bride's mother that if she permitted such a marriage, she would be damned.

"I heard that she said it was bad enough not having sons to light the funeral pyre, but to have made sure that there were no Brahmin grandsons to do that either!"

"Did she actually say that? What a thing to say! What about her own daughter? I heard that *her* marriage was a love match too. She was just lucky that her daughter fell in love with a Brahmin boy, that's all."

"I heard that two Brahmin couples have refused to come to the wedding."

"Are you sure that's the reason? I heard they were offended because the wedding invitation hadn't been personally delivered. I went twice to their house to hand them the invitation, but they were out both times. So I left it with the servant. With the price of gasoline what it is, I just couldn't go back a third time, you know."

"Well, good riddance to bad rubbish," said a convent-educated younger cousin of the bride. "Aren't you glad, Babloo-didi, that you married a foreigner? When I grow up I want a kind husband like Clark-da."

"Ah, don't we all want to be like Babloo and Clark, the love birds! I envy all the attention he pays her."

The day before the wedding it rained very hard. We stood in the hallway and watched the rain swirl in the gutters of the inner courtyard. Water dripped off crows and pigeons that nestled under the overhanging roof. It stayed in muddy puddles in the veranda.

The aunt who was rumored to have been upset about future funerary difficulties climbed the steep, wet staircase to the entrance of the flat, squeezed water out of her soggy sandals by pressing hard with the balls and heels of her feet, and said very seriously, "The weather seems unpropitious. We have to do something about the weather."

Only the unmarried girls had time to help her plot against the weather. The rest were still quarreling over the menu, still calling friends on the telephone to make sure there would be enough cars to run last-minute errands, and still collecting cans of cooking oil for the hired cooks. The ground floor of a house and its large adjoining garden had been rented for the wedding. People shuttled between the two houses complaining about the rain and cursing the Chembur strikers who were responsible for the absence of my father.

"This rain is going to ruin everything. It's just our luck to get such rains this week."

I wandered from the hallway to the living room which was rarely used and had the appearance of a storage room. A woman sat with her hips pushed against a rolled-up Kashmir rug and checking the wedding menu. "They should have had the dinner catered. This is going to be ridiculously expensive. My daughter's was catered, and did any guest complain about the quality of the food or of the service?" Then without looking up at me she said as if to acknowledge my presence, "Wear a red sari tomorrow, and lots of gold jewelry. We'll pretend you're the second bride since you didn't have a gala Hindu wedding in America."

A woman with curly hair and puffy eyes added, "I agree, the dinner should have been catered. At my eldest niece's wedding, I ordered the mutton from a trusted butcher but I still had to throw the whole thing out because it tasted just a little randy. The caterers are responsible. After all, they've their reputations to keep."

"Besides these people are too busy with other things. I hate to say all this in front of Babloo but do you know what I've heard? These people aren't as simple as they make out. They all go to Park Hotel. They keep bottles of liquor in their bedroom cabinets."

"I think you're mistaken," I ventured. "I've been in the room when they've opened up their cabinets and I've certainly never seen any liquor."

"I've heard what I've heard," she said, triumphantly shutting her puffy eyes.

A chubby young girl in pants poked her head through the open doorway and shouted, "The car should be back in about fifteen minutes. Does anyone here want to go to the wedding house in the next shift?"

We declined the trip to the *biyebari*. The women continued to gossip in their shrill, childish voices. There was no relief from gossip; it seemed to be the secret purpose of all family reunions. I continued to sit on the arm of a cracked leather chair. Like the rolled-up rug and the glass-faced bookcase with a complete set of the *Book of Knowledge*, the chair reminded me of a faded era.

"Why is her mother making such a fuss about the girl leaving for another city after the wedding? It's not as if the bride and groom are strangers. Who is she trying to fool with that story about it being an "arranged marriage?"

"In my opinion, it's a good thing that it's a love match. My daughter had seen the groom only twice before her wedding, and he whisked her off to Kalamazoo three weeks after the wedding."

I scrutinized the women as they scrutinized their list. They had thick, pleasant faces which they swiveled on thick necks hung with gold chains when they wanted to express their feelings.

The bride's mother, wearing gold bangles that jangled against her wrists and forearms, brought in a tray of unmatched teacups filled with hot tea premixed with milk and sugar.

"What a pity Bert and Baarnie can't be here," she said to me with tears in her eyes. She handed me a sloshing cup and saucer, then broke down completely, "How can I live without my daughter? She'll be in a faraway city."

The women made her sit on the floor with them and drink a cup of hot tea. "You're going to make yourself sick if you go on like this. A wedding is a happy occasion. You'll be able to visit your son-in-law and daughter anytime you want to, and probably soon there'll be grandchildren for you to play with."

"She's such a good girl," the bride's mother cried. "She's so obedient and submissive. Whichever way you want her to turn, she will turn. I just want her to be happy."

I heard the men in the hall outside, so I went to talk to them. One of the men said, "Two of the three borrowed cars should be back any minute. Why don't you go and take a look at the *biyebari* and tell us what you think of it?"

The bride's father was sitting in a corner of a sofa in the hall. He had large eyes which now looked suspiciously tearful. He said to me, "You are a writer. You must write about the good Bengali girls with middle-class training. Bengali girls are like foster children—you bring them up with love but they belong to someone else actually. After tomorrow, who will come to me and say, 'Daddy, here are your slippers,' when I come home from the office?"

The woman who had been checking the list darted out of the living room to say, "Babloo, I hope you're planning to spend the next two nights with us. Let Clark go back to the Ramakrishna Mission. This place is crowded and too full of mosquitoes for him. But you must stay with us, and join in all the fun."

I explained that I would not spend the night but that I would come very early in the morning and leave very late at night.

"Oh, it is because of the bathroom," the woman said, laughing. "Bert and Baarnie have no trouble with the Bengali toilets, but their mother doesn't like it!"

I made my way to the next room where an old woman was lying on her side on a hard four-poster and looking out of a window through which she could see only the rain-washed steep staircase and the neighbor's courtyard full of wet saris hanging on the line. I sat on the bed beside her and massaged the exposed oval of her shoulder. "Everything is going quite smoothly," I told her. "No major problems so far. They'll carry you into the *biyebari* tomorrow morning so you won't miss out on the fun."

"Flying is a dangerous job," she sighed. "If I were her father I'd have objected to pilots, soldiers, and sailors." She heaved her bulk to face me, then settled the pillow underneath her drooping cheek. She said, "Your hands are too warm. It's bile. I know it's an imbalance of bile. My father had it, the servant has it. You should eat two little pieces of raw turmeric every morning before breakfast."

After a while, the bride's aunt, who had been sitting just outside the bedroom and plotting with her daughters to change the weather, called out to me, "How about you, Babloo? Don't you have any bright ideas?"

I had to confess that I did not. I did not confess, however, that inclement weather made me feel helpless, and slightly resentful. She seemed pleased that I had offered no solution.

"I've heard that a sure way to stop the rains is to steal *choon* and hide it where it can't be found by the owner," she said, speaking slyly. *Choon* is a white solution with an astringent taste that is used to flavor *pan*.

"Well, since lots of people eat *pan* in this house, there's got to be a jar of *choon* also," said her youngest daughter.

"That's no good," cried the woman. "It's got to be stolen, not taken."

She devised a plan; she would steal it from Sambhunath, who had once been a servant in the house but who had now become a mild-mannered semiprosperous *pan*-shop owner in Ballygunge.

"But that's no good either," cried her daughter. "If you steal his pitcher of *choon*, he'll lose a day's business."

"Well, I suppose, when the car comes back I could have the fellow drive me to Bhowanipur and I could steal some *choon* from my friend's house. I could steal it and hide it among the potted plants in the veranda."

"Babloo," called the old woman from inside the bedroom. I parted the hand-loom curtains and saw her try to prop herself up on the pillows. "Don't eat the turmeric. You've been away so long, who knows perhaps your stomach can't tolerate raw turmeric anymore. Don't take any risks. Canada has a nice climate. Go back there as soon as you can. Otherwise your body will rot like ours."

Perhaps a new scheme for stopping the rains was hatched by the ingenious mother and daughters. I do not know. I was called downstairs by the prettiest of the unmarried girls, who told me that one of the cars had returned, and that she would like me to accompany her on her expedition to get two cans of cooking oil from an aunt who had long expressed her feelings of alienation by staying away from family gatherings. The two of us dashed through the rains and into the parked car, and I was surprised that the borrowed chauffeur who came with the borrowed car did not get out in the rain to hold the door open for us, let alone rush to the front door with an open umbrella. When I was with Anjali or Nirmala, the staff was invariably obsequious. But in other parts of the city, the staff was obviously capable of arrogance, or narrow self-interest.

We stopped by the *biyebari*. The pretty girl's father stood in an uncanopied and muddy garden, arguing with the team of professional cooks. "Hurry up and get the cooking oil," he ordered his daughter. "The oil was supposed to have been here long ago. So was the firewood. How can there be any success if I'm the only one doing a decent job?"

The pretty daughter's face looked mean. She said, enunciating clearly, "Don't shout at me. Shout at the people who let you down."

The cooks stared impassively. The father said finally, "Take the car to your aunt's and bring her, the kids, and the cooking oil as soon as you can. Don't dawdle. We can't proceed with our work until you bring the oil here."

On the way back to the car, I asked what her father had meant by bringing back the aunt and her kids. The last time I had talked to that aunt she had vowed undying enmity toward all members of the pretty girl's family. The pretty girl smiled at me and explained that

the situation had changed (in Calcutta situations are always changing and it is impossible to tell enemy from friend) and that the aunt
had conceded sufficiently to tradition to spend the night in the wedding house. "We're going to be one big happy family. Only you are
holding out, Babloo-didi. I know the toilet doesn't flush properly in
this rented house but at least it's your kind of Western-style bathroom."

We intended to stop at the alienated aunt's house only long
enough to pick up the cooking oil, the aunt, and her children. But
while the aunt was still debating whether she should spend the night
at the wedding house after all, and pointing to an enormous trunk in
which she had packed the overnight clothes and wedding-party finery
for herself and her daughters, her widowed uncle-in-law sent word
through his servant that he wanted us to stay for tea. Her uncle-in-
law was a very famous man, very rich though now retired. He was
not a man one could refuse.

"You must stay and have tea," said the aunt, fiddling with the
clasps of the trunk. "Otherwise I'll never hear the end of it. He's not
doing it for my sake. It's for Babloo. You know how colonial he is,
he's decided she's half *memsahib*."

"But what about my father," wailed the pretty girl. "He wants us
back immediately. Let's drink the tea as fast as we can. Remember,
girls, if you don't want to get me in trouble, swallow that tea in two
minutes."

So we stayed for tea, and I was made to sit at the elderly gentleman's right and to hear his lecture on the decaying moral fiber of the
city. The youngest of the children spilled her tea and there was a
tense scene as the gentleman's gentleman tried but failed to rinse
out the brown spreading stain from the white tablecloth. We were
very late bringing over the promised cooking oil, and the pretty girl
received an unkind scolding from her father.

I stood apart from the others in the inner courtyard where the actual wedding ceremony was scheduled to take place the next evening. The rain had not yet stopped. There were pools of water everywhere. Even the walls appeared damp and water-stained. Through
the narrow front door and beyond the private alley, I could see a tiny
wet rectangle of green garden where the groom was supposed to sit
and where the guests were supposed to be fed. Pariah dogs wandered

in and were shivering in the alley. An occasional beggar walked in and quickly walked away. It did not seem likely to me then that the professional decorators could string up enough lights and hoist enough canopies to make the house, courtyard, and garden a dry and cheerful enough place for a wedding.

It did not seem likely to me then that the next day I would hear Professor Ali and his band play the *shanai* in the inner veranda, that I would see the private bodyguard brought in to keep an eye on the bride's jewelry give up his chair to Clark, that a man who claimed to be a distant relative would ask me to put him up for a month in Montreal during the 1976 Olympics, that I would hear the lone Marwari guest praise Bengali women as "very cultured, very faithful to their peoples," and that the wife of the man who had invited himself to Montreal would caution me against touching any religious vessels since I was no longer "full Brahmin," and that a mother would ask me to find her daughter a scholarship at McGill or Harvard.

But in Calcutta the assurance of future magic is never totally absent. On the day of the wedding, the rain dwindled to a drizzle, and finally ceased. The canopies went up, and the lights went on. And the wedding was a raucous, joyous, vulgar, typically Bengali festival.

*EPILOGUES*

# CLARK BLAISE

After Jaya's wedding, our vacation from parenthood began to weigh on us guiltily. Bart and Bernie, who'd been staying in Chembur since a September holiday in Kashmir, had run out of books. They had no friends, no stimulation. Calico Colony was surrounded by strikers; an executive had died and his secretary been scarred in a fire-bombing of his car just outside the factory gates. No tutor could be sent in, and the children could not be allowed outside. The moment we'd left Kashmir they'd started fighting with each other, stopped eating, and were regressing in every way. Never robust, they now looked sickly. Always independent, they'd become whining and helpless. The things that made India fascinating for us were, of course, the very things middle-class Indians spent their lives trying to avoid. The cluttered, demanding, and exhausting street life of Calcutta could only bore and confuse an average pair of Canadian kids.

And so I'd sent away to the Swiss embassy in New Delhi for boarding school brochures, and during those quiet November and December afternoons in the mission, after the morning visits and the

Park Street lunch, and before the evening plays and parties, we'd applied ourselves to the selection of a French-speaking boarding school for the next six months, signing away that accumulated mound of unspent dollars from our double income.

On December 30, then, jacketless, the boys and I left Bombay for Tulu's in Hamburg. She met us at the airport with winter clothes and we spent the rest of New Year's Eve in Hamburg buying ski sweaters, pants, and ice skates. Then we flew on to Geneva where another parent met us and drove us back to Montreux and on up to Caux. The school was housed in a small châlet three thousand feet above Lake Geneva, in permanent view of Mont-Blanc across the lake, on the steep brown slopes of the Swiss-side Alps. The snows began another thousand feet higher and were descending by the day; there would be skiing every day. No one spoke a word of English.

I found a cheap room in an old folk's *auberge* a few miles on the unfashionable side of Montreux. I was the youngest boarder by a good forty years. I served as a bread breaker on nights when the hard rolls proved exceptionally crusty; I patiently held the swinging doors to the dining room, the automatic doors to the elevator, the cubicle doors in the shared men's room. Every night, the palsied tapping of fifty soup spoons against the sides of the hostel's crockery sounded strangely like an overture to a geriatric demonstration. The waitresses—ruddy Swiss-German girls practicing their French—snickered in the kitchen. One old lady died during the month.

In the mornings I watched my kids skiing with their schoolmates at the top of the funicular run at Rochers-de-Naye; by night I wrote letters to Bharati in Chembur, read Simenon novels, and went to Bruce Lee movies dubbed in French, with German subtitles. In the front rows, the waitresses from the *auberge* would be smoking dope and necking with motorcycle toughs in leather jackets. Somehow, it didn't seem Swiss. I worried about the children, lost in a strictness they'd never known. They screamed for release after each of my visits; finally the *directrice* asked me not to come. I wrote lies to Bharati: the great times the kids were having, the *rightness* of the decision, even if it meant we'd come back to Canada broke and without a house. We had condemned the kids to an idyllic hell, rather than keep them with the most loving, protecting grandparents in the world. They were skiing, speaking French, gaining weight.

*What the hell*, I told myself, they'd survive. Do them good, in fact. I was rich and heedless for the first time in my life, shipping my children off to people I didn't know and probably didn't like because, frankly, *they were inconvenient*. After all, the Swiss schools understand such kids and such parents; that's what they're for.

Released from daily visits, I prowled the bookstores of Geneva in those unreal January fogs, stocking up on new American paperbacks, mailing back to Calcutta the new Travis McGee and Lew Archer titles. I flew up to Basel and toured the museums. One night I direct-dialed my mother in Canada. Europe was nothing, after Calcutta, an old shoe. That same night I flew back to Bombay. The stewardess gave me a copy of *Le Figaro*. Watergate, according to their American correspondent, was a left-wing, intellectual plot. The American intelligentsia had never forgiven Nixon, Rebozo, and Abplanalp for the sin of having become rich after having been born poor. I was thankful for *Le Figaro*, Bruce Lee and the waitresses, the dismal fogs of a Swiss January. It eased the pain of leaving Europe.

We went back to Calcutta immediately, but something had changed. There'd been a shake-up in the month we'd been away from the mission. No one in the front office knew us or had any record of our earlier stays. Our old room-sweeper vouched for us, as did Charles, the Australian sarodist. The rest of the staff was out on strike. The manager of the guest house had been fired for picketing some rents, and the swamis had taken over direct control. Group Captain, Shirt Ad, Super Slurp, and all the other attractions had been cleaned out. We had to present documents in order to stay on as scholars; we dug out publishers' letters, our books, our project statement, old receipts. We were interviewed by the new managerial staff. It was as though we'd been away five years.

We were given a room on the ground floor, in the nearly deserted International wing. It was February 1974, just a year after our fire. On that first afternoon back in Calcutta, I made my way across Gol Park to Ganguram's Sweetshop and bought our usual clay *bhars* of sweet yoghurt. We had to eat them inside, since the winter mosquitoes made even the afternoons unbearable. I threw the empty clay pots out the back window, just inside the iron grates, where they shattered. A few minutes later, one of the pariah dogs squeezed

under the grate to lick the shards. Crows darted down to scoop up
the smaller pieces. A few minutes after that, a beggarwoman sent her
tiny daughter between the black iron slats, where she fished out the
larger fragments. Then, holding them in both hands in front of her
face, the way children eat orange or coconut sections, she licked
them with gusto before passing them out to her mother, who also
gave a dispirited lick before dropping the fragments into the street.

Our social life picked up immediately. The winter "season" was at
its late-January, February zenith, when the titled codgers from England, those who'd made their fortunes in tea and jute in the old
days, would return to Calcutta for a month's shooting, riding, and
socializing. The palatial homes of Ballygunge seemed almost in competition with their strings of lights on the hedges, spotlights on the
lawn, bands, caterers, and extra retinues of liveried servants, as each
night a different Sir and Lady were entertained in the same gracious
manner. In the winter of 1973–74, with England reduced to candlelight because of the oil embargo, and India facing predictions of the
absolute collapse, there was a frenzied, Weimar gaiety to the season;
everyone spoke of it as perhaps the last of the old-time parties. We
drank, we joked; the British were speaking as wistfully now of the
vanished days and of the uncertain future as Bengalis always had.

We couldn't keep up with the invitations. They were coming at
the rate of six a week, then ten, then three a day. They grew more
extravagant; cocktail parties before the races, at eleven in the morning. Discotheque parties in the Park Hotel; private dinners with
black money barons, with movie czars and actors from Bombay. At a
noon-hour Sunday cocktail party, I overheard a loud young journalist
explaining to a group of accountants the nuances between Ehrlich-
man's behavior and Haldeman's, how "Bud" Krogh's honesty ranked
with John Dean's. He also admitted responsibility for an *Amrita
Bazar* headline earlier in the week: MINISTER'S PROCESSION STONED.
"Yeah, man," he said to me, "were they ever!" I asked him how high
the grass was growing these days and he said, "To the board room,
man, right to the editor's desk."

He invited us to "the Party" as he called it, at an address I could
not be given in advance, for fear of a raid or gate-crashers. Just meet

at his house half an hour before, and his wife would drive us. Yes, I said, of course.

The party turned out to be in a high rise near one of the jails where hundreds of political prisoners, it was said, were still interned. The journalist disappeared into a bedroom. The living room (it was in the apartment of a Muslim advertising man; we were beginning to move in slightly alienated, rootless circles) was filled with elegant young women, some in saris but mostly in pant-suits, smoking, drinking, and playing cards. The men were in serious games, tossing their crumpled twenty-rupee notes into plates in the middle of the table. The smoke was thick, but it was familiar old tobacco smoke, nothing else.

People started drifting into the bedroom, and smiling, looking satisfied. I waited for more noise, then went in. A roulette wheel and a craps table had been set up. My man was a croupier, with green eye-visor, sleeve garter, and Monte Carlo French at his command. "*Faites vos jeux, mesdames et messieurs!*" he kept repeating, and now the men deserted the rupee ante games in the front and were buying their chips from "the Bank" with hundred-rupee notes.

I drew close to the Bank, a young man who'd driven over with us with the croupier's wife. He was hip, with the vocabulary, jeans, shades, hair, beads, and a cool manner that would ingratiate himself in any company. He identified the players for me, gave soul-slaps to some, spoke to everyone in whatever Indian language he was spoken to. Even I could recognize some of the players: some Hindi movie stars, the same ones whose pictures we'd seen in *Stardust* or on street posters on every urban light standard in India; some tiny, muscular Anglo-Indians who had to be jockeys; and some of the elaborately dressed, double-knitted, sideburned, white-shoed, and white-belted scions of Marwari and Gujarati fortunes, now following a predictable Western pattern of dissolution; various younger brothers and ex-wives of the wealthier Maharajahs; two redneck Americans—tall, crew-cut acneed youths who soul-slapped the Bank, blurted out their "Hey, baby, what's comin' down?" to him, then caught my watching intently and said (one to the other), "No *dices nada*." They were marine guards at the United States consulate; they'd been in the corps for seven years, posted first in French-speaking Africa, then Guatemala, and now, since they liked so-called "hardship postings" (only place to be; no one watches and you make extra bread), Calcutta. They spoke more fluent and colloquial Hindi than Bharati. Clever Ivy League CIA plants? Smart, hustling rednecks? Or just a twentieth-century American version of the kind of displaced young brigand Calcutta has always attracted?

I had delivered a series of public lectures for the USIS on the form and language of the contemporary American short story, and now I was being driven back to the mission through those narrow streets lined with bookstalls and further congested by parked cars, cows, and hundreds of milling students who read and browsed as they skirted the impacted gutters of the street. My companion in the back seat was a woman my age who'd been attending the lectures; she lived in Bhowanipur and was to be dropped on the way to the mission. She too wrote stories and poems, though in Bengali; some had been published in *Desh*.

"I suppose it is easier for the sexes to mingle in the West, is it not?" she said.

I said that I supposed it was, in many ways, but that Calcutta was a marvelously open city.

"I mean sexually," she said. "It is easier for married people to have sexual congress outside of their mutual marriages, is it not? At least one reads that it is so."

I told her she was probably right.

"I am not offending you by asking, am I?"

"Certainly not."

"A gentleman such as yourself—you would have many extra-marital relationships, would you not?"

"Many men in my position—writers, professors—do," I admitted. I could not yet tell if the next question was up to me; if I were merely a sociological resource, or an obvious target of her affections. "There are many who do not, of course," I said.

I couldn't tell, because all the social clues that would accompany such questions at home—gestures, voice, occasion—were so different. I could not tell if this woman—attractive but not done up, a mainstream middle-class Bengali Hindu, not smoking, not wearing her hair down, not in pants or even a silk sari—was asking me in the most direct way I'd ever been asked, to go home with her; or if she was using me as a safe, sexless respondent. Perhaps my whiteness had rendered me *hors de combat*. Perhaps my whiteness was an irresistible attraction.

It was then that I became aware of a persistent hammering noise from the street outside. It came from a tram, speeding toward us down the center of the street. The metal grate that attached its second car had been twisted perpendicular; it flared three feet out into the traffic flow, and the cars approaching it couldn't swerve into the mass of pedestrians to avoid it. And so we inched trustingly forward, hemmed by the crowd on one side and the cars on the other. *Thwack, shatter:* Each car in its turn had its right-side headlight and grillwork smashed, and a car-length metal furrow screeched along the fenders and doors. Our waxed, black government-issue car was, in its turn, slammed hard enough to rock it, as the indestructible grate chewed its way through the doors and fenders. I asked my companion to tell the driver, in Hindi, that I would write a note testifying to his innocence. She didn't bother, and the driver only turned to us and smiled. I decided, at the same time, that she was only a curious housewife, unaware of how touching, how brash, her questions sounded. Thank God I hadn't misinterpreted.

She told the driver to let her off in a building just off Chowringhee. Strangely enough, it was the building occupied on the third floor by the Doctors Sengupta. Her business was with the consulate on the second floor; her husband's passport had been left there for visa-stamping. "He will be leaving for Europe in a few days," she told me. As we pulled away, I mentioned that we knew some people in that same building. "Dr. Sengupta," she said, "he has published some of my poetry in his magazine." We drove on to Bhowanipur, past the gold stores and cinema halls that I knew so well, turning into a fashionable side street off Elgin Road. We passed the house of an uncle of Bharati's, and she began to tell me a story about his daughter, a story I already knew. We passed an even bigger home nearby. "A tragic man lives there, all alone," she said, and she related the tale of a lonely young woman married to a rich old gentleman, and her decision, long before such things were fashionable, to leave her husband. My companion had written it as a story, but it was true. I knew it was true, because the lonely gentleman was an in-law of Bharati's youngest aunt; he'd been to Jaya's wedding. We passed a block near her flat, where I'd been inside nearly every house: a Tata man, a film editor, a painter, an editor, two relatives, a city politician. *Ink blots, ink blots:* They were linking up. I realized too there were many strong, bold women who, as usual, I had failed to understand.

I recalled the final line of a favorite Updike story, one that I hadn't quoted in the lectures, and one that I wanted to deliver from a bashed-in car on a Bhowanipur street. *Dear Vera Glavanakova,* Updike's imaginary writer Henry Bech writes to the Bulgarian poetess he must soon be leaving, *It is a matter of earnest regret for me that you and I must live on opposite sides of the world.*

In our last week in Calcutta, I ran out of tape for the various interviews I still wanted to complete. My Uher 3000 ran best on BASF reel-to-teel tape; BASF was, by definition, a smuggled item in India. And for smuggled electrical items, one goes to the general area behind New Market, a Muslim quarter of great crowdedness, where every corner contains radio or phonograph shops.

The shops were generally open to the street, with the shopkeeper and his assistant, plus a *chokra* or two, all standing behind a greasy glass display case of dusty tubes and radios.

"You have tape?" I asked from the broken sidewalk in front of his shop.

"Tep, *saab.*" He nods vigorously. "*Hanh.*"

"BASF?"

Another swivel of the head, the quick flick of the wrist, as though unscrewing an imaginary light bulb, accompanied with a radiant smile of recognition. "BASF, *saab. Hanh.*"

"BASF reel-to-reel?" I asked, now stepping under his wooden awning, resting my arms on his case. "You have BASF reel-to-reel?"

"*Hanh, saab.* BASF reel-to-reel." He would stand, smiling, but not offering to bring it out.

"How much is it? *Kitna he?*"

"*Kitna?* How much is what, *saab?*"

"BASF tape."

"No have tep, *saab.*"

"No BASF?"

"What is BASF?"

A *chokra* presented me with a package of Indian tape, the size of a Benson & Hedges pack. "Forty-three rupee, *saab*."

"High quality?"

"High, high, *saab*. Very high. Best tep."

I left it, crossed the street, and repeated the whole charade. BASF, I soon learned, they took to mean "Good day," which they courteously repeated. The intricacies that followed, reel-to-reel, must have seemed only an elaboration. From that first store, *chokras* had fanned out across the quarter, so that by my third shop I was first greeted: "BASF, *saab*."

"You have?"

"*Hanh*, I have."

"May I see it?"

"See what, *saab*?"

I walked a five-block square, tramping through the black-market haven of Calcutta, in hopes of finding tape, getting nowhere but feeling myself somehow *in the spirit*, enjoying it hugely. I was a known quantity; my fame had spread so quickly that a gentleman in a rickshaw, under an umbrella, and wearing a business suit, peered down at me from the high perch of the rickshaw seat and said, "Young sir, the BASF reel-to-reel you seek is available one block in that direction and half a block in. *Sattar and Sons*. They will have."

And, for slightly over twenty dollars, they did.

It is a blessing that I arrived in Calcutta by plane; it is a blessing that I did not see Howrah Station, Calcutta's rail terminus, until I was ready to leave. Howrah is the center of life and the end of hope, the place of arrival and surrender; it is Calcutta at its densest and most paradoxical. It is where village India arrives every day by the uncountable thousands and where others manage to return, but not escape. It is more like a circle of hell than any place on earth that I can imagine.

The entire family went down to the station to see us off. The cross-country train was to leave at 5 P.M., but because of a knifing of a guard and subsequent strike of policemen, it did not pull out till midnight. Eight hours in Howrah Station is the closest any foreigner is likely to come to experiencing Calcutta like a native.

We engaged two porters to carry our metal trunks and suitcases.

The men seemed in their sixties; their professional porterage equipment consisted only of a turban which, placed as a fulcrum in the center of the head, cushioned the scalp while providing a sufficient platform. Each trunk weighed well over one hundred pounds; we also had five suitcases packed to the brim. Since we had engaged the porters in time for the scheduled departure, they were obliged to remain with us during the eight-hour wait. Seeing we were foreign, they had fought other porters for our patronage; now, according to the cousins, they were grumbling about the wait, the lost revenue, the meals they'd missed, their families who were expecting them. "Such impudent fellows! They expect to be paid and the train hasn't come—as if you will engage more porters to do the same work twice." The girls were incensed; they were on our side. I yearned to bestow a handful of sweaty notes on each of them, dismiss them for meals and a good night's rest, but that too, I realized, would be an impudence. A betrayal.

I couldn't take the platforms; the families of beggars, the toddlers who clamped onto the legs of travelers, white men especially, smearing their greasy bodies against your pants, dropping the coins you give them, for fear of losing their grip. You will not touch them not because of the dirt, but because of the smallpox craters in the scalp that are still pink. Furiously, you shake your leg, ready to kick them onto the tracks if they won't let go. I offer the child a tangerine, dropping it in his hand, and he lets it drop as though I'd offered him the clearings of my nose. "Don't go that side, Clark," say the relatives. "All professional beggars."

In the main waiting rooms, all the benches are taken by sleepers. A boy with an enormous water bag strapped to his back spurts water on the floor, as a man follows with a wide broom to wash the floors. The floor sleepers don't even wake as the waves of filthy water, papers, and excrement wash around them. Another more finicky man follows in the wake of the water and selects his sleeping area in a place just cleaned; he unwraps his *dhoti* and fans the concrete until it dries. A young girl of eight or so, with her naked potbellied brother of perhaps less than three, squats beside him and whispers, "*pss, pss,*" until he lets go a long thin yellow jet and a slightly more solid yellow spray from the rear.

But on the platform just behind our lugguage, where I return, a quite attractive young mother of sixteen or so and her naked baby, who is old enough to sit on the platform and smile, are playing games with their fingers for the entire eight hours. The baby grabs her fingers and she pretends to be hurt and the baby giggles. She has a second, much younger baby, sleeping in a sling wrapped around one shoulder and under one breast. When it wakes, she feeds it. She never asks for a thing from us, nor is anything offered. The two babies never cry. I roll four tangerines to her; she and the older baby devour them on the spot, but nothing is said, nor acknowledgment passed.

Belpahar, Hingir, Dahgora, Kelo, Raigarh, Champa Junction, Jairam Nagar, Bilaspur, Nipania . . . it would take color film to shoot the March landscape of Bihar just to show how colorless it is. Thirty hours of unrelieved dust, shrub-pocked hills, cattle grazing where not even a fuzz of green is evident. Three calendar days of travel across India, and not a single tractor, not a single productive farm, is seen. An American dreams, watching India pass by, of ten-thousand-acre communes, of pumps, irrigation, of the San Fernando Valley, he dreams of the ground water that cannot be raised, of the monsoons that may not come, and he thinks if only he had the training instead of his useless flair for writing short stories, his absorption into literature, that if he were wanted, he would devote himself to this place. He dreams of vast tracts being electrified, irrigated, and fertilized while all the absentee landlords and *jotedars* are driven away, the tenancy laws are finally enforced. One waits for a sign. Then, five hours out of Bombay, the soil turns suddenly lush, green, brown, and planted. Groves bursting with fruits for the bazaars of Bombay. The pebble-toss pattern; the wealth of Bombay has reached this far.

A few weeks later we were in Teheran, tramping through snows. The hotel room boasted an Italian refrigerator, German fire extinguishers, Swiss elevators, and American Armed Services Network television. Pictures of the Shah hung in every room. Down in the bar, Ali Mustapha's "Red River Ramblers" played country and western music for the Bell Helicopter engineers. The country created nothing, produced nothing, could afford to import it all. India never looked better than it did from the lobby of a Teheran hotel.

We were sitting with a middle-aged American couple, watching reruns of *Bonanza*. We were off to Turkey in the morning; they'd been due to leave for Karachi. But they weren't going through with it, they said; they'd just been to Lufthansa to cancel their tickets. And they'd just placed a call to their children in California, warning them they'd be home in another two days. Their travel agent had told them it would be this way, they said, east of Athens, but they hadn't believed him. People weren't friendly, you couldn't trust them, couldn't trust the food, they didn't speak English, they were only out to make a buck. "We know when we're not wanted," the man said. "We'll get a good night's sleep for once and be back in Rome tomorrow."

"Rome was very nice," his wife agreed.

# BHARATI MUKHERJEE

## 1

In January, while Clark was in Switzerland putting Bart and Bernie in boarding school, I saw a ghost. Nothing in my adult life had prepared me for seeing ghosts. I knew that I was prone to miscalculation, but I had not suspected this susceptibility to the supernatural.

My bedroom was in a pleasant-enough, split-level row house in a colony of hierarchically arranged row houses and apartment buildings overlooking a chemical plant. The colony itself had been hacked out of unyielding hills and jungles. Here the vegetation was a little too exuberant, and the monsoon sometimes washed down baby cobras destined to be killed by house servants in someone's car porch. In retrospect it seems the right kind of thickly curtained room in the right kind of row house for trapping a ghost.

In a country like India where metaphor and reality continually change places, ghosts are serious business. This ghost did not come to me in a dream. It stood at the head of my bed and breathed warm, sweet shafts of air on my face and pillow. The sound of its breathing was soft, scratchy, like lizards speeding across the cement floor. It did not speak to me; it simply stood in one spot, discomfiting me. I recalled a childhood trick to keep away evil or frightening things: Repeat the word "Vishnu" as quickly and as often as possible. In Loreto House, the nuns had taught us to mix a few Hail Marys with our apparently intractable Vishnus. So I hurled Vishnu novenas at the ghost. After a while, it withdrew.

I do not know why the ghost disappeared. It appeared, then it was gone; that was all. Much later in the night, because I could not convince myself that nothing unusual had occurred, I slipped off my bed—I was alone in a room that held three beds, also two metal Godrej cabinets, a desk, a chair, and a trunk that served as a coffee table—and awoke my mother who was sleeping with my father in a smaller room that housed the icons of Hindu gods.

"Whose ghost was it?" my mother wanted to know. My father snored.

I told her whose ghost I thought it was. That of an uncle who had died of gastric ulcers years before. I had rarely seen him in Calcutta in the "good old days" of which my mother and I liked to talk.

"Oh, him?" she laughed. "That's all right then. You don't have to worry. He was such a quiet, mild person, I'm sure he won't give you any trouble. Even as a ghost." Then, perhaps because I still seemed nervous, she added, "You know, soon after *thakuma* [my father's mother] died, your father was off on a business trip and I slept in this house all alone. I didn't have any trouble."

That was all ghosts were to my mother: potential troublemakers to be coped with, or outwitted. Itinerant specters, mental telepathy, and premonitions were not extraordinary. She had not been saddled as a schoolgirl with all the ethical apparatus—pocket-size books on moral science and year-long courses in religious knowledge—of the nuns of Loreto House. She and her mother and my father's mother could recount funny or chilling stories about irrational forces, often involving male ghosts and female ghosts.

I have never been excited by spiritual kinesthetics, by holy men's abilities to pull diamond rings, gold lockets, and Omega watches out of thin air. But the ghost, I had to concede, was a symptom of the frailty of my reason. Until its appearance I had approached India through the viewfinder of Clark's Nikon. What the viewfinder had framed, it had framed almost by accident, and sometimes in spite of my intentions. I had pretty shots of decently confined emotions. Then the ghost had come and shown me that there were forces present which could not be photographed at all.

After the night of the ghost I became a little too easily irascible, and found that irascibility reflected more intensely all around me. There were too many violent labor disputes, factory sieges, fire-bombings, starvation deaths, and assaults on Harijans. Then there were the minor confusions. I heard a beautician complain that she could not operate her salon because her imported equipment had broken down and no one could repair it. I heard a tailor lose his temper because his assistants had gone on strike making it impossible for him to deliver my cotton hand-loom pant-suit on schedule.

My parents and I argued more than usual. My mother and I argued about the newspaper reports of clashes between the Dalit Panthers and the police. Our arguments always ended with my mother pumping angry air into her satiny cheeks and saying, "What you don't understand is that it's all political, it's not a caste battle." My father and I argued about projected trips downtown. These ended with my father citing the price of gasoline and the sacking of South Indian Udipi hotels in the city as sufficient cause to restrict us to the house.

During the month that Clark was away, my mother and I made only one trip to downtown Bombay, and that was to drop me off for a USIS seminar on contemporary American writers such as Saul Bellow and Bernard Malamud. Even that trip nearly did not come off. It was as if my father sensed that if he let go of his family again, this time the parting would be irrevocable. And so he used the threat of street violence to hold us all together under the tiled roof of the row house. Nostalgia, for the way we had once been, and for the way the entire country had been: It was nostalgia that I had to battle.

I did not go to the seminar to hear the invited Indian professors talk about American literature. I went because I had to escape crushing parental love. And I went because one of the invited Indian professors, Dr. Ranu Vanikar of Baroda University, was my younger sister, whom we had thought of as the only rebel in the family when we were growing up, and who had been the only one of us three sisters to settle in India after marriage. She had come from Baroda in spite of heavy street fighting in her neighborhood and a city-wide curfew. We shared a hotel room, and sat up talking late into the night, every night of the conference. She was full of amusing stories about her infant son, her in-laws who lived in a separate bungalow in the family compound, her ancient but efficient part-time maids, her students and colleagues. I wished I could see her more often.

At the end of the seminar my father as well as my mother came to the hotel to take me back to Chembur. I suggested we delay the return until Ranu and the Baroda contingent had left for the railway station. But my father said that there were rumors of a serious street battle and that we had to leave at once. We quarreled in the hotel lobby. An Englishwoman in tourist clothes directed a brief and scornful stare at us for quarreling in public. My father won. We left my sister with her colleagues and drove the long and angry way home. We witnessed no riots that evening.

"But something bad might have happened," my father insisted. "You know you can't ever be too careful. You've been back long enough to see how it is."

What he said was true. Some disaster could easily have occurred. I was glad I had left India, not because I wanted to avoid disaster but because I wanted to avoid the crippling prudence that comes with living too close to imminent disasters. The year in India had forced me to view myself more as an immigrant than an exile.

## 2

Do ghosts exist, or don't they? That debate is dull and meaningless; the interesting point is that in India different perceptions of reality converge without embarrassing anyone. My year in India had showed me that I did not need to discard my Western education in order to retrieve the dim shape of my Indian one. It might have been less painful if I could have exchanged one locked trunk of ethics for another, but I had to admit that by the end of the year in India I no longer liked India in the unreal and exaggerated ways I had in Montreal. Certainly I had more friends in India, and I loved these friends more deeply. And I was glad to be racially invisible. But I believed that if I stayed on, the country would fail me more seriously than I had failed it by settling abroad. I had come carrying a childish memory of wonder and promise, unsoiled by summer visits to my parents, of the mood of Independence Day, 1947. Now, on the eve of my return to Canada, I was an irritable adult who sensed in the procession of postures at the post offices, railway stations, restaurants, races, factories, and middle-class living rooms, crushing dismay and cynicism.

Not everyone had lost faith; it is impossible to escape at least the cultural jaws of Hinduism. In a country the size of India, even minorities constitute vast populations. But those who believed, in God or government, did so out of their mammoth need to believe. Without some inviolable area of faith, daily life, even the simplest chores, prove impossible to bear.

As I prepared to leave Bombay for the slow flight westward, I realized that for me there would be no more easy consolation through India. The India that I had carried as a talisman against icy Canada had not survived my accidental testings. I would return, of course, but in future visits India would become just another Asian country with too many agonies and too much passion, and I would be another knowledgeable but desolate tourist. I would never again flit inside the cool dark mansions of cultivated Bengali housewives like Anjali and thrill to teatime intimacies and tamely revolutionary ideas. I would never again share lemonade and chocolate cake with a celebrated Marxist editor and be told—with the same conviction that he heralded the socialist millennium—that my *Newseek* photo was deceiving, and that I was not quite as pretty as his granddaughter. Never again to be in the presence of, or under the protection of, the playfully sullen Ballygunge middle class. Next time I would probably get to know the official India better: the hotel waiters, the baggage carriers, the functionaries and smiling P.R. men of Delhi and Bombay.

It was hard to give up my faintly Chekhovian image of India. But if that was about to disappear, could I not invent a more exciting—perhaps a more psychologically accurate—a more precisely metaphoric India: many more Indias?

Writers are free to demolish and reinvent. But to be a woman writer in North America, to be a Third World woman writer in

North America, is to confine oneself to a narrow, airless, tightly roofed arena. In a dust-jacket photograph such a writer is usually in full dress, and appears uncommonly composed, elegant, and mysteriously forbearing. But I am not what I want my dust jacket to suggest I am. Instead, I am anxious and querulous, convinced that every aspect of the writing profession—finding an authentic voice, an audience, a publisher, knowledgeable reviewers—weighs heavily against me because of my visibility as a stereotype. Though in my fiction I may now be ready to construct new metaphorical Indias more real to me than the literary stereotypes, I must first persuade North American readers that the stereotypes are also—if only partially—correct. Because of my readers here, I cannot take the same liberties with India, even with a private India of my imagination, that a Bellow or Malamud can take with America.

To me, the problem of voice is the most exciting one. Born in Calcutta and educated initially in Bengali, I now live in Canada and write in English about Indians living in India or in the United States. My aim, then, is to find a voice that will represent the life I know in a manner that is true to my own aesthetic. But my aesthetic has emerged during my education and stay in North America. I am of the first generation of Indian writers to be influenced by American life and fiction, to have been exposed in my impressionable years to writers such as Djuna Barnes, Flannery O'Connor, John Hawkes, John Cheever, John Updike, William Gass, and Thomas Pynchon. Even our sons are named for our friends, John Bart Gerald and Bernard Malamud. My aesthetic, then, must accommodate a decidedly Hindu imagination with an Americanized sense of the craft of fiction. To admit to possessing a Hindu imagination is to admit that my concepts of what constitute a "story" and of narrative structure are noncausal, non-Western. A Hindu writer who believes that God can be a jolly, potbellied creature with an elephant trunk, and who accepts the Hindu elastic time scheme and reincarnation, must necessarily conceive of heroes, of plot and pacing and even paragraphing in ways distinct from those of the average American.

The works of Hindu writers writing in English about Hindu characters often read like unpolished, self-conscious translations. To avoid this ornateness, other writers opt for limpid naïveté: simply narrated stories about simple village folk. Complexities the voice

cannot encompass are simply left out. But for me, an accidental immigrant, the brave and appropriate model is not R. K. Narayan, but
V. S. Naipaul. In myself I detect a pale and immature reflection of
Naipaul; it is he who has written most movingly about the pain and
absurdity of art and exile, of "Third World art" and exile among the
former colonizers; the tolerant incomprehension of hosts, the absolute impossibility of ever having a home, a *desh.* I am content that
my only stability is the portable world of my imagination.

I am content. I realize, only after the return to India, that I never
had the genteel sensibility of Loreto House girls, nor can I restrict
myself to the conventional perimeters of Anglo-Indian fiction: romance and cultural clash if done with dignity and good humor; spir-
itualism, maharajahs playing cricket, village virgins clinging to their
purity. Even more than other writers, I must learn to astonish, even
to shock.

But I am content. Most Indian women do not give up easily.
What foreigners perceive as forbearance is really a secretive love of
revengeful survival. Most writers do not give up easily. What died,
that year in India, was my need for easy consolation. What has survived is the stubbornness to go on.

# BHARATI MUKHERJEE

May 1995

I write to discover ideal worlds so that I may live to repair ruined ones. I didn't know this about myself twenty years ago. There's so much I didn't guess, or maybe didn't want to know. When I set out with Clark and our two children for that year in India, I still believed what I'd been told all my girlhood: that my "Bengaliness" was erosion-proof; that the monolithic identity based on land and language, which I had inherited by accident of birth into the Mukherjee family of Faridpur, would resist all wear and tear, no matter how far from that phantom ancestral place I eventually settled.

What astonishes me now are my inadvertent and unregistered disclosures. For instance, that I always suspected my "I" was made up of fluid identities.

I thought I was setting out to write a communal autobiography of the women of my age and my vanishing class who had stayed on in the riot-pocked hometown and made their survivalists' peace with Marxist revolution. Once upon a time they and I, sentimentally schooled women, had shared a "Benglish" vocabulary and convent-educated BBC accent, tried and discarded the same hobbies, avoided the same sweat-inducing sports, confessed to similar, modest dreads and dreams. I'd looked forward to an exercise in nostalgia. I'd visualized memory as a suspension bridge connecting my two separate cultural incarnations.

But the "real" story that I ended up writing—in spite of myself—was about North America, not India; about the choice to stay away rather than to stay on. Leaving is easy in our new diasporic age, but staying away and fashioning "home" among hostile people in a strange landscape was, even then, my urgent subject.

In a sense, my right to *feel* Indian had already been challenged by an Ottawa-based bureaucrat of the Indian government. In the late sixties, when I was officially a citizen of India with "landed immigrant status" in Canada, I was warned quite sternly by a member of the Indian High Commission to Canada that since I had willfully married a non-Indian man, I had no right to request that he renew my Indian passport.

In writing this accidental autobiography, I completed the painful, risky journey from exile to settler and claimant. I could finally acknowledge to myself that not only was it no longer possible for me to go back to India to live, but that I did not want to. I would not barter my decision-making rights for physical comfort and unearned dignity. I had lived as a privileged member of the dominant community in a caste- and class-conscious society, and I had lived—was still living—as a despised and discriminated-against minority in a race- and color-conscious society. I had been bestowed terrifying and intimate knowledge of the anatomy of power and of the consequences of its abuse. The victimizer turned victim makes a relentless, fearless champion of freedom.

The urgent drama that I began to play out centered on making a choice between two distinct New World myths of nationhood. The Canada I was a mother/wife/teacher/writer in during the mid-seventies claimed for itself a racial and cultural tolerance that I, as a Canadian citizen of Indian origin, did not experience; on the contrary, that Canada, in spite of its professed love for a culture of ethnic mosaic was creating new official phrases—"visible minority," "absorptive capacity," among others — to marginalize its non-white citizens exclusively on the basis of race. Over the years I spent in Canada—1966 to 1980—I experienced racial harrassments in increasingly crude forms, forms I associated with the segregation-era Deep South I'd read of or seen in Hollywood films. They included removal to a seat in the back of an inter-city bus, not being served in stores, and racial slurs in Toronto's Rosedale subway station.

Worse, because in those years Canada was a "Dominion" of Great Britain pledging ultimate loyalty to the British crown, it did not yet have its own constitution, let alone an enforceable bill of rights. The United States in which I'd been a student on scholarship, and then a bride, had already been compelled by civil rights activists to confront its racism. The debate in the U.S. didn't focus on "Are we racist?" but how do we—through law-suits, sit-ins, rioting in the streets—cleanse ourselves of complicity? In my anguish, "America" and "Canada" swelled into Proustian metaphors, con-crete with memory and insubstantial with desire.

I made my choice; I shouldered my way into the country in which I felt minority discourse empowered me rather than enfeebled me. This time I was crossing a border because I wanted to cross it. This time I was repos-sessing a "homeland" I had willed into existence, not inherited. Giving up a tenured full professorship at McGill University and leaving for the U.S. meant that I was demanding of Clark, Bart and Bernard that they choose either penniless and nomadic living *with* me or tension-free, financially comfortable life in Canada where they felt they belonged and for which they could summon great affection and loyalty. No wife or mother has the right to force such a decision on her family. And no nation should have the permission of its citizenry to force such decisions on its minority commu-nities. For Clark the costs of continued companionship with me have been greater than I might have found myself willing to pay.

Poverty debases more than it ennobles. There were too many occasions in the eighties when we came close to being jobless and hungry. I found out the insomniac's way that I wasn't a bourgeois writer at all, but one who is impassioned, entranced, obsessive. All the same, I want to think that our story—Clark's, our sons', and mine, braided together—is a happy one. Happy because we made our fates out of the many possibilities offered us by destiny. We built our "homeland" out of expectation, not memory. We came "home" to sweetness and light within.

This much I know. Ghosts not only exist, but they endure. They visit me when I most need to be reminded of the invisible wonders all around me that I shan't ever have time to explore.